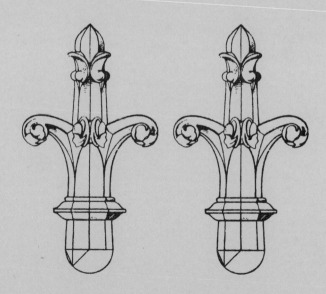

CITIES BUILT TO MUSIC

CITIES BUILT
TO MUSIC

Aesthetic Theories

of the Victorian Gothic Revival

Michael Bright

OHIO STATE UNIVERSITY PRESS : COLUMBUS

The photograph of the Royal Courts of Justice, London, used as the frontispiece is a detail from figure 12.

Library of Congress Cataloging in Publication Data

Bright, Michael, 1942–
  Cities built to music.

  Bibliography: p.
  Includes index.
  1. Gothic revival (Architecture)—Great Britain. 2. Romanticism in literature—Great Britain—Influence. 3. Aesthetics, Modern—19th century—Influence. 4. Ut pictura poesis (Aesthetics). I. Title.
NA967.B74   1984   720'.941   83-23651
ISBN 0-8142-0355-8

CONTENTS

ILLUSTRATIONS

PREFACE

This book is interdisciplinary, and its title indicates the three disciplines that it encompasses: literature (the main title is adapted from Tennyson), aesthetics, and architecture. Aesthetics is the meeting ground of the other two. That is, on a concrete or practical level literature and architecture have little in common, and one would have difficulty in drawing correspondences between, say, a poem and a church. However, on the abstract or theoretical level of aesthetics, literature and architecture begin to converge, and one can perceive interesting and enlightening similarities between the two. Thus it is that though the poem and the church set side by side may appear to have little in common, the artistic theories upon which poet or architect—or any kind of artist, for that matter—bases his work frequently are similar if not identical. Everything that rises must converge, and this book focuses on the point of convergence, the apex of an artistic pyramid.

Of these three disciplines I came first to literature, the primary subject of my formal education. My interest in aesthetics began during an NEH summer seminar at UCLA directed by G. B. Tennyson. I am, therefore, indebted to the NEH for offering the seminar and to Professor Tennyson, who has since that time continued to encourage my work on this project and to help in various ways with it. His support has been of great value throughout the years that went into the preparation of this book.

I was led to architecture through an interest in the Medieval Revival, for the more I learned about the Revival the more I came to see that architecture is the most important manifestation of the Victorians' fascination with the Middle Ages. I have pursued this interest for the most part independently, with the exception of having attended the Victorian Society's summer school in England. I should like to acknowledge the Society for offering this splendid program and to thank Christopher Forbes for providing me with a scholarship.

Most of the research for the book was done at the Crabbe Library of Eastern Kentucky University and at the Cambridge University Library. The staffs of both of these libraries have been unfailingly helpful and courteous, making my work all the more pleasant. I have used as well the libraries of the University of Kentucky, the University of Michigan, and UCLA, and I am obliged to all three for help and hospitality.

Eastern Kentucky University granted me a sabbatical leave in 1981, which allowed me to spend more than half a year in England, reading, and then writing part of the manuscript. This leave, for which I am very grateful, was of crucial importance to the completion of the book. The research committee of the University also generously provided travel funds that were essential to the gathering of the photographs.

In addition to institutional support, I have benefited from the help of individuals. Ashby Bland Crowder, of Hendrix College, and A. J. Mangus, of Eastern Kentucky University, have made useful suggestions about the text and the photographs. Kristine Ottesen Garrigan, of DePaul University, has read the manuscript carefully and given excellent advice for its improvement. Ann Townley guided me through St. Augustine's, Ramsgate, kindly sharing her knowledge of the church. My wife, Catherine, proved an invaluable helpmate in assisting with the photographs. Jim Cox, of Richmond, Kentucky, developed most of these photographs and took others of them. At the Ohio State University Press, Weldon A. Kefauver, director, and Robert S. Demorest, editor, have been the patient, considerate, and able partners any author might wish for. Finally, I should like to express my obligation to my father, an architect who instilled in me a love for buildings, by dedicating the book to his memory. Sharing in this dedication are my wife and two children—Catherine, Taylor, and Marion—who were with me in England and who in their special ways lent support to my work.

CITIES BUILT TO MUSIC

INTRODUCTION

> But it is nonetheless true that there are few authors who have considered
> architecture from the artistic point of view; what I mean is that few authors
> have attempted to study in depth that side of architecture that I term art,
> in the strict sense of the word. (Etienne-Louis Boullée, *Architecture, Essai sur
> l'art*)

Writing in 1907, Howard Maynadier introduced *The Arthur of
the English Poets* by observing that because the Middle Ages had
exerted such a powerful appeal from the time of Chatterton to
the present "mediaevalism is likely to be one of the phenomena
of the century just passed which will most attract the attention
of historians and critics in the centuries to come." Maynadier
shared the self-conscious preoccupation of Victorians with
what the future would think of the present, and also like them
accurately perceived the dominant tendencies of the age, but
he has proved no more capable than they in predicting either
what would occur in the future age or what that age would
think important about the nineteenth century. In those
"centuries to come," Maynadier's prophecy might well come
true; but, for the present, modern writers have failed to be
properly interested in a phenomenon that Maynadier correctly
described as being such an extraordinarily important and pervasive feature of Victoria's reign.

As befits a phenomenon that is essentially historical in nature, modern historians have perhaps dealt more fully with the
nineteenth-century Medieval Revival than have scholars in
other fields, and a fine example of recent historical scholarship
is Mark Girouard's *The Return to Camelot*. Yet even here the
interest has been mainly limited to historiography and has not
reached as far as is required to such areas of influence as, for
example, the Young England movement. In religion, despite
the voluminous scholarship devoted to the Oxford movement,
relatively little has been said about its medieval aspect; and
although James F. White has provided in *The Cambridge Movement* a thorough account of the connection between the Revival
and the church for the middle and late parts of the century,

there remains much to be done on this matter for the writers of the tracts themselves. Art historians have been even more neglectful, for, apart from Roy Strong's recent book, *Recreating the Past*, they have paid scant attention relative to the importance of the subject to medievalism in Victorian painting, and even Strong's book treats the matter only partially. The influence of the Middle Ages on the Pre-Raphaelites has been but indifferently dealt with, and we are left with discussions that are either incomplete or superficial. In literature Alice Chandler has done much in *A Dream of Order*, yet her book, like Strong's, is limited in its scope and does not begin to cover the total range of medievalism in nineteenth-century literary works. In brief, the Medieval Revival was of such vast significance to the century and so permeated the entire substance of British society that our full understanding of it is in very early and tentative stages.

With the Gothic Revival, which term I shall use in contradistinction to the Medieval Revival in order to differentiate between the specifically architectural manifestation of medievalism and the generally cultural aspects of it, the case is somewhat different, as one would expect since architecture is at once the most visible and important expression of medievalism in the nineteenth century. Indeed, as early as 1872 Charles Eastlake wrote his *History of the Gothic Revival*, and in the next year T. G. Jackson followed with *Modern Gothic Architecture*. Since that time there has been a continuing stream of books on the subject, with no doubt the most popular being Kenneth Clark's *The Gothic Revival* although it is a somewhat biased account (Clark admits that he does not much like the style). Yet, for all this study of the Revival, Nikolaus Pevsner could write in his contribution to Peter Ferriday's *Victorian Architecture* that "as far as the knowledge and appreciation of architecture goes, the Victorian Age is the most neglected of all ages." That was in 1963. During the interval between then and the present, there have appeared as many books on Victorian architecture, all of them dealing necessarily with the Gothic Revival, as there are years since Pevsner made the statement, and this number of books does not include those devoted to individual architects. We are, therefore, rather better off with architectural scholarship than we are with other areas influenced by medievalism, and we can be more optimistic about the study of Victorian architecture than Pevsner was twenty years ago.

However, it is nonetheless true that the majority of these books, by being either historical or descriptive, tend to ignore the theoretical principles that formed the foundation of the Revival.[1] In saying this I do not mean to deprecate these approaches to nineteenth-century architecture, for both are essential to our understanding of it. We must know the historical sequence and circumstances in order to survey the whole and to see the relationship of its parts. We must have descriptions in architecture above all arts since a building cannot be placed before a student as can a poem, and neither can it be reproduced as adequately by illustrations as can a painting. History and description are, then, basic and essential first steps in our understanding of architecture; but they are, I suggest, first steps only, which by themselves fail to go the whole way. It strikes me that in our understanding of the Gothic Revival we are rather curiously at the same stage as the Revivalists themselves were toward the beginning of the nineteenth century in their understanding of the medieval Gothic, which is to say that we have pretty well mastered the facts but have yet to grasp the principles. This deficiency Pugin set about to put right then, and this deficiency we should attempt to correct now.

I propose, further, that such a study should aim at an etiological explanation of the Gothic Revival since our understanding of any such cultural phenomenon lies to a great extent in its origins. What is it about the nineteenth century, one should ask, that led so many of its foremost architects back to a style of building whose heyday was some five hundred years distant? But the attribution of origins in the history of ideas is a treacherous affair, for there is a reciprocal relationship between ideas and their outward manifestations that often prevents one from knowing how far the idea determined its manifest expression and how far the expression reciprocally affected the idea. In short, and more specifically, when one is dealing with ideas and their artistic forms, does the idea create the form or does the form influence the idea? Which is the cause, which the effect? I dare say it is impossible to be sure in answering the question, and to be somewhat safer, although by no means avoiding the problem entirely, I shall equivocate by substituting the word "popularity" for "origins" and conclude with the proposition that an understanding of the popularity of the Gothic Revival in the nineteenth century is the chief goal toward which one should aspire.

Perhaps the most apparent explanation for its popularity is a religious one. James Fergusson advocated this theory in *History of the Modern Styles of Architecture*, and the intimate relations between Revival architects and Ecclesiologists, as well as between Pugin and the Roman church, surely argue forcefully for it. Had not the Church Building Act of 1818 provided one million pounds for the erection of 214 churches, 174 of which were in the Gothic style, and thus given occasion for architects to work with the type of building traditionally associated with Gothic, the Revival might never have made headway. Had not, further, the Tractarians returned to pre-Reformation doctrine and had not their followers restored pre-Reformation forms of worship, architects would not have been called upon to furnish churches suitable for the old ways. In fact, the original Gothic had its source in the church, and the neo-Gothic continued to derive its most steadfast and nourishing support there. George Gilbert Scott, principally, sought to extend the Revival to encompass secular architecture, but in the end it was always the church that carried the movement and made for its success.

The next most widely accepted explanation is a literary one. Eastlake, William Morris, and Clark believe that the groundwork for the Revival was laid by poets and novelists; and without exception they, along with others afterward, regard the immense popularity of Sir Walter Scott as in large part responsible for the mania about all things medieval, architecture among them, that characterized the century. Scott it was, more than anyone else, who reversed the neoclassic prejudice against the Middle Ages as a rude and barbarous era and who thereby created in the general population a favorable and receptive climate in which Gothic architecture might flourish.

These two explanations, as well as a number of other less far-reaching ones, are valid enough; but they are only partially satisfactory, for with them all there is something either wholly missing or else but briefly touched on, and that is the matter of taste.[2] After one has reviewed the religious explanation or the literary one, the historical or the social, the political or the whatever, one still asks oneself, "But why, aesthetically, did Gothic architecture appeal to the Victorians?" These various other explanations are insufficient to account for the popularity of the Revival, for no matter how compelling they may have been, if a people do not find a particular style artistically pleasing no amount of other motives will induce them to accept it. No age other than our own, so far as I can determine, has set about to produce quite consciously art that is ugly; and thus it seems to me inconceivable that Victorian artists, architects, and the people who appreciated their works could embrace so enthusiastically a style of art incompatible with their tastes. Much has been made of the ugliness of Victorian art, of Butterfield's churches, for example; but, as Paul Thompson has said in his recent biography of the architect, Butterfield did not think his churches were ugly, nor, we may add, did the majority of others. Certainly there were such charges made by Butterfield's contemporaries, but these amount to little more than the criticism all artists who attempt new things have always endured, and to take them as a starting point in arguing that no one at the time found these churches beautiful is to impose modern aesthetic values on art that follows entirely different rules.

I begin, therefore, with the simple assumption that Victorians liked Gothic architecture—liked it, that is to say, because they found it artistically pleasing—and my task becomes the discovery of how this particular style fulfilled their artistic expectations. The rhetorical approach demanded by the purpose is comparative: to assess on the one hand the fundamental and common aesthetic values of the age, and on the other to eval-

uate the theories behind the Gothic Revival, at each point drawing parallels between the two. By this method I hope to show
that the architectural theories correspond quite closely to the
aesthetic theories of art in general, that architects were trying to
do in buildings what writers and painters were attempting in
their special modes, and that the audience approved Gothic
architecture for the same reasons it responded to contemporary literature and painting.

In discussing nineteenth-century aesthetics, I have relied
principally upon literary examples. In addition to knowing
more about literature than about the other arts and having the
references more readily at hand, I have done so because architecture in the nineteenth century seeks out poetry as an artistic
analogy far more frequently than any other art form, even than
its traditional sister arts of painting and sculpture. Since chapter 2 is largely a matter of supporting this point, I shall not
dwell on it here other than to remark that Ruskin's *The Poetry of
Architecture* is but one example of many in which architecture is
likened to poetry and seen to have similar ends. Because of this
popularly conceived kinship between the two art forms, it
seems logical to choose literature as the primary reference in
explaining aesthetic theory. The main title of the book is meant
to suggest this relationship between the two, requiring only that
the reader accept the common equation of poetry and music.
"The Poetry of Architecture" would have been a less misleading title, but it was unacceptable as having a meaning too restricted by use in the eighteenth and nineteenth centuries.

An interdisciplinary study of this kind is basically a comparison and as such may be likened to figurative language, also
basically comparative. In both cases the writer must concern
himself with the essence or general truth of the objects before
him rather than with their accidents or peculiarities. When,
therefore, Shakespeare describes the barren limbs of trees as
"bare ruined choirs where late the sweet birds sang," he is
drawing upon immediate and predictable impressions of the
two parts separately. So too here I have tried to outline the
essential ideas of architecture on the one hand and of literary

and artistic theory on the other. It has not really been my purpose to discover troves of new material in either area, if such exist, although I hope the reader will perhaps encounter unfamiliar matters within his special field of knowledge. This has not been my purpose because a comparison must necessarily treat its two parts in this way, for its success depends upon the subservience of the parts to the whole. The success of Shakespeare's metaphor relies not on new insights into the separate natures of choirs and trees, insights of little value to the ecclesiologist and botanist alike, but instead on the combination or synthesis of the two. Here is where the delight in the metaphor springs, and here, in the mutually reflecting light of the two parts, one with the other, do we come to see each in a new way. It is this kind of mutually informative relationship that I have attempted to create in joining architecture and literature.

In dealing broadly with architectural theory, I am not, then, interested in pointing out exceptions to the generalizations with which I work as long as they truly remain relatively insignificant exceptions and do not assume the proportions of a major opposition. Neither am I concerned with variations on an idea that may appear in several writers or within one writer, for I am interested in common and widespread principles, not with individual writers and architects. Nor should the reader expect much about the buildings themselves since the subject is architectural theory rather than architectural practice. At the same time, the approach is not so abstract as Roger Scruton's *The Aesthetics of Architecture*, taking, as it were, a kind of middle course between heaven and earth. Chronologically I have taken liberties by drawing upon writers who lie somewhat beyond the final limits of the Revival—Ralph Adams Cram, for instance. The inclusion of Cram reveals, furthermore, that I have allowed myself some geographical license in using foreign sources. Such liberties may be justified in that the influence of the Gothic Revival extended far beyond chronological and geographical boundaries, and when the ideas of those so influenced accord as nearly to principal tenets of the Revival and

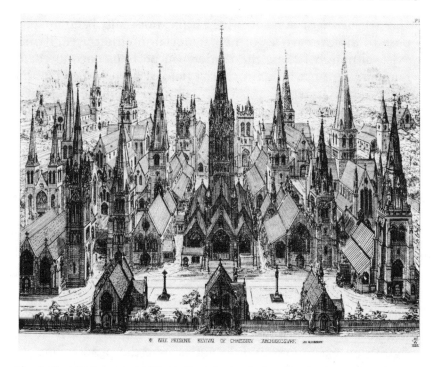

Fig. 1. Frontispiece to A. W. N. Pugin's *An Apology for the Revival of Christian Architecture*—a city built to music.

are expressed as articulately as are Cram's, then I have no
qualms about a liberal policy. The reader will notice, in addition, that I have sometimes violated the limits of the Revival
itself by using statements from writers antipathetical to Gothic
architecture; but such writers—James Fergusson, for
instance—quite frequently shared certain ideals with the Revivalists even while being opposed to their ultimate goal; and
when, therefore, I have found the ideals to be common, I have
employed these statements not only because they are apt illustrations but also because they indicate the pervasive influence
of the Revival. In brief, I have attempted throughout to present
the central and dominant ideals by which the architects of the
Gothic Revival were guided, and have not always demanded

that my sources be card-carrying members of the Revival if
their beliefs correspond to these ideals.

The first two chapters are introductory. Chapter 1 shows that
the dynamics of the Revival, that is, the basic motives for artistic
retrospection, were as much aesthetic as historical, religious, or
social. In other words, there was a specific and urgent aesthetic
reason for returning to the Gothic style that explains the initial
impulse of the Revival as satisfactorily as the various other
causes that have been traditionally put forward. Chapter 2 has
two introductory purposes. The first is to justify the method of
the entire book by pointing out how, during the nineteenth
century, it was an ordinary practice to draw analogies between
the different art forms and to say, for example, that architecture was like poetry, or like painting, or like music. Since the
Victorians themselves were in the habit of seeing correspondences between the various art forms, my attempt to place architecture within the general aesthetic context by indicating similarities between architectural theory and the theories of the
other arts employs the point of view of Victorian artists and
critics. My object here, in Coleridge's words, "is to enable the
spectator to judge in the same spirit in which the artist produced, or ought to have produced" ("On the Principles of Genial Criticism"). The second purpose is to introduce the organizational principle of the subsequent chapters by basing this
discussion of artistic analogies on the aesthetic categories suggested by M. H. Abrams in *The Mirror and the Lamp*. I have
chosen this organizational approach, first, because it provides
considerable latitude and, second, because Abrams developed
it to explain the same Romantic aesthetic theories with which I
am dealing. Chapter 3, therefore, has to do with the theory of
art original with Romanticism and overridingly important to it,
expressionism; chapter 4 concerns the traditional theory of
mimesis; and chapters 5, 6, and 7 discuss the subdivisions of
pragmatism: pleasure, instruction, and function. I have added
the last of these subcategories to Abrams's scheme in order to
accommodate the special nature of architecture as an applied
art.

Wishing to keep the footnotes to a minimum, I have not annotated some quotations, literary for the most part but also from well-known aesthetic works, beyond title references within the text. The general reader will likely be familiar with most of them, and, also, they do not constitute the focal point of the book. On the other hand, I have used footnotes for most direct references to architecture, less famous works on aesthetics, and all modern books and articles.

I. THE AESTHETIC MOTIVE
OF REVIVALISM

I. ARCHITECTURAL AND SOCIAL CONFUSION

> The breaking up of this wretched state of things has naturally produced a
> complete convulsion in the whole system of arts, and a Babel of confusion
> has succeeded to the one bad idea that generally prevailed. (A. Welby
> Pugin, *Apology*)

> [Authority] is being dethroned in our day, and is being supplanted by a
> babel of clashing, irreconcilable utterances, often proceeding from the
> same quarters, even the same mouths. (Alfred Austin, *The Bridling of
> Pegasus*)

> And we are here as on a darkling plain
> Swept with confused alarms of struggle and flight,
> Where ignorant armies clash by night.
> Matthew Arnold, "Dover Beach"

In August of 1861 an artistic congress convened at Antwerp to
consider why the nineteenth century had no distinctive
architectural style. Whatever resolutions the congress may have
drawn up are less important than that the simple fact of its
meeting indicates a profound and widespread dissatisfaction
with the present state of European architecture. In England the
chief spokesman against the riotous motley of architectural
styles had been A. W. N. Pugin, who in 1843 declared that
architecture, along with the other arts, was passing through a
transitional period following the dissolution of Renaissance art,
and that in this aesthetic wasteland anarchic individualism prevailed:

> The age in which we live is a most eventful period for English art. We
> are just emerging from a state which may be termed the dark ages of
> architecture. After a gradual decay of four centuries, the style,—for style
> there was,—became so execrably bad, that the cup of degradation was
> filled to the brim; and as taste had fallen to its lowest depth, a favourable
> re-action commenced.
> The breaking up of this wretched state of things has naturally produced
> a complete convulsion in the whole system of arts, and a Babel of confu-
> sion has succeeded to the one bad idea that generally prevailed.
> Private judgment runs riot; every architect has a theory of his own, a
> beau ideal he has himself created; a disguise with which to invest the

building he erects. This is generally the result of his latest travels. One
breathes nothing but the Alhambra,—another the Parthenon,—a third is
full of lotus cups and pyramids from the banks of the Nile,—a fourth from
Rome, is all dome and basilica; while another works Stuart and Revett on a
modified plan, and builds lodges, centenary chapels, reading-rooms, and
fish-markets, with small Doric work and white brick facings. Styles are now
adopted instead of *generated*, and ornament and design *adapted to*, instead of
originated by, the edifices themselves.

This may, indeed, be appropriately termed the *carnival* of architecture:
its professors appear tricked out in the guises of all centuries and all
nations; the Turk and the Christian, the Egyptian and the Greek, the Swiss
and the Hindoo, march side by side, and mingle together; and some of
these gentlemen, not satisfied with perpetrating one character, appear in
two or three costumes in the same evening.

Amid this motley group (oh! miserable degradation!) the venerable
form and sacred detail of our national and Catholic architecture may be
discerned; but *how* adopted? Not on consistent principle, not on authority,
not as the expression of our faith, our government, or country, but as one
of the disguises of the day, to be put on and off at pleasure, and used
occasionally as circumstances or private caprice may suggest.[1]

I have quoted this lengthy passage in its entirety because it
deals rather completely with the problem that was to be considered by the Antwerp congress and that was central to
nineteenth-century architecture as well as to the Victorian age
in general. Here we see the notions of a transitional age, of
runaway eclecticism, of lawless individualism, of artificiality, of
shams and disguises, all apparent in the displays of the Great
Exhibition of 1851 and in the statements of other writers, but
not as explicitly or as fully developed as in this passage.

Seven years later Edward Lacy Garbett treated one aspect of
the problem when he attributed the architectural chaos to the
democratization of art. As adamantly antidemocratic as Carlyle,
Garbett took the elitist view that art succeeds only when dominated by an enlightened minority. "Some regret," he wrote,
"that we have (as they think) no national style. Alas! the woe is
that we *have* a national style,—a national shame, as all national
styles ever will be. . . ." The old styles were not national but the
creations of "classes, priesthoods, and corporations," and "this
was the very essence of their success,—that they were the exclusive production of the thinking few, uninfluenced by the
thoughtless multitude; though universally admired, yet totally

unpopular, un-national."[2] If Garbett runs counter to one of the central doctrines of the Gothic Revival, which is that architecture expresses national character and that Gothic is the national architecture of England, he at the same time conforms to the Romantic concept that art is the product of the gifted few. In this respect he presents an architectural parallel to a subject E. D. H. Johnson has treated in *The Alien Vision of Victorian Poetry*: the growing distrust of nineteenth-century poets for the tastes of those whom Arnold was to call "Philistines."

Fifteen years later, and four years after the Antwerp congress, William Burges dealt with another aspect of the problem. The absence of a single and distinctive architectural style, according to Burges, is the greatest impediment to progress in art because the architect is required to master half a dozen styles, a clear impossibility, instead of just one as in former times. From the point of view of the student, then, the multiplicity of styles is the bane of architecture:

> If we take a walk in the streets of London we may see at least half-a-dozen sorts of architecture, all with different details; and if we go to a museum we shall find specimens of the furniture, jewellery, &c., of these said different styles all beautifully classed and labelled. The student, instead of confining himself to one style as in former times, is expected to be master of all these said half-dozen, which is just as reasonable as asking him to write half-a-dozen poems in half-a-dozen languages, carefully preserving the idiomatic pecularities of each. This we all know to be an impossibility, and the end is that our student, instead of thoroughly applying the principles of ornament to one style, is so bewildered by having the half-dozen on his hands, that he ends by knowing none of them as he ought to do. This is the case in almost every trade; and until the question of style gets settled, it is utterly hopeless to think about any great improvement in modern art.[3]

Burges's description of the plight of the contemporary architect is particular proof of John Stuart Mill's contention in "The Spirit of the Age" (*Examiner*, 1831) that "the grand achievement of the present age is the diffusion of superficial knowledge. . . ." Clearly the day was past when an Admirable Crichton could master the realms of all learning.

Apparently the problem became somewhat less acute as the century matured and the number of available styles decreased. In 1841 Richard Brown had listed in *Domestic Architecture* sixteen different styles appropriate for the Victorian domicile, omitting only Gothic since it "exclusively belongs to sacred architecture and not to domestic."[4] In 1865, as we have seen, Burges set the number at half a dozen; and in 1884 Robert Kerr declared that there were three current styles: Gothic, Modern European (Renaissance), and Queen Anne. However, the long-sought one style never developed; and after the turn of the century, Ralph Adams Cram could walk the streets of New York, just as Burges had walked those of London fifty years earlier, and gain a similar, "indelible impression of that primal chaos that is certainly without form, if it is not wholly void."[5] The transitional chaos lasted longer than the Victorians anticipated, so that Cram in 1914 still looked forward to the birth of a new age. Cram speculated that historical epochs occurred in five-hundred-year cycles, one having come into being between 450 and 550 A.D., a second between 950 and 1050, a third between 1450 and 1550, and a fourth due in 1950. Thus, like Yeats, who wrote that "the centre cannot hold," Cram believed that the current disintegration of the old epoch would give way to the birth of a new:

> As mediaevalism was centripetal, so is modernism centrifugal, and disintegration follows on, faster and ever faster. Even now, however, the falling wave meets in its plunge and foam the rising wave that bears on its smooth and potent surge the promise and potency of a new epoch, nobler than the last and again synthetic, creative, centripetal.[6]

In this time of transition from one epoch to another, the duty of art lies

> in giving expression to all that is worth preserving in an era so fast becoming history, and in bridging the inevitable chasm now opening between one definte epoch and the next. . . . In his work, whatever it may be, he [the artist] must record and preserve all that was and is best in a shattered era, that this may be carried over into the next and play its new part, no longer of conservation but of re-creation.[7]

A hundred years had passed since Shelley's "Ode to the West Wind," and spring was still tantalizingly not far behind.

In addition to these direct descriptions of the confused and unsettled state of architecture, another approach that gives insight into the problem is through the Victorians' concept of

how their architecture would appear to future generations. Peter Collins has written that "architectural historians were dominated by one notion, and one notion only; namely, that a modern building was essentially a collection of potential antiquarian fragments which one day would be rediscovered, and studied by future historians with a view to determining the social history of the Victorian age."[8] This is putting it rather too categorically, but the Victorians were acutely self-conscious and very much concerned about the image they bequeathed to posterity. Also, we find that a projection into the future served them as a sort of rhetorical device by which to comment on the present in much the same way as Pugin, Carlyle, and many others used the past to criticize the present. Furthermore, whenever a writer uses this device, he almost surely embodies the future in the figure of a New Zealander, drawn from Macaulay's comment in "Ranke's History of the Popes" (*Edinburgh Review*, 1840) that the Catholic church may still exist "when some traveller from New Zealand shall, in the midst of a vast solitude, take his stand on a broken arch of London Bridge to sketch the ruins of St. Paul's." Although Macaulay may have taken the image from a letter Horace Walpole wrote Sir Horace Mann in 1774, everyone attributed it to Macaulay and used it as a symbol for the collapse of English civilization. Gustave Doré illustrated the New Zealander in *London: A Pilgrimage* (1872), and Anthony Trollope entitled a book, written in 1855–56 though unpublished till 1972, *The New Zealander*. Of the many references, one will suffice to illustrate how the New Zealander was used to foretell England's fall and to comment on the confused state of contemporary architecture. Writing in the *Builder* in 1862, T. Mellard Reade made this prediction:

> If the inevitable New Zealander who is to sketch the ruins of St. Paul's from London-bridge should be anything of an antiquary, he will be sorely troubled to eliminate the history of the English nation from its writings in brick and stone. If the history of architecture be the history of the human mind, his researches will indicate a very chaotic mental state on the part of the present generation.[9]

The New Zealander may yet come, but if he stands on that London Bridge the sands of Arizona will present him with a

THE NEW ZEALANDER

Fig. 2. Gustave Doré's version of Macaulay's New Zealander. From Gustave Doré and Blanchard Jerrold, *London: A Pilgrimage* (1872; rpt. New York: Dover Publications, 1970).

spectacle closer to the one viewed by the traveler in "Ozyman-
dias" than to the ruins of St. Paul's. One need not, however,
quibble about bridges or wait for the New Zealander to attest to
the essential truth of Reade's claim that there was little unity of
aim among Victorian architects or in the larger society to which
they belonged.

In *The Present State of Ecclesiastical Architecture in England*,
Pugin had argued that "architecture to be good must be consistent";[10] and in *An Apology for the Revival of Christian Architecture in England*, he uses the word *consistent* over and again. In
the last chapter of *The Seven Lamps of Architecture*, significantly
entitled "The Lamp of Obedience," Ruskin refers to liberty as a
"treacherous phantom," and maintains that the principle of
creation "is not Liberty, but Law." The practice of architecture
must be brought under control, Ruskin says, for it "never could
flourish except when it was subjected to a national law as strict
and as minutely authoritative as the laws which regulate religion, policy, and social relations. . . ."[11]

At the end of the century, there was an attempt to impose
restrictions when a bill was presented to Parliament in 1891
requiring the certification of architects by examination. Several
leading architects opposed the bill by writing essays against it in
a volume entitled *Architecture: A Profession or an Art*, but the bill
was not really what Ruskin had in mind and would have had
little effect upon the proliferation of styles since its main purpose was to eliminate from practice the unqualified. If architecture could not, and for many architects should not, be subjected to external controls, then at least there might be some
less formal agreement as to the direction in which architecture
should go. On the classic side of the Battle of the Styles, James
Fergusson argued that the renovation of art requires "some
high and well-defined aim towards which it may strive," and
Samuel Huggins called for a "unity of aim and action among
architects" as was the case in former days.[12] On the Gothic side,
George Gilbert Scott urged his colleagues to "unite, one and all,
in one steady, unflinching effort,—constant, untiring, and in
the same direction."[13] Later, as president of the Institute of

British Architects, he emphasized to the members "the great necessity of a singleness of aim, of a devotion to and community of effort in the advancement of art, above all individual and personal considerations. . . ."[14] The formation of the Institute of British Architects in 1834, to receive a royal charter as the R.I.B.A. in 1837, further indicates a desire for concord among the architects of the time.

In a passage quoted above, T. Mellard Reade applies the nineteenth-century maxim that architecture reflects the society from which it springs by saying that the New Zealander of the future will regard the ruins of London architecture as evidence of "a very chaotic mental state on the part of the present generation." So it does reflect it, although not in ruins; for, as I have already suggested, there is a close parallel between the architectural problem and the troubled state of Victorian society at large. In fact, the parallel is so apparent that it is impossible to read these architects and not be instantly reminded of familiar statements by their more celebrated contemporaries. For example, the general confusion in architecture corresponds to the well-known description of Victorian uncertainty at the end of "Dover Beach": "And we are here as on a darkling plain/Swept with confused alarms of struggle and flight,/Where ignorant armies clash by night." Tennyson develops the image more fully in "The Passing of Arthur" with the "dim, weird battle of the west" wherein "even on Arthur fell/Confusion, since he saw not whom he fought." The individualism Pugin held accountable for "the *carnival* of architecture" meets equal disapproval in Arnold's "Doing As One Likes" from *Culture and Anarchy*. Garbett's attack upon democracy in art and his contempt for "the thoughtless multitude" run parallel to Carlyle's scorn for the mob and his fear that "the Niagara leap of completed Democracy" will lead England over the precipice into a political and social maelstrom (*Shooting Niagara: and After?*). The factionalism of the Battle of the Styles reflects Arnold's description of the "Servants of God": "Factions divide them, their host/Threatens to break, to dissolve" ("Rugby Chapel"); and in the popular hymn "The Church's

One Foundation" (1866), Samuel John Stone portrays the Church as "By schisms rent asunder,/By heresies distrest."

The social critics quite often attributed this restlessness, uncertainty, and confusion to the transitional nature of the Victorian age just as the architectural critics believed that architecture was passing through a time of change. In *Sartor Resartus* Carlyle shows that after rejecting the mechanistic philosophy in "The Everlasting No," Teufelsdröckh must experience the difficult and trying search of "The Center of Indifference" before arriving at the affirmation of dynamic organicism in "The Everlasting Yea." In *The Rime of the Ancient Mariner* and *The Prelude*, Coleridge and Wordsworth describe similar trials when the soul is on dead center, unable to move in any direction. The problem is one of a moral and philosophical vacuum, for, as Carlyle writes in "Characteristics," "the Old has passed away: but, alas, the New appears not in its stead. . . ." Mill says almost exactly the same thing in the same year: "The first of the leading pecularities of the present age is, that it is an age of transition. Mankind have outgrown old institutions and old doctrines, and have not yet acquired new ones" ("The Spirit of the Age"). The idea is often repeated throughout the century as the momentum of change, far from slowing to a settled condition wherein new and universal values obtained, accelerated with the rapidity sensed by Thomas Arnold in his comment that "we have been living, as it were, the life of three hundred years in thirty" ("Letter II," *13 Letters on Our Social Condition*). Twenty years later his son still speaks of "Wandering between two worlds, one dead,/The other powerless to be born" ("Stanzas from the Grande Chartreuse"); and as late as 1884 William Morris told the seventh annual meeting of the S.P.A.B., "Let us admit that we are living in the time of barbarism betwixt two periods of order. . . ." In 1920 Yeats was still awaiting the Second Coming, and today, bewildered by the vagaries of Future Shock, we wait for a Godot who will never arrive, at least not in the way expected by Carlyle, Mill, Arnold, and Morris.

As we have seen, Ralph Adams Cram thought that it is the duty of the artist to preserve his art until the new epoch arrives and society once again provides a congenial climate in which culture might thrive. Similarly, Arnold writes that if the turbulent age makes it impossible "to think clearly, to feel nobly, and to delineate firmly," then the poet should transmit to his successors "the practice of poetry, with its boundaries and wholesome regulative laws, under which excellent works may again, perhaps, at some future time, be produced . . ." ("Preface to First Edition of *Poems,*" 1853). The phrase "wholesome regulative laws" echoes Ruskin's belief that the principle of creation "is not Liberty, but Law" and recalls that liberalism threatened with anarchy poetry as well as architecture. Indeed, in society at large no less than in poetry and architecture, there was an absence of common goals. Samuel Huggins, in a passage quoted above, called for a return to the "unity of aim and action among architects" of earlier days, and Arnold tells us that the great advantage of the Scholar-Gipsy over "this strange disease of modern life,/With its sick hurry, its divided aims" is that he "hadst *one* aim, *one* business, *one* desire." For Arnold, culture would afford the unity needed to hold in abeyance the threat of social anarchy; for Pugin, Scott, and others, the answer to the corresponding architectural problem lay in the revival of Gothic.

II. THE GOTHIC REVIVAL AS A SOLUTION TO THE PROBLEM OF STYLISTIC CONFUSION

> We must *look* backwards under all circumstances, *go* backwards as soon as we find that we have got upon the wrong road. (Augustus Reichensperger, *Die Kunst Jedermanns Sache*)

> No one could have guessed that of all the arts it was architecture that was destined to be the first to emancipate itself from its degrading thraldom, the first to retrace its steps to the right path, and the first to enter upon a new career of sound and legitimate development (Benjamin Webb, "The Prospects of Art in England")

One explanation for the Medieval Revival in the nineteenth century is that it offered a therapeutic escape to those suffering from the "strange disease of modern life," or, if not an escape, at least a nostalgic ideal of a golden age of order, faith, and

meaning directly opposite to a modern world so lamentably
deficient in those virtues. As Alice Chandler has written in *A
Dream of Order*, which takes this point as its theme:

> But behind all these varying expressions of a medievalizing imagination
> lay a single, central desire—to feel at home in an ordered yet organically
> vital universe. The more the world changed, and the period of the medi-
> eval revival was an era of ever accelerating social transformation, the more
> the partly historical but basically mythical Middle Ages that had become a
> tradition in literature served to remind men of a Golden Age. The Middle
> Ages were idealized as a period of faith, order, joy, munificence, and
> creativity.[15]

At times the seductiveness of the Middle Ages corresponds to
the escapist element in Romanticism. Horace Walpole wrote
Montagu that "there is no wisdom comparable to that of ex-
changing the realities of life for dreams. Old castles, old his-
tories, and the babble of old people, make one live back into the
centuries, that cannot disappoint one. One holds fast and
surely what is past" (5 January 1766). A youthful Edward
Burne-Jones praised Tennyson's "Sir Galahad" to his friend
Cormell Price, saying that Tennyson is "the only poet worth
following far into dreamland." Tennyson, for his part, found
delight in the past more from the equally Romantic notion that
"distance lends enchantment to the view" than that it is an
avenue of escape. In explaining "Tears, Idle Tears," Tennyson
wrote James Knowles that "it is what I have always felt even
from a boy, and what as a boy I called the 'passion of the past.'
And it is so always with me now; it is the distance that charms
me in the landscape, the picture and the past, and not the
immediate to-day in which I move." Whatever the motive, the
Middle Ages held an enormous appeal during the course of the
century as a charmed land of dreams. Even such an inveterate
classicist as Matthew Arnold was not immune from its allure.
His fond and well-known description of Oxford as "whispering
from her towers the last enchantments of the Middle Age"
("Preface," *Essays in Criticism, First Series,* 1865) is reinforced by
a letter to his youngest sister in which he wrote, "I have a strong
sense of the irrationality of that period, and of the utter folly of
those who take it seriously, and play at restoring it; still, it has

poetically the greatest charm and refreshment possible for me"
(17 December 1860).

The growing appreciation for the Middle Ages brought
about by the romance of the past created an atmosphere quite
naturally conducive to the advancement of Gothic architecture.
As Charles Eastlake has said,

> The Mediaeval sympathies which Scott aroused were enlisted less by refer-
> ence to the relics of Pointed architecture than by the halo of romance
> which he contrived to throw around them. The fortunes of the Dis-
> inherited Knight, the ill-requited love of poor Rebecca, the very jokes of
> Wamba and the ditties of the Bare-footed Friar, did more for the Gothic
> Revival than all the labours of Carter and Rickman.[16]

Or, as Peter Collins has remarked, Gothic architecture made it
possible for readers to live out fantasies elicited by Gothic
novels and so make more real and vivid the vicarious pleasures
of fiction.[17]

If, however, the Medieval Revival were nothing more than a
vehicle for escape or an enchanting prospect charmed by the
passage of years, it would never have developed into other than
a plaything, as trivial and frivolous as Strawberry Hill or the
Eglinton Tournament, as artificial and exotic as the Royal
Pavilion at Brighton. But for those who were mainly responsible for it, the Revival was a matter of utmost seriousness; and
for those who now look back, it seems a natural, almost inevitable, phenomenon. Without some profound and fundamental
need for such a revival, without some sympathetic identification of the one age with the other, interest in the medieval
period would never have become the dominant cultural force
that it was. There must be more to it than an object of curiosity
for dreamers and antiquarians; there must be something inherently responsive in the Victorian imagination for a large
segment of the population to embrace with such pleasure and
dedication the revived institutions and art of the Middle Ages.
In his *History of Civilisation in England* (1856–61), Thomas
Buckle wrote,

> There must always be a connexion between the way in which men con-
> template the past, and the way in which they contemplate the present; both

views being in fact different forms of the same habits of thought, and therefore presenting in each age, a certain sympathy and correspondence with each other.

This important principle of historiography suggests not only that the Victorian era and the Middle Ages shared certain things in common but also that one may learn much about the Victorians by studying how they regarded their medieval forebears. Roy Strong, who quotes Buckle in *Recreating the Past*, has recently shown how historical painting reveals nineteenth-century attitudes, and I am developing somewhat the same premise through architecture in this book. More to the point, Buckle implies that an interest in history and, by extension, in the revival of historical modes is not capricious or shallow. And more explicitly, Ralph Adams Cram insisted upon the importance of the Gothic Revival by declaring that

> the inception and growth and culmination of the new Gothic mode is not a whimsey of chance, a sport of erratic fancy; it was and is a manifestation in art forms of a world impulse, as fundamental as that which gave itself visible form in the Renaissance, as that which blossomed in the first Gothic of the twelfth century, as that which created Aya Sophia or the Parthenon. It meant something when it happened, it means something to us to-day, it will mean more to our children. . . .[18]

What does it mean to us and what does that meaning explain about its origin and popularity? One answer is that the Gothic Revival, and the entire Medieval Revival of which it is a part, was a result of Romanticism and especially of those aspects that were to bring about the inception of modern historical inquiry: dynamic organicism, primitivism, material progress, nationalism, and particularity, among the more important. To unravel and explain all these extraordinarily complex determinants would go far beyond the aesthetic limits of this book and be more the task of a historian, but to understand the context of the Revival, we must take a brief though necessarily superficial look at the influence that the study of history bore upon it.

At its worst the new historical consciousness manifested itself in the snobbish vanity of those who wished to establish pedigrees imbued with the aura of antiquity. In *Rural Rides* William Cobbett ridiculed Fonthill Abbey and William Beckford's claim to be lineally descended from seventy-eight knights: "Was there ever vanity and impudence equal to these!" Others, like Tennyson's uncle Charles, who changed his name to d'Eyncourt and sought a peerage throughout his life, adopted Norman names and built castellated mansions in their pretensions to gentility. Often this sort of thing was harmless enough, even amusing. There is, for example, nothing reprehensible in Walpole's self-conscious and flippant remark to Henry Conway that he writes "from Strawberry Castle" where he gives himself "the airs, in my nutshell, of an old baron" (23 September 1755). It is no less difficult to take seriously the change from Jeffrey Wyatt to Sir Jeffrey Wyatville in light of the remark of his chief patron, George IV: "Veal or Mutton, he could call himself what he liked."

Far more importantly, these elements in Romanticism conjoined to develop an awareness of the differentness of the past. As long as the notion of general nature, especially in the sense of human nature, dominated, there existed the corollary that there was no essential difference between people past and present. In the words of R. G. Collingwood,

> the eighteenth-century historians . . . assumed that human nature had existed ever since the creation of the world exactly as it existed among themselves. Human nature was conceived substantialistically as something static and permanent, an unvarying substratum underlying the course of historical changes and all human activities. History never repeated itself but human nature remained eternally unaltered.[19]

While this attitude lasted, there could be little advantage in studying human nature obscured by the mists of time when the very same traits were so much more readily apparent in the present. Nor could curiosity be piqued by the strange or unusual. When, however, the Romantic historian came to view past epochs as distinct and individual, then there simultaneously arose an interest in what had gone before.

This change in historical perspective is more readily apprehensible in its ontogenetic application than in its phylogenetic. It is something of a cliché that eighteenth-century parents looked upon their children as miniature adults,

undeveloped perhaps but sharing basic traits common to all
ages. Rousseau, on the other hand, was one of the first to maintain that the child was different and should be treated as such.
Blake was to divide sharply childhood and maturity in *Songs of
Innocence and Experience*, and Wordsworth was preoccupied
with the distinct stages of life in such major poems as *The Prelude*, "Tintern Abbey," and the "Intimations Ode." In minor
poems, too, like "We Are Seven" and "Anecdote for Fathers,"
Wordsworth explores the difference between the way children
perceive the world and the way adults do. Now there is a direct
parallel between the attitudes toward childhood and those
toward early historical epochs, for, as Shelley says in "A Defence of Poetry," "the savage is to ages what the child is to
years."[20] It is no accident, then, that the cult of childhood in the
Victorian era should occur simultaneously with the Medieval
Revival, that interest in the childhood of an individual should
coincide with interest in the childhood of the race. Furthermore, it is no accident that the glorification of a child as an
innocent and blessed creature, "trailing clouds of glory,"
should be cotemporaneous with the idealization of the Middle
Ages as a golden age, since childhood, whether of an individual
or a race, was considered to be not only different from maturity
but superior to it as well. The "Intimations Ode" and *Contrasts*
are but different versions of the same idea.

Nevertheless, readers will recall that though Wordsworth distinguishes between the stages of a person's development, he
also stresses the organic continuity of them—"The Child is
father of the Man"—and it is no less true phylogenetically that
historians came to be interested in their nation's origins for
what those origins embryonically revealed about the mature
society. The first step in this process, though, was to overturn
the neoclassic bias that conceived the Middle Ages to be savage
and barbarous times, "tedious years of Gothic darkness" as
Cowper puts it in *Table Talk*.[21] This was accomplished by innumerable writers, among them Bishop Hurd in *Letters on Chivalry and Romance* (1762) and Sharon Turner, whose *History of
the Anglo-Saxons* (1799–1805) reversed the concept of the de-

struction of the Roman Empire "as a barbarization of the human mind; a period of misery, darkness, and ruin" by claiming instead that the Germanic triumph was "a new and beneficial re-casting of human society in all its classes, functions, manners, and pursuits."

Once this battle had been won, historians were prepared to establish the Germanic origins of English society. John Kemble, for example, wrote in *The Saxons in England* (1849) that "the Englishman has inherited the noblest portion of his being from the Anglo-Saxons. In spite of every influence, we bear a marvellous resemblance to our forefathers." In their attempt to prove that English character and institutions were primarily Germanic, Kemble, who also edited *Beowulf*, along with Bishop William Stubbs and Edward Freeman, both Regius Professors of Modern History at Oxford, met opposition from the Romanists, as the Battle of the Styles was waged in the theater of history in addition to those of architecture and painting.

Although it is interesting and worthwhile to note how widespread was the classic-Gothic controversy, the pertinent point is that by retracing their cultural, social, and political streams back to the fountainhead, the Victorians sought a better understanding of themselves and of their future. In other words, this retrospection is in part both symptom and anticipated cure for that loss of identity suffered by the Victorians as they searched for meaning and values in a world of change and confusion. To understand where they had come from might explain who they were and where they were headed just as the seed or embryo holds the secrets to the plant or animal. In "The Spirit of the Age," Mill writes that the future may be learned in the present: "And since every age contains in itself the germ of all future ages as surely as the acorn contains the future forest, a knowledge of our own age is the fountain of prophecy—the only key to the history of posterity." In "English Architecture Thirty Years Hence" (1884), Robert Kerr justifies a historical review before discussing the future with this statement:

> Now we pretty well understand in these scientific days that all continuous enterprises of human industry or skill, or of social or intellectual activity ... are found to be subject to the government of certain laws of progression; so that it is the critical study of the past that becomes the only means of forecasting the future.[22]

Finally, one might note that in 1879–82 Walter Skeat published his *Etymological Dictionary* and that in 1879 James Murray began to compile the *O.E.D.* "On Historical Principles," both works reflecting this same tendency toward definition by origin.

Once we understand the retrospective habit of mind among the Victorians, we are naturally led to question why they should focus on the Middle Ages. All of them, of course, did not. The Classical Revival in architecture, painting, and sculpture; the Romanist group in history; and the classical subjects popular with Tennyson, Arnold, and Swinburne, all testify to the persistence of another tradition throughout the period.[23] But for a large number of others, the question remains a valid one. For some of these the return to the Middle Ages was simply a matter of harkening back to an immediately preceding age that had come to a close around the end of the eighteenth century. Walter Houghton has pointed out that for many Victorians the institutions and ways of life that had been lost in the Romantic revolution and that left the Victorians between two worlds were essentially feudal. To this effect, Houghton quotes from Baldwin Brown's *The Revolution of the Last Quarter of a Century* (1869–70): "Until quite recently our modes of thought and speech, our habits of action, our forms of procedure in things social and political, were still feudal."[24] We must remember, too, that the precise and analytical Linnaean categorization of history was foreign to people who were accustomed to dividing history into three epochs: ancient, medieval, and modern. This tripartite division is, after all, what explains why the eighteenth century coined the terms "medieval" and "middle ages" to define a historical segment between two others. When a Victorian looked back, therefore, he had but the two choices we see reflected in the primary revivals during the century.

On the other hand, the scientific analysis by which modern historians so precisely dissect the past into many and distinct groups had made inroads among some Victorians, who came to regard their own age as distinct and to employ the term "Victorian" in reference to themselves. As Mill says in "The Spirit of the Age," "Before men begin to think much and long on the peculiarities of their own times, they must have begun to think that those times are, or are destined to be, distinguished in a very remarkable manner from the times which preceded them." Not only, however, did they regard their own time as having been separated from the past by Romanticism, the Industrial Revolution, democracy, or whatever, but they also came increasingly to fix the end of the Middle Ages not so much at the advent of their own time as at the Renaissance, much as we do now. For these men, then, who recognized a major cultural break coinciding roughly with the Tudor dynasty, a return to the Middle Ages represented a reversion to the penultimate historical epoch instead of to the last. In seeking to revive certain medieval traits, they were involved in what W. Jackson Bate has explained as "the 'leapfrog' use of the past for authority or psychological comfort: the leap over the parental—the principal immediate predecessors—to what Northrop Frye calls the 'modal grandfather.'"[25] In other words, the Medieval Revivalists rejected the parental influence—that is to say, the neoclassic—by appealing to the grandparental authority of the Middle Ages. Believing that with the Renaissance things had begun to go wrong and that the predicament of modern times was largely due to the false steps taken at that period, the Revivalists sought in the Middle Ages, the wise and true grandparent, answers to their questions, solutions to their problems, values for their void of them, order for their chaos. Young Englanders sought political solutions in the feudal rapport of lord and serf, Tractarians sought religious solutions in an unreformed church, Pre-Raphaelites sought artistic solutions in the unconventionalized naturalism of early Christian painting, and Gothic Revivalists sought

architectural solutions in a Christian, national, and un-
corrupted style.

The leading Goths were as unequivocal in their scorn for the
cultural parent as their forebears had been of the Middle Ages.
John Mason Neale and Benjamin Webb, founders of the Camden Society, derided the neoclassic architecture of Georgian
England as "that ne plus ultra of wretchedness,"[26] and Pugin
wrote from Rome in 1847 of earlier examples: "The Sistine
Chapel is a melancholy room, the Last Judgment is a painfully
muscular delineation of a glorious subject, the Scala Regia a
humbug, the Vatican a hideous mass, and St. Peter's is the
greatest failure of all."[27] Even as the Tractarians, especially
Hurrell Froude, regarded the Reformation as the great calam-
ity for the church, so did others consider it disastrous for art.
Following Pugin, the Ecclesiologists believed the ruin of art was
precipitated by the renaissance of classical design that accompanied the upheaval in the church: "About the time of the
Reformation, the partial recurrence to classical forms, induced
by the vitiated and unhappy taste for Italian architecture, completely corrupted the pure Pointed style by giving birth to various anomalous compositions, generally termed Debased."[28]

It is especially important that we understand their attitude
toward the Reformation, for it is in large measure both justification and explanation for the Revival. The Revivalists have
continuously been blamed of attempting to thwart the natural
course of art by imposing artificially on the present a worn-out
style from the past. In their own age *The Times* charged in the
1840s that the study of the Middle Ages was "a foolish in-
terference with the natural progress of civilization and prosper-
ity." The Revivalists held, to the contrary, that the introduction
of classical art in the Renaissance was the false and unnatural
interruption in the progress of art. As the *Builder* states in 1850,
"Subsequent to the Reformation a new element was introduced
in Europe—that of copying antecedent and dead styles; progress was unknown, retrocession the fashion. . . ."[29] For the exponents of Gothic architecture, therefore, the art against which

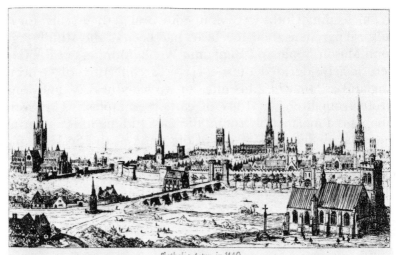

Catholic town in 1440.

1. St Michaels on the Hill. 2. Queens Cross. 3. St Thomas's Chapel. 4. St Maries Abbey. 5. All Saints. 6. St Johns. 7. St Peters. 8. St Albans &c. 9. St Maries. 10. St Edmunds. 11. Grey Friars. 12. St Cuthberts. 13. Guild hall. 14. Trinity. 15. St Olaves. 16. St Botolph.

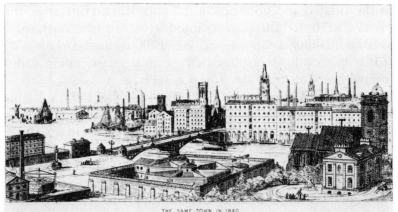

THE SAME TOWN IN 1840.

1. St Michaels Tower rebuilt in 1750. 2. New Parsonage House & Pleasure Grounds. 3. The New Jail. 4. Gas Works. 5. Lunatic Asylum. 6. Iron Works & Ruins of St Maries Abbey. 7. St Evans Chapel. 8. Baptist Chapel. 9. Unitarian Chapel. 10. New Church. 11. New Town Hall & Concert Room. 12. Wesleyan Centenary Chapel. 13. New Christian Society. 14. Quakers Meeting. 15. Socialist Hall of Science.

Fig. 3. The modern degradation of taste. From A. W. N. Pugin, *Contrast*, 2d ed. (1841; rpt. New York: Humanities Press, 1973), n.p.

Fig. 4. Contrast from King's Parade, Cambridge. To the left is James Gibbs's Senate House, 1722–30; to the right is Alfred Waterhouse's Gonville and Caius College, 1868–71.

they were rebelling was artificial, pagan, foreign, and dead, whereas the style they favored was natural, Christian, national, and vital, not exhausted and fossilized, as George Edmund Street emphasized, but having existed in a state of suspended animation from which he and others now meant to resuscitate it.[30]

By reviving the Gothic style of the cultural grandparent, these men would turn architecture back to the true and natural course from which it had been diverted, and in so doing would lead the art of building out of the chaotic morass in which it was presently mired. This is the practical goal of the Revivalists that makes them something more than "dreamers of dreams born out of due time"; this is the aesthetic aspect of that larger motive impelling the Young Englanders and the Tractarians. We see this most important motive in George Gilbert Scott, who writes in mid-century:

> I am no mediaevalist; I do not advocate the styles of the middle ages as such. If we had a distinctive architecture of our own day worthy of the greatness of our age, I should be content to follow it; but we have not; and the middle ages having been the latest period which possessed a style of its own, and that style having been in part the property of our own country, I strongly hold that it has greater *prima facie* claims to be used as the nucleus of our developments than those of ancient Greece or Rome.[31]

It is typical of later neo-Gothic architects to disclaim dedication to Gothic per se and to profess instead devotion to architecture and art in general. For them Gothic architecture is not necessarily and absolutely the best style, but the Gothic is best for restoring architecture to the condition from which its natural progress might resume and lead to other forms. As T. G. Jackson says later in the century:

> The real and proper end of the revival of a bygone style is an indirect result from it; namely, the recovery of that artistic temper by which men will be led to express themselves in their work with truth, force, and feeling, just as their forefathers once did by means of that style which is now adopted for revival. The task that is set before us of the nineteenth century is not the revival of this or that particular style; it is something far wider than that: it is nothing less than the revival of art itself. We have to learn once more to look to art as a ready outlet for ideas, and a natural vehicle for thought; to regard it as an instrument to be used, not a curiosity to be

looked at; the equal heritage of all men, not an appanage of wealth and learning.[32]

There is at the end of this passage, incidentally, that democratic element which played so large a part in justifying the Gothic as expression and property of all the people instead of an aristocratic few, which had been the case with neoclassic art.

Finally, we see the motive quite explicitly stated after the turn of the century by Ralph Adams Cram, who asks,

> What is the meaning of the return to Gothic, not only in form, but "in spirit and in truth"? Is it that we are pleased with its forms and wearied of others? Not at all. It is simply this, that the Renaissance-Reformation-Revolution having run its course, and its epoch having reached its appointed term, we go back, deliberately, or instinctively,—back, as life goes back, as history goes back, to restore something of the antecedent epoch, to win again something we had lost, to return to the fork in the roads, to gain again the old lamps we credulously bartered for new.[33]

It is not the intent of the Revivalists, Cram says, to "re-create an amorphous mediaevalism and live listlessly in that fool's paradise," but rather, like a man faced with the obstacle of a narrow stream, to back up, get a running start, and clear the barrier at a bound: "We are getting our running start, we are retracing our steps to the great Christian Middle Ages, not that there we may remain, but that we may achieve an adequate point of departure; what follows must take care of itself."[34]

In view of these statements by Scott, Jackson, and Cram, we should reassess the usual attitude toward the Gothic Revival, common from its beginning to the present, that it is essentially retrogressive.[35] One might claim, to the contrary, that many of the exponents of the Revival believed as fully in the new idea of progress, especially evolutionary progress, as those who accused them of being perverse and musty antiquarians; for although it is true that they went backward, they did so only that they might move architecture off its dead center and propel it forward once more. In *The Prelude*, when Wordsworth describes the terrible despair into which his soul had fallen, he tells us that he regained his spiritual health only by recalling certain "spots of time" from his youth. By means of retrospection he was able to emerge from his "Center of Indifference" and to continue with his growth; no less did the leaders of the Gothic Revival mean to move architecture forward out of its malaise by first going backward. There is really nothing inconsistent in Pugin's motto, *"En Avant."*

III. ARCHITECTURAL ANTIQUARIANISM—THE PROBLEM OF COPYING

> The more progressive artists of the day are denounced by mere antiquaries as rash innovators, and by their opponents as mere archaeological copyists. The truth is, that their advance is made from a new starting-point which they could only reach by a preliminary retrogression. (Benjamin Webb, "The Prospects of Art in England")

> It may be that many among our revivalists keep too long in leading strings, and that we want an occasional spur to make us strike boldly forward and develope for ourselves, and to make the revived art more decidedly our own; but this is a very different thing from decrying all we are doing as mere blind servility. (G. G. Scott, "Copyism in Gothic Architecture")

At the very beginning of *A Laodicean* (1881), Thomas Hardy introduces his protagonist, the young architect George Somerset, engaged upon a sketching tour in which he is copying down the details of ancient buildings. Since Hardy told a friend that this novel "contained more of the facts of his own life than anything else he had ever written," one may assume that Hardy's architectural apprenticeship, like that of so many other Victorian architects, was similarly employed in learning his craft from the rich heritage of his country's buildings. Paul Thompson reports that for William Butterfield "the examination of old buildings was by far the most valuable part of an architect's education, and he had begun his own career with an intensive study of this kind."[36] In a sort of Victorian version of Wordsworth's "The Tables Turned," the *Builder* counsels that "Gothic architecture is not to be learnt from books and illustrations, but from examples themselves. . . ."[37] The sight of a young architectural student busily sketching away before an old Gothic pile must have been a fairly familiar part of the Victorian landscape, for if Gothic was to be revived, it must first be learned from what had survived the ravages of time and Cromwell.

Behind these students stood the age-old artistic habit of learning from predecessors. Horace had advised in *On the Art of Poetry*, "Give your days and nights to the study of Greek models." In the preface to *Annus Mirabilis*, Dryden proudly acknowledged his debt to Virgil: "I have followed him everywhere, I know not with what success, but I am sure with diligence enough; my images are many of them copied from him, and the rest are imitations of him." And we know from the scores of "Imitations" surviving in the works of English poets that students well into the nineteenth century were taught to write by modeling their compositions on Greek and Roman authors.

But was not copying incompatible with the Revivalist doctrine, and with Romantic theory in general, as evidenced by "The Tables Turned," that art should derive immediately from nature? Did copying not commit the same sin of artificiality with which neoclassic art was charged? In the field of literature, the accusation had been made by Henry Mackensie in *The Lounger*: "another bad consequence of this servile imitation of the ancients . . . has been to prevent modern authors from studying nature as it is, from attempting to draw it as it really appears; and, instead of giving genuine descriptions, it leads them to give those only which are false and artificial" (10 October 1785). In painting Holman Hunt chose as an epigraph for chapter 6 of *Pre-Raphaelitism and the Pre-Raphaelite Brotherhood* this quotation from Leonardo's *Trattato della Pittura*: "I say to painters, Never imitate the manner of another; for thereby you become the grandson instead of the son of Nature." For many others, however, the problem had been solved long ago by Pope. Pope no less than Wordsworth believed that the chief rule for the artist was to "follow Nature," although he of course understood the word in a different way, and he had in *An Essay on Criticism* reconciled the dictum with the equally potent tradition of following the ancients by maintaining that classical authors were in much closer touch with nature than writers in more civilized times and that, as Virgil discovered, "Nature and Homer were . . . the same." Therefore, he can recommend,

"Learn hence for ancient rules a just esteem;/To copy Nature is to copy them." Although George Gilbert Scott does not make as complete an identification between the two, he nevertheless believes that they are closely related when he advises architects to learn from old buildings, "not studying Nature *through* them, but only using them as *helps* in the study and application of lessons learned from the fountain-head. . . ."[38]

Despite Dryden's claim to have followed Virgil so closely, there was in his time, even when originality had not attained to the inflated premium of the nineteenth century, a clear difference between the unimaginative and servile practice of copying and the freer adaptation of imitating. Pope wrote his mentor Walsh on this matter: "I would beg your opinion, too, as to another point: it is how far the liberty of borrowing may extend? . . . A mutual commerce makes poetry flourish; but then poets, like merchants, should repay with something of their own what they take from others; not, like pirates, make prize of all they meet" (2 July 1706). In the middle of the next century, Ruskin echoed almost exactly these words, even using the same image, in *The Seven Lamps of Architecture*: "It is no sign of deadness in a present art that it borrows or imitates, but only if it borrows without paying interest. . . ."[39] Finally, George Edmund Street applied the advice more directly to architecture and the practice of sketching as a way of learning:

> The value of ancient examples for educational purposes cannot be overestimated. But they must be used and not abused; for individuality is a necessity in a great artist, and copyism is the almost infallible sign of a bad one. This, however, does not make it any the less advisable for the architect to register in his memory or in his sketch-book the beauties which are all around him. . . .[40]

That Street should feel it necessary to issue this warning indicates that architects were borrowing "without paying interest," and there is plenty of evidence to support the view that in their zeal for correctness many Revivalists adhered narrowmindedly to precedent. At the very outset of the Revival, this had not been true. Walpole's Strawberry Hill, which Beckford deprecated as "a Gothic mouse-trap," was so free in its adaptation of Gothic designs that T. G. Jackson could later deny its importance in the history of the Revival: "There was, therefore, no more chance of Strawberry Hill bringing about a revival of Gothic than of the Pavilion at Brighton introducing the general use of Hindoo architecture, for one was as little Gothic as the other Indian."[41] But after Thomas Rickman had classified the several stages of Gothic style in *Attempt to Discriminate the Styles of English Architecture* (1819), and after the elder Pugin and E. J. Willson furnished correct models in *Specimens of Gothic Architecture* (1821), and after the Revival had developed into a serious cause, correctness became an architectural watchword. The Reverend Alfred Barry, son of Sir Charles, wrote that during the thirties and forties "'correctness' was everything, and any innovations were ruthlessly hunted down as heretical."[42] At about the same time (1845), a writer to the *Builder* complained that "there seems to be a general feeling against every thing new in architectural design; and unless we have a precedent for what we do, it is not correct and does not please."[43]

The antiquarian spirit, which played so influential a part of the Revival in its early stages and which, as Geoffrey Scott has pointed out, "attaches an undue importance to detail,"[44] manifested itself no less conspicuously in other areas as part of the developing historical conscience of Victorian England. Roy Strong has commented that in historical painting an anachronism became "little short of a crime against art itself," and offers support in Sir Samuel Rush Meyrick's statement in 1836 that "an anachronism in an historical picture is as offensive to the eye of taste as is an imperfect metaphor or a defective verse to the ear."[45] In 1850 Ford Madox Brown wrote in the *Germ* that the historical painter should become thoroughly familiar with the times he seeks to depict so that all the details may be accurately portrayed ("On the Mechanism of a Historical Picture," February 1850). In literature Walter Scott based descriptions on actual buildings and insisted upon the historical accuracy of his novels in prefaces and notes. J. W. Mackail in his biography of William Morris attributed the failure of "Sigurd the Volsung" to Morris's being "bound by an almost impossible loyalty to his original," Morris apparently forgetting the advice he once gave his daughter, "When you are using an old story, read it through, then shut the book and write in your own way." In the theater Charles Kemble and Charles Kean performed Shakespeare in accurate costumes. William Burges objected to an actor's holding his shield on a straight arm instead of properly on a crooked arm and concluded that because of this and many other examples "a theatre is not quite the place to make an antiquary happy."[46]

If architectural correctness owed something to antiquarianism in general, it also was associated with the scientific exactitude of paleontology whereby ancient buildings become fossils and architects comparative anatomists. As he toured de Stancy castle with its new owner, who wished to restore it, the young architect George Somerset "pointed out where roofs had been and should be again, where gables had been pulled down, and where floors had vanished, showing her how to reconstruct their details from marks in the walls, much as a comparative anatomist reconstructs an antediluvian from fragmentary bones and teeth" (Hardy, *A Laodicean*). Arthur Edmund Street remarked that his father's knowledge of old buildings enabled him to reconstruct them even "as some learned man will construct an entire prehistoric animal from a fossil footprint" and quoted Thomas Drew, a Dublin architect, on Christ Church Cathedral: "To Mr. George E. Street's marvellous instinct for the comparative anatomy, as I may term it of an ancient building, and profound architectural erudition, we owe the recreation of the perfect and unique twelfth and thirteenth century church from the merest shreds of evidence."[47] Applying this skill in a somewhat different area, Street was one of the first to suggest the purpose of the walls in the Colosseum floor, which archaeologists had recently uncovered. Interestingly, so popular was the Victorian fascination with fossils that the analogy was extended to literature as well. In his *History of English Literature* (trans. 1873), Hippolyte Taine compared an old piece of writing to "a fossil shell, an imprint, like one of those shapes embossed in stone by an animal which lived and perished"; and in "The Critic as Artist" (1891), Oscar Wilde claimed that "criticism can recreate the past for us from the very smallest fragment of language or art, just as surely as the man of science can from some tiny bone, or the mere impress of a foot upon a rock, recreate for us the winged dragon or Titan lizard. . . ." My chief point here is that these analogies reflect the antiquarian approach to architecture, which valued so highly detailed correctness, but we might notice at the same time that they signify two other important features of the Revival. First, the associated interests in paleontology and archaeology help explain the Victorian concept of modern buildings as future fossils and ruins to be examined by the New Zealander who would come in some distant age. The acute awareness of the mutability of all things, revealed in FitzGerald's "Rubaiyat" and Pater's "Conclusion" to *The Renaissance*, caused Ruskin and Browning to warn that England's greatness would fade no less surely than that of Venice, and led the Victorians to believe that their own monuments would remain to be studied even as they themselves studied the relics of earlier times. Second, these analogies point up the subject of chapter 3, which deals with the aesthetic doctrine of expressionism. The Victorians believed, as did the Romantics before them, that art reflects the character of an artist and his society. It follows, therefore, that a work of art is an index to the artist and his age just as surely as the fossil reveals the animal. It is not simply, then, that the Victorians were concerned about what posterity would think of the buildings in themselves but about what posterity would think of the Victorians as they were revealed in those buildings.

In addition to the historical and scientific trends reflected in architecture and the other arts, there are specifically aesthetic causes for antiquarianism in building. Nikolaus Pevsner has suggested that one of these lies in the materialistic and ignorant Victorian public, which was incapable of appreciating art for any reasons other than its accuracy. In Pevsner's words, "Accurate copying of period detail could appeal strongly. . . . For whereas to risk verdicts on artistic merit seemed unsafe and also a little dubious, accuracy could be checked and hence evaluated."[48] I must admit to some skepticism about this argument, for it is doubtful that the Victorians of whom Pevsner speaks could draw fine distinctions between middle pointed and perpendicular, or that many would, like Burges, object to a shield held on a straight arm.[49] A more convincing reason may be derived from T. G. Jackson's statement that "the first danger that besets the revival of a dead style arises from an excessive regard for precedent; from that blind imitation of the letter or outward form of the adopted art, which is so much more common because it is so much easier than the intelligent study of the spirit and principles which once animated it. . . ."[50] What we may infer from this passage and from the prevalence of copyism at the beginning rather than at the end of the Revival is that the preoccupation with precedent and the insistence upon correctness were necessary first steps in learning an art that had been lost. After all, one learns any skill by copying, and it is only after the apprentice at last becomes master that he perceives the principles behind the forms and gains the confidence to break rules the beginner is wise to follow. So it was with the exponents of the Gothic Revival in its earlier stages— they kept very meticulously to precedent because Pugin had not yet taught them the "True Principles." When Pugin announced in *Contrasts* that "the mechanical part of Gothic architecture is pretty well understood, but it is the principles which influenced ancient compositions, and the soul which appears in all the former works, which is so lamentably deficient,"[51] the time had come to progress to the next stage wherein the old forms might be adapted with more originality and freedom. The intolerant views of "preterpluperfect Goths," the limited abilities of lesser architects who could never grasp principles, and the meretricious opportunism of other architects who cared nothing for those principles all collaborated to make antiquarianism tenaciously resistant to the progress Pugin called for, but its responsibility for the unimaginative and sometimes foolish resurrection of old forms should not blind us to the important and absolutely necessary part it played in the Revival. It rescued Gothic from the rococo frivolity of Strawberry

Hill and laid a groundwork that allowed later architects to develop a style based upon "true principles" and that we now acknowledge to be distinctively Victorian. As Sir Joshua Reynolds had recognized earlier, "A confidence in the mechanick produces a boldness in the poetick. He that is sure of the goodness of his ship and tackle puts out fearlessly from the shore; and he who knows, that his hand can execute whatever his fancy can suggest, sports with more freedom in embodying the visionary forms of his own creation" ("Discourse XV").

IV. THE METHOD OF IMITATION—PRINCIPLES AND SPIRIT, NOT RULES AND FORM

> Hitherto, in this country, at least as far as we know, there has not been the slightest attempt to teach architecture on any other basis than that of precedent; and the consequence is, that the minds of most architects are incapable of tracing effects to first principles. . . . (J. C. Loudon, "Forms, Lines, Lights, Shades, and Colours")

> Utter, O some one, the word that shall reconcile Ancient and Modern!
> Arthur Hugh Clough, *Amours de Voyage*

In his survey of the Gothic Revival, Charles Eastlake divided modern Gothic architects into three groups: (1) the Traditional or Correct, who attempted literal reproduction; (2) the Adaptational or Artistic, who modified for modern requirements; (3) the Independent or Eclectic, who believed in a free and unrestrictive application of the style. We have just seen how the first of these three was most influential in the early stages of the Revival; however, in its refusal to give way to the other two, it became the most vulnerable to censure. Looking back from the perspective of 1909, Charles Spooner found that "the greatest mistake [of the Revival] was the attempt to revive the letter of mediaeval art rather than the spirit of it—to reproduce what had been done, rather than to learn the underlying principles. . . ."[52] Furthermore, there was a long-standing prejudice against imitation. Johnson's Imlac had said that "no man was ever great by imitation" (*Rasselas*); A. W. Schlegel had written that "in the fine arts, mere imitation is always fruitless" (*On Dramatic Art and Literature*); and Holman Hunt told Millais in

1846 that "Revivalism . . . is a seeking after dry bones" (*Pre-Raphaelitism and the Pre-Raphaelite Brotherhood*).

But, since one could not disregard precedent altogether, a solution was found in the advice to emulate the artist rather than to copy his work. So in 1759 Edward Young gave this counsel in "Conjectures on Original Composition": "Must we then, you say, not imitate ancient authors? Imitate them by all means; but imitate aright. He that imitates the divine *Iliad* does not imitate Homer; but he who takes the same method which Homer took for arriving at a capacity of accomplishing a work so great." Sir Joshua Reynolds approved of this advice and added that "it is not by laying up in the memory the particular details of any of the great works of art, that any man becomes a great artist, if he stops without making himself master of the general principles on which these works are conducted" ("Discourse XI"). A. W. Schlegel maintained that what we borrow from others must "be born again within us" (*On Dramatic Art and Literature*).

The very same advice—to follow the spirit rather than the letter of earlier artists—was given by the leaders of the Gothic Revival and by none so insistently as Pugin, whose greatest contribution to the Revival may well lie in his delineation of the principles of pointed architecture. At the same time, no other architect was as misrepresented as Pugin, whose eminence attracted the lightning bolts of such enemies as James Fergusson, who, like Ruskin, opposed Pugin on religious grounds but who, unlike Ruskin, compounded his animus with an anti-Gothic bias. Fergusson wrongly accused Pugin of being one of those who attemped to revive the letter of the Gothic style by comparing his architectural work to the theatrical productions of Charles Kean: "What Kean did for the stage, Pugin did for the church. The one reproduced the drama of the Middle Ages with all the correctness and splendour with which it was represented at the Princess's Theatre, and with about the same amount of reality as the other introduced into the building and decoration of the Mediaeval churches of the nineteenth century. . . ."[53] In making these charges Fergusson chose to ignore the title of one of Pugin's books, *The True Principles of Pointed or Christian Architecture*, and the many statements throughout his other books to the effect that one must imitate in spirit only. Pugin fully realized that Gothic architecture was not to be revived by simply re-creating the forms and details of the old style. As he says in *Contrasts*:

> And now I cannot dismiss this subject without a few remarks on those who seem to think, that, by restoring the details and accessories of pointed architecture, they are reviving Catholic art. Not at all. *Unless the ancient arrangement be restored*, and the *true principles carried out*, all mouldings, pinnacles, tracery, and details, be they ever so well executed, are a mere disguise.[54]

Like Young and Reynolds, Pugin believed that the answer lay in emulating the artist, not in copying the work: *"for we do not wish to produce mere servile imitators of former excellence of any kind, but men imbued with the consistent spirit of the ancient architects, who would work on their principles, and carry them out as the old men would have done, had they been placed in similar circumstances, and with similar wants to ourselves."*[55]

Later in the century T. G. Jackson was to make the same appeal. It is no more desirable nor possible, Jackson said, to restore Gothic art in its exact form than it is to bring back the Crusades or trial by ordeal. In attacking what he calls "Formalism and Purism," Jackson singled out those who "mistake superficial features for essential elements" and held, as had Pugin before him, that "traceried windows and pointed arches did not make Gothic architecture then, nor will they now." Instead, then, of obeying the letter of the style, architects should "catch the spirit of the old work" and "master the principles which made it what it was. . . ."[56] Others, too, followed Pugin's advice. Scott, Street, Burges, and Butterfield all gave the principles of medieval design precedence over exact models, indicating, as I have suggested, that antiquarianism in architecture continued after it had served its purpose of establishing correct precedents not in the hands of the leaders of the movement but in those of its lesser, unremembered followers.

In other areas there is a similar insistence on the importance
of spirit over letter in the use of precedent. One of Owen
Jones's propositions for the decorative arts is, "The principles
discoverable in the works of the past belong to us; not so the
results. It is taking the end for the means."[57] In literature
Arthur Henry Hallam as early as 1831 made the same point in
commenting on Tennyson's "The Ballad of Oriana":

> We know no more happy seizure of the antique spirit in the whole compass
> of our literature. . . . The author is well aware that the art of one genera-
> tion cannot *become* that of another by any will or skill; but the artist may
> transfer the spirit of the past, making it a temporary form for his own
> spirit, and so effect, by idealizing power, a new and legitimate combina-
> tion. ("On Some of the Characteristics of Modern Poetry and on the Lyri-
> cal Poems of Alfred Tennyson")

Swinburne, who had objected to the license with which Tennyson adapted the Arthurian legends in *The Idylls of the King*,
nevertheless maintained in his essay on Hugo's "L'Année terrible" that the artist should treat the past "not by mechanical
and servile transcript as of a copying clerk, but by loving and
reverent emulation as of an orginal fellow-craftsman."

With their belief in following the spirit rather than the letter
of the Gothic style, it is not surprising that many of these
architects fell into that category defined by Eastlake as "Adaptational or Artistic." Not only was the modification of the old
style a matter of artistic integrity for an architect whose creative
instincts would not be satisfied with mere copying, but also it
was a matter of practical expediency since these men were
quick to realize that unless the neo-Gothic could fulfill the functional needs of modern people and provide them with the comfort to which they were fast growing accustomed, it would
never gain the popularity required for its success. In *A Laodicean* Dare tells his father, Captain de Stancy, that the Captain's
failure to win the hand of the newly rich Paula Power means
the end of their family line: "We de Stancys are a worn-out old
party—that's the long and short of it. We represent conditions
of life that have had their day—especially me. Our one remaining chance was an alliance with new aristocrats; and we have

failed. We are past and done for." When, at the end of the novel, Dare burns down de Stancy castle, now owned by Paula Power and recently restored by her, Hardy implies that the old architecture will perish along with the old families unless it too can somehow be married to the new and vital. However, when George Somerset suggests to Paula that they plant ivy about the charred ruins and build a new house on eclectic principles, the reader surmises that Hardy is pessimistic about the chances for a union between old and new.

Others were no less skeptical about the adaptability of Gothic to modern conditions, and many of these opposed the Revival on religious grounds, feeling that the old, Gothic arrangements in churches were Catholic in design and ill-suited for Protestant worship. Alfred Barry tells us, for example, Sir Charles "felt strongly that the forms of mediaeval art, beautiful as they are, do not always adapt themselves thoroughly to the needs of a service which is essentially one of 'Common Prayer.' Deep chancels, high rood-screens, and (in less degree) pillared aisles, seemed to him to belong to the worship and institutions of the past rather than the present."[58] Barry adds in a note that his father and Pugin not surprisingly disagreed on this matter. James Fergusson found Gothic unsuitable for Protestant services, as he found it unsuitable for all other purposes; and Ruskin, who attempted to reconcile the Gothic with the Protestant, was compelled to admit that Gothic was more appropriate to Catholic worship. Representative of the ordinary citizen's distrust of Gothic as tending toward Rome is a letter to the *Builder* in which Thomas Goodchild writes that churches should be designed "for seeing and hearing," leaving off "the fopperies of image worship" as out of place in "an enlighted nation adoring the Great One."[59] Some, on the other hand, objected to Gothic on functional grounds, feeling that the old forms simply would not satisfy modern requirements. Richard Norman Shaw, who had begun his career in Gothic architecture, later explained his rejection of it by saying that "it is totally unsuited to modern requirements. When it came to building, especially in places like the City, we found it would not answer."[60]

However, those faithful to the Revival—Burges, Butterfield, Webb, Jackson, Scott, Pugin, Ruskin, Street, Viollet-le-Duc in France, Cram in America—all believed that Gothic could be adapted to modern needs, even as on the other side Charles Robert Cockerell believed that classical could be practically applied. Pugin belies his reputation as a narrow-minded zealot when he writes that "any modern invention which conduces to comfort, cleanliness, or durability, should be adopted by the consistent architect; *to copy a thing merely because it is old, is just as absurd as the imitations of the modern pagans.*"[61] Ruskin similarly recommended that one who borrows from the past do so with audacity, by which he means "the unhesitating and sweeping sacrifice of precedent where precedent becomes inconvenient."[62] But more than any other writer, George Gilbert Scott championed Gothic as a flexible and universal style of architecture. In *Remarks on Secular and Domestic Architecture*, Scott sought to remove from the Revival the stigma of antiquarian impracticality by demonstrating that Gothic was perfectly suitable to modern times; and, further, he attempted to secure for the style a broader application and acceptance by claiming its appropriateness for buildings other than ecclesiastical. In the introduction to the book, Scott declares that pointed architecture is " pre-eminently free, comprehensive, and practical; ready to adapt itself to every change in the habits of society, to embrace every new material or system of construction, and to adopt implicitly and naturally, and with hearty good will, every invention or improvement, whether artistic, constructional, or directed to the increase of comfort and convenience."[63] And with the belief that Gothic was not only receptive to modern developments in building but also was adaptable to secular purposes, Scott spoke against "the absurdity of the theory that one style is suited to churches and another to houses," arguing against the prevailing opinion that Gothic was proper for churches, but classic was the style for public buildings. The choice for domestic houses was more open, but Italian Renaissance was making inroads there as we see in Osborne House, designed in 1844 by Thomas Cubitt and Prince Albert.

Fig. 5. An example of how the Gothic style could meet contemporary requirements. This office building has obvious Gothic features yet a surprisingly modern appearance. Oriel Chambers, Liverpool, by Peter Ellis, 1864.

The Goths having pretty well won the Battle of Styles on the ecclesiastical front, Scott at the height of the controversy in the late fifties and early sixties intended to extend the influence of the Revival by making claims on secular and domestic buildings. The one great victory behind him was the New Houses of Parliament; ahead lay the successes of Waterhouse's Manchester Assize Courts and the New Law Courts, although the latter was personally disappointing to Scott, who was passed over in the competition in favor of Street. But more immediately loomed the crushing defeat of the Foreign Office at the hands of Palmerston, a defeat only partially assuaged by having his way with the Gothic design of the St. Pancras Hotel at the end of the next decade. There was greater success with domestic buildings, and Tennyson's explanation in 1892 of his preference for Gothic—"It is like blank verse; it will suit the humblest cottage and the grandest cathedral" (*Tennyson and His Friends*)—witnesses to the durability and pervasiveness of the idea. Scott's book, therefore, and the Revivalists' emphasis on the adaptability of Gothic that it reflects, should be considered as an offensive in the Battle of the Styles as well as a reaction to the literal copyism of antiquarians within their own ranks.

Before proceeding to the third category of architects Eastlake established, we might conclude by asking how precisely the old could be adapted to the new. One area that gives insight into the matter is windows—how could the pointed arches of casement windows be made to accommodate the far more convenient sashes that had been developed in the seventeenth century? Ruskin addressed the problem in *The Stones of Venice* by saying there was no reason a sash could not be fitted into a pointed arch. "There is not the smallest necessity," he argued, "because the arch is pointed, that the aperture should be so. The work of the arch is to sustain the building above; when this is once done securely, the pointed head of it may be filled in any way we choose."[64] T. G. Jackson, however, less dedicated to the pointed arch as an essential feature of Gothic architecture and freer in his application of the old style, felt there was no need for the compromise since a sashed window in an arched

Fig. 6. Philip Webb's Red House, Bexleyheath, Kent, 1859–60. Reproduced by permission of the National Monuments Record, London.

frame is a sham and, besides, weakens the arches. One simply should use a lintel and forget about arches.[65] In the house he built for William Morris, Philip Webb utilized both methods, designing some of the windows of Red House according to Ruskin's advice and some according to Jackson's. But whatever the approach, for all three Gothic was capable of incorporating the advantage of a sash window.

The third school of architects designated by Eastlake, the Eclectic, was yet more liberal than the Adaptational in its treatment of Gothic although it, like both the Adaptational and the Traditionalist, attempted to find a solution to "the carnival of architecture." But though Eclecticism was similar to the other two groups in seeking an answer to the problem, it was different in that its fundamental approach to art had been in large measure responsible for the problem in the first place. Had the Victorians not had something of an eclectic temperament, they would never have been so hospitably receptive to the several styles that struggled for recognition and that added to the artistic confusion of the age.

There are at least two forces behind the eclectic proclivity of the Victorian period: one is diversitarianism and the other is the proliferation of knowledge. Of the first of these, Arthur O. Lovejoy has written that "the shift from the uniformitarian to the diversitarian preconception [is] the most significant and distinctive single feature of the Romantic revolution. . . ."[66] As we have already seen, the shift from the uniformitarian outlook to the diversitarian played an important part in changing historical studies. In aesthetics the turnabout was no less influential. The neoclassicist tended to apply universal and absolute aesthetic values, believing along with Johnson's Imlac that the poet "must consider right and wrong in their abstracted and invariable state; he must disregard present laws and opinions, and rise to general and transcendental truths, which will always be the same . . . " (*Rasselas*). Practically, this meant an appreciation of the ancients, who were close to Nature, and a disapproval of medieval times when the atrophy of reason blinded men to the precepts of Nature. When the change described by Lovejoy occurred, people began to apply relative standards out of a belief that each age is unique and must be evaluated on its own special terms. Practically, this meant an appreciation of medieval artists, who came to be regarded not as having deviated from the universal rules of General Nature but as having followed the principles of a particular and mutable Nature peculiar to their own times.

With this aspect of Romanticism, or with that of any cultural movement for that matter, manifestations appear long before the trait reaches full bloom; and as far back as Dryden, one may find evidence of relative standards. During the last quarter of the seventeenth century, Dryden wrote in *Heads of an Answer to Rymer* that "the climate, the age, the disposition of the people, to whom a poet writes, may be so different, that what pleased the Greeks would not satisfy an English audience." In 1754 Thomas Warton defended *The Faerie Queene* with the opinion that "it is absurd to think of judging either Ariosto or Spenser by precepts which they did not attend to" ("Observations on the Faerie Queene of Spenser"). Eight years later Bishop Hurd made a similar defense of Spenser in *Letters on Chivalry and Romance* and argued for Gothic architecture on the same principles:

> when an architect examines a *Gothic* structure by *Grecian* rules, he finds nothing but deformity. But the *Gothic* architecture has its own rules, by which when it comes to be examined, it is seen to have its own merit, as well as the *Grecian*. The question is not, which of the two is conducted in the simplest or truest taste: but whether there be not sense and design in both, when scrutinized by the laws on which each is projected.

With the coming of Romanticism, eclectic values become a typical feature of criticism. In the first decade of the new century, A. W. Schlegel echoed the opinions of Warton and Hurd in *On Dramatic Art and Literature*:

> We will quarrel with no man for his predilection either for the Grecian or the Gothic. The world is wide, and affords room for a great diversity of objects. Narrow and blindly adopted prepossessions will never constitute a genuine critic or connoisseur, who ought, on the contrary, to possess the power of dwelling with liberal impartiality on the most discrepant views, renouncing the while all personal inclinations.

At the end of the century, writers were still proclaiming the eclectic ideal. Walter Pater based his belief "that in literature as in other matters it is well to unite as many diverse elements as may be" ("Postscript," *Appreciations*) on his earlier statement in the preface to *The Renaissance* that for a critic "beauty exists in many forms. To him all periods, types, schools of taste, are in themselves equal. In all ages there have been some excellent workmen, and some excellent work done." Similarly, Oscar Wilde wrote under Pater's influence in the last decade that the true critic "will seek for beauty in every age and in each school . . . " ("The Critic as Artist").

With so much emphasis upon catholicity of taste, it is no wonder that architects were influenced toward an eclectic approach; but there was a second determinant at work leading in the same direction, and that was the proliferation of knowledge. Superficial it may have been, as Mill commented in "The Spirit of the Age," but profuse as never before it nonetheless was. "We live," Robert Kerr observed in 1864, "in the era of *Omnium-Gatherum*; all the world's a museum, and men and women are its students." The aptness of the metaphor is borne out by the number of museums erected during the course of the century, and the availability of so much new information made eclectism almost inevitable. Kerr goes on to say that the architectural style of the present is one of "miscellaneous connoisseurship,—the style of instinct superseded by knowledge,—a state of things characteristic of our age as no other state of things could be characteristic of it."[67] Others also attributed eclecticism to the diffusion of knowledge. Pater spoke of "an intellectually rich age such as ours being necessarily an eclectic one" ("Postscript," *Appreciations*), and *The Builder* perceived an "Eclectic revival" replacing the revivals of classic and Gothic and owing its rise to the fact that "the vast extension of modern art-knowledge has brought about a possession of almost world-wide forms of art, which with astonishing and the most elastic adaptation have appeared in recent architecture. . . ."[68]

As I have already said, eclecticism both contributed to the architectural confusion and provided a way out of the labyrinth. It contributed simply by making available a plethora of styles such as had never before perplexed architects, who had but one style from which to choose and for whom the question of style was meaningless. An eighteenth-century architect would have as naturally and unhesitatingly chosen Palladian as a medieval one chose Gothic, but when Hardy's George Somerset was beginning his career, he had been unable to decide which of the architectural styles "that were coming and going in kaleidoscopic change was the point of departure for himself. He had suffered from the modern malady of unlimited appreciativeness as much as any living man of his own age" (*A Laodicean*). Robert Kerr wrote that current architecture "exists in utter bewilderment. Much learning hath made it mad."[69] And it was bewildering not only for the architect, who must choose and execute, but also for the client, who must determine which style best suited him. In an imaginary dialogue with a perplexed client who wants only "a Plain, substantial, comfortable *Gentleman's House*," Kerr's architect offers these choices:

> You can have *Classical*, columnar or non-columnar, arcuated or trabeated, rural or civil, or indeed palatial; you can have *Elizabethan* in equal variety; *Renaissance* ditto; or, not to notice minor modes, Mediaeval in any one of its multifarious forms, eleventh century or twelfth, thirteenth or fourteenth, whichever you please,—feudalistic or monastic, scholastic or ecclesiastic, archaeological or ecclesiologistic, and indeed a good many more.[70]

Such a cornucopia of architectural riches might drive the most omnivorous dilettante in search of simpler fare.

At the same time, however, that it was partially responsible for the architectural chaos of the era, eclecticism sought a solution to the problem in a new style that would be a composite of the old ones. If returning to an old and lifeless style was out of the question and if no wholly new style was possible until constructional technology produced one, then this approach was indeed the only alternative remaining. In refuting Coleridge's distinction between the fancy, which combines, and the im-

agination, which creates, Poe had argued that "all novel con-
ceptions are merely unusual combinations. The mind of man
can imagine nothing which has not really existed . . . " ("Fancy
and Imagination"). This attitude is the basis of the Eclectics'
faith that a new style could—in fact, could only—be derived
from combinations of the old ones. T. L. Davidson, professor
of architecture at University College, London, put the solution
most clearly when he said in 1842 that "we are wandering in a
labyrinth of experiment and trying by an amalgamation of certain features in this or that style of each and every period and
country to form a homogeneous whole with some distinctive
character of its own, for the purpose of working it out into its
fullest development, and thus creating a new and peculiar
style."[71]

How this solution might be practically effected, however, was
a matter of much less general agreement, and one could hardly
expect otherwise of a group of liberal-minded men whose very
philosophy rested on individualism. Nor, despite their protests
of impartiality, did they propose an eclectic style as distinctive
as they desired, for old prejudices invariably intruded in the
form of one style dominating the composition. Fergusson advocated Italian, Jackson recommended Gothic, and Ruskin, Scott,
and Kerr foresaw a merger of Gothic and classic, which for
Ruskin and Scott would be preponderantly Gothic and which
for all three would have the added advantage of resolving the
Battle of the Styles. But the truce was never signed, and about
the only agreement between the Gothicists and Classicists was
founded on their mutual disapproval of the one, distinctive
eclectic style, the Queen Anne. Mark Girouard has described
the development of this style in the 1870s by such architects as
George Frederick Bodley, J. J. Stevenson, E. R. Robson,
Richard Norman Shaw, and William Eden Nesfield; its affilia-
tion with the Art-for-Art's-Sake movement; and its eventual
eclipse at the turn of the century.[72] A mixture of Queen Anne,
Dutch, and Flemish; espoused by young, apostate Goths who
preserved a distrust of symmetry; sometimes called "Free
Classic"; Queen Anne architecture was the only truly eclectic

Fig. 7. Richard Norman Shaw's New Zealand Chambers, Leadenhall Street, London (1871–73). An early example of the Queen Anne style. Reproduced by permission of the National Monuments Record, London.

style of the age. But if this particular style did not survive the century, the eclectic principle that fostered it did. Looking back from the perspective of his old age in the early twentieth century, T. G. Jackson remarked, "We are now become eclectic and smile at the simple and narrow enthusiasms of our callow age."[73] Today the choices offered by Kerr's architect to his client shrink in comparison with those offered a prospective home-builder, who no doubt wonders why his Victorian forebears made such a to-do about style.

V. THE BURDEN OF THE PAST

Poeta nascitur, non fit.

> The Waterbeetle here shall teach
> A sermon far beyond your reach:
> He flabbergasts the Human Race
> By gliding on the water's face
> With ease, celerity and grace;
> *But if he ever stopped to think*
> *Of how he did it, he would sink.*
>   Hillaire Belloc, "A Moral Alphabet"

When people talk most about Work of Art, generally speaking at that period they do least in art. (William Morris, "The English Pre-Raphaelites")

Diverse though the three schools of architecture may have been in the means by which they meant to solve the problem confronting them, the ultimate goal for all of them was the same: to establish a distinctive style of architecture, and to do so, moreover, by returning to the past either as a point of departure or as a quarry from which to mine elements that were to be newly combined. Their retrospection was supported by the artistic tradition of using precedents, a Romantic love of remoteness, and a sense of insecurity requiring an acknowledged authority for guidance. As we have seen, the knowledge they culled in their antiquarian research recoiled upon them in that although it provided them with the necessary material, it also aggravated the problem by contributing to their uncertainty and confusion. But the abundance of architectural precedents militated against the success of their goal in another way, too, for the Revivalists found themselves hooked on the Romantic dilemma of a twin emphasis on precedent and originality that W. Jackson Bate has discussed in *The Burden of the Past and the English Poet*. Fuseli's *The Artist Moved by the Grandeur of Ancient Ruins* or Keats's reaction to the Elgin Marbles summarizes Bate's theme that, caught in the Romantic conflict between revering the past and being original, the poet came ambivalently to regard the past both as help and as burden. No less did the Victorian architect find himself caught in the same trap, discovering that the end was thwarted by the means.

In its early and more radical form, the problem of knowledge for the artist is that everything has already been done and there remains nothing left to do. Addison gives a good example of this attitude in the *Spectator* when he writes, perhaps with La Bruyère's "Tout est dit" in mind, "It is impossible for us, who live in the latter ages of the world, to make observations in criticism, morality, or in any art or science, which have not been touched upon by others" (20 December 1711). More than a hundred and fifty years later, John Stuart Mill was daunted by the same prospect. Like a young Alexander fearful that his father would leave no worlds to conquer, Mill despaired that there were no undiscovered realms of music:

> I was seriously tormented by the thought of the exhaustibility of musical combinations. The octave consists only of five tones and two semitones, which can be put together in only a limited number of ways, of which but a small proportion are beautiful: most of these, it seemed to me, must have been already discovered, and there could not be room for a long succession of Mozarts and Webers, to strike out as these had done, entirely new and surprisingly rich veins of musical beauty. (*Autobiography*, 1873)

What Mill could not anticipate, and what would scarcely have made him more optimistic, is that once musicians abandoned the standard of beauty, the number of combinations increased and made originality once more possible. The overshadowing achievements of the past loomed over architects as well. George Edmund Street's son, himself an architect, wrote,

> The field of discovery in architecture is exhausted. It is undeniable, as Ruskin tells us, that no principle of construction has been discovered for

centuries. My father thought that Gothic architects had left nothing to be found out worth the finding in construction, and he scoffed at the idea, which some have been bold enough to entertain, that a brand-new Victorian style might be invented, whose birth should rival that of Athene—springing fully armed from the brain of some king of architects.[74]

If nothing new were possible in the arts, what was possible? Refinement was the usual answer. After observing that no new discoveries are possible, Addison concludes that "we have little else left us, but to represent the common sense of mankind in more strong, more beautiful, or more uncommon lights" (*Spectator*, 20 December 1711). Pope, who had been advised by his friend Walsh that he could excel only in correctness, wrote in the same year as Addison his famous lines in *An Essay on Criticism*, "True Wit is Nature to advantage dress'd,/What oft was thought, but ne'er so well express'd." This attitude toward art in the Augustan age furnished Peacock with his description of it in "The Four Ages of Poetry" as the age of silver that followed the golden age of Shakespeare. If matters had rested there, the Revivalists would have found confirmation for their theories and could have been content endlessly refining and correcting the features of Gothic architecture. Unfortunately there is another aspect to this attitude that was to make for serious problems because, while finding solace in the elegance of their compositions, neoclassic writers acknowledged that refinement was both inferior to invention and antithetical to it as well. Addison relied upon the authority of Longinus in saying, "The Productions of a great Genius, with many Lapses and Inadvertencies, are infinitely preferable to the Works of an inferior kind of Author, which are scrupulously exact and conformable to all the Rules of correct Writing" (*Spectator*, 2 February 1711). Pope stressed the observation of rules in *An Essay on Criticism*, but he also admitted that bold writers sometimes "snatch a grace beyond the reach of art"; and in the preface to his translation of *The Iliad* (1715), he recognized that Homer's genius rested on his originality: "It is the invention that in different degrees distinguishes all great geniuses. The utmost stretch of human study, learning, and industry, which master everything besides, can never attain to this." Later in the century Joseph Warton turned the tables, damning Pope with the faint praise that he was "one of the most correct, even, and exact poets that ever wrote" and therefore a lesser poet than Spenser, Shakespeare, and Milton ("An Essay on the Genius and Writings of Pope," 1782). On the one hand, a belief in the superiority of earlier writers based upon a valuation of genius over rules could justify Gothic architecture as the work of a golden age in the same way that it explained the excellence of Shakespeare; but on the other hand, it created a sense of inferiority and hopelessness among writers and architects alike. Romantic primitivism attempted a solution by seeking through a return to nature the restoration of those conditions that made originality possible in a golden age. Although gaining partial success, the attempt was inherently futile, as Coleridge makes clear in faulting Wordsworth's precept of simple language and as Byron shows in "The Island." Once lost the innocence of paradise could not be regained; the wisdom and experience of ages could not be suddenly forgotten, and the nineteenth century found itself condemned to bear the burden of the past.

When Sir Joshua Reynolds claimed in "Discourse VI" that the mind of the artist is inspired and fed by the ideas of his predecessors, he was continuing a tradition that stretched at least as far back as Longinus, who had similarly held that "many authors catch fire from the inspiration of others" (*On the Sublime*), but he was running directly counter to the growing tendency to regard learning as antithetical to originality. Seven years before Reynolds made these claims, William Duff had argued to the contrary that, instead of nurturing creativity, knowledge of other writers makes originality impossible:

> Another effect of learning is, to encumber and overload the mind of an original Poetic Genius. . . . For as no man can attend to and comprehend many different things at once, his mental faculties will in some cases be necessarily oppressed and overcharged with the immensity of his own conceptions, when weighed down by the additional load of learning. The truth is, a Poet of original Genius has very little occasion for the weak aid of Literature: he is self-taught. He comes into the world as it were completely accomplished. ("An Essay on Original Genius," 1767)

Eight years before Duff, Edward Young had objected to learning as an impediment to originality on the slightly different
ground that a study of early writers stifles individuality:

> Illustrious examples engross, prejudice, and intimidate. They engross our
> attention, and so prevent a due inspection of ourselves; they prejudice our
> judgment in favor of their abilities, and so lessen the sense of our own; and
> they intimidate us with the splendor of their renown, and thus under
> diffidence bury our strength. ("Conjectures on Original Composition,"
> 1759)

Ben Jonson had faulted Shakespeare for having "small Latin
and less Greek," that is to say, little formal education. Young
suggested that Shakespeare is preeminent precisely because he
did not labor "under the load of Jonson's learning," and further proposed that "if Milton had spared some of his learning,
his Muse would have gained more glory than he would have
lost by it."

The doctrine of natural genius, especially as put by Duff,
gathered greater force as it flowed into the next century, where
it vitalized so many different features of Romanticism. Like
Young, Macaulay felt that Milton's great learning was a hindrance to his poetical genius but believed that he triumphed
over the handicap and became a great poet in spite of his
education ("Milton," *Edinburgh Review*, August 1825). Some
years later Ruskin wrote in *The Stones of Venice* that Raphael
"painted best when he knew least."[75] As the doctrine spread
into the nineteenth century, it reached out to inform the principles of architecture as well. Street believed that the architects of
old buildings had the advantage of being "much less hampered
and restrained by self-imposed rules than we are."[76] Scott
thought that "our knowledge of all arts which have existed.
. . . absolutely precludes us from generating a perfectly new
art, spontaneously growing as a plant from its seed, as has been
the case in former periods."[77] In advocating the use of Gothic
for domestic buildings, Scott admitted that there were very few
medieval houses left for examples, most of the remains being
churches. But instead of presenting a difficulty to an architect
who has little to copy, the lack of precedents is actually an
advantage since "it leaves more to the imagination and in-

ventive powers of the architect, and leaves him more un-
fettered by precedent to strike out freely such developments as
the practical conditions prescribed to him may suggest."[78]
Finally, Burges reflects something of the Romantic yearning
for an age of innocence when he remarks impatiently, "If some
kind fairy could make a clean sweep of all our existing buildings and all our books on architecture, to say nothing of the
architects, being then left to our own resources we might do
something of our own."[79]

Frequently, the villain in the dissemination of knowledge so
antagonistic to natural and spontaneous genius is criticism, for,
as Matthew Arnold had said, the aid of criticism is *"to learn and
propagate the best that is known and thought in the world"* ("The
Function of Criticism at the Present Time"). But criticism was
antithetical to art in another way, too, for in addition to over-
burdening the natural genius of the artist with the heavy weight
of knowledge, restricting his flight with the shackles of rules,
and daunting his courage with examples of insurmountable
attainments, criticism threatened imaginative creativity with rationalism. I am not talking here about the quarrels between
artists and critics that are so common and well known. Rather, I
mean the opposition of the critical, rational faculty of mind to
the creative, imaginative faculty that is so persistent a theme in
Romantic poetry. On a wider scale than poetry, Carlyle found
that criticism in this sense was as destructive to society at large
as Keats's Apollonius is to Lamia or the man from Porlock to
Coleridge's memory. "The healthy Understanding," Carlyle
wrote in "Characteristics" (1831), "is not the Logical, argu-
mentative, but the Intuitive; for the end of Understanding is
not to prove and find reasons, but to know and believe." The
disease of religion, literature, and society as a whole is attributable to a dependence on the logical instead of the intuitive:

> Never since the beginning of Time was there . . . so intensely self-
> conscious a Society. Our whole relations to the Universe and to our fellow-
> man have become an Inquiry, a Doubt; nothing will go on its on accord,
> and do its function quietly; but all things must be probed into, the whole
> working of man's world be anatomically studied.

This last phrase brings us back to those architects who, by their thorough knowledge of past styles and by their scientific approach, could reconstruct an old building as a comparative anatomist might re-create a prehistoric lizard from the merest shred of evidence. Could it be possible, as some maintained, that the architects who analytically dissected architecture into its many different styles and then subdivided each into its several different phases after the best modern way, were in fact murdering the very creature they meant to revive? Such at least was the opinion of John Sedding, who wrote that before the breach with artistic tradition in the early part of the nineteenth century, "there was no scrutiny, for the simple reason that there were no critics. They did not talk art then, they made it, and enjoyed it as it came. There was no scrutiny, for there was no anxiety; no annual fingering of the nation's art-pulse; no malady to combat. . . ."[80] Carlyle had written in "Characteristics" that "self-contemplation . . . is infallibly the symptom of disease"; but the symptom had developed yet another malady as the analysis that was to find a cure impeded the only true healer—the creative imagination. As architecture entered the twentieth century, Ralph Adams Cram continued the warning against rational analysis, reminding his readers that "the curious inquiries of Calvin wrought hopeless havoc with the heavenly vision of St. Augustine,"[81] but his is one of the last utterances from the deathbed of Romanticism.

Cram's protest is out of date because both functionalism and the change in constructional techniques dictated by the use of new materials had brought about a corresponding shift of emphasis from architecture as an art to architecture as a science. As long as architecture was regarded primarily as an art, it belonged appropriately to the domain of the imagination; but by developing into more of a science, it became the prerogative of analytical reason. Furthermore, as long as architecture was considered mainly as art, the Revivalists found support for their doctrines since architecture could no more be expected to keep up with the giant strides of material progress than could any of the other arts. In 1814 William Hazlitt set down the

primitivistic theory, well established by that time and to be repeated later in Macaulay's "Milton," that whereas science pro-
gresses and therefore flourishes in civilized societies, art often
thrives among more primitive people since it depends on natural genius instead of accumulated learning. In "Why the Arts
Are Not Progressive" (*Morning Chronicle*, 1814), Hazlitt denies
the parallel between art and science by this reasoning: "What is
mechanical, reducible to rule, or capable of demonstration, is
progressive, and admits of gradual improvement: what is not
mechanical or definite, but depends on genius, taste, and feeling, very soon becomes stationary or retrograde, and loses
more than it gains by transfusion." Some years earlier Blake,
who shared the common Romantic notion that geniuses are
born not made, jotted down in his copy of Reynolds's *Discourses*
that if art were progressive, "we should have had Mich. Angelos
& Rafaels to Succeed & to Improve upon each other. But it is
not so. Genius dies with its Possessor & comes not again till
Another is Born with It." The Revivalists employed this sort of
thinking in defense against the growing number of voices calling for a new style befitting an age of scientific developments.
As late as 1886 Henry Van Brunt argued that "architecture is a
fine art upon a basis of science; if it were a pure science, we
could emulate the electrician, the geologist, the political eco-
nomist, the naturalist, the civil engineer. . . ."[82]

Such arguments were becoming more untenable as the century drew to a close, but perhaps they were never really very
effective against a population that expected progress in all
things and that was increasingly impatient with revivalism in
any form. The Gothic Revival, then, came to be threatened
externally by modernism even as it was threatened internally by
the burden of the past. The latter was ironically its own
creation; the former was beyond its control and ultimately
more damaging.

Sir John Soane once sued a man for the libelous accusation
that Soane had introduced a new order of architecture in Re-
gent Street houses. The Gothic Revivalists were less dogmatic,
but they, too, considered the creation of an entirely new style as

"the philosopher's stone of architecture" and blamed the demand for such a thing upon a foolish craving for novelty. Despite their protestations the desire for originality in art was not to be put off, and T. Blashill could count on popular support for his statement in the *Builder* that if modern architecture is to interest future generations, "we must, besides being honest and learned, be original."[83] Nor were all convinced that art and architecture should not be expected to progress along with science. To the contrary, some writers maddeningly persisted in making art answerable to the laws of progress and in wondering why it was perversely disobedient to them. For example, T. Mellard Reade wrote in the *Builder* (1862) that although "giants in science, we are pigmies in art," and eleven years later another architectural critic wrote in the same journal,

> Nature and philosophy, as well as the evaluation of civilization itself, point to a *law of progression*, or a process of education which must be accepted, which Comte, Dr. Spurzheim, Herbert Spenser [*sic*], and a host of our foremost thinkers of modern times have laid down and are elaborating; a process to which modern art and religious thought curiously stand, forsooth, in strange and direct opposition. . . .[84]

The idea of progress undermined the uniqueness of art by denying the regressive theory of a golden age and by repudiating natural genius through its corollary, utilitarian rationalism. For Bentham, Mill, Arnold, and increasing numbers of others, education was the solution to all problems—a man and a society became great because of their learning, not in spite of it. As James Fergusson said, great art, or greatness in any area, depends on the gradual accumulation of knowledge rather than the sudden flash of genius: "The only means by which man ever did any thing great, either in the useful or fine arts, was by this aggregation of experiences. . . . A thousand little steps of a thousand little men, if in advance of one another, will surpass the stride of the greatest intellectual giant the world ever saw. . . ."[85] Another Victorian who believed in artistic progress was Dickens, who in the following year attacked the Pre-Raphaelites for ignoring the lessons to be learned from the past three hundred years of painting ("Old Lamps for New Ones," *Household Words*).

A slightly different perspective on the assimilation of art into the aggregate of human endeavor might be taken by asking how it could now be possible for art to stand beyond the laws of progress when its creators were themselves moving ever upward. In *In Memoriam* Tennyson writes of mankind's spiritual improvement, in *Culture and Anarchy* Arnold speaks of realizing our best selves, and in *An Historical Inquiry* Fergusson says that we should "progress and perfect ourselves, for this is our true mission on the face of the globe. . . ."[86] If man was progressing toward perfection and if, according to the expressive theory, art reflects the man, then it follows that art should be advancing, too. At times, however, it was doubtful that man's moral and spiritual development was any more in step with the abundantly clear material progress than art was, for an age that Carlyle and Arnold described as diseased could hardly be on the path to perfection. Tennyson suggested a resolution to the paradox when King Arthur consoles Sir Bedivere after the fall of Camelot with the words, "The old order changeth, yielding place to new, / And God fulfils himself in many ways . . ." ("The Passing of Arthur"). Perhaps the turbulence of modern life was a necessary transitional moment in the long-range evolution forward. Samuel Huggins holds out the same hope in the midst of architectural chaos: "The dissolution of old styles may have been but preparation for new and more glorious ones, and not the general decline of architecture in the world."[87]

The idea of progress naturally restored self-confidence to artists, who had long suffered from a sense of inferiority imposed by the regressive theories of a golden age. We see, for example, a self-assertive pride in William Richard Lethaby's boast that "an age that can produce Watts' Physical Energy, Madox Brown's Manchester paintings, and the Forth Bridge, should be able to produce anything. . . ."[88] The pendulum of opinion was swinging back to the attitude of a hundred years earlier that the Middle Ages were savage and barbaric. Mark Twain's Connecticut Yankee, for instance, shows the superiority of modern ingenuity and mechanical know-how by making fools of King Arthur's superstitious louts.

The better-informed and more realistic supporters of the medieval ideal, like Carlyle and Morris, never pretended that the Middle Ages were utopian; but they did believe that, with all its flaws, the time was nonetheless superior to the modern world. Twain reversed that opinion, and others less bold argued that the days of King Arthur were at least no better than those of the nineteenth century. Elizabeth Barrett Browning pointed out the folly of idealizing the past in *Aurora Leigh*: "And Camelot to minstrels seemed as flat / As Fleet Street to our poets."

A final argument employed against the Revivalists turned their own most effective weapon against them. Ever since Pugin had charged neoclassic art with being a sham and had launched a crusade against architectural dishonesty, truth in building became a Revivalist catchword and deceit anathema. Pugin may very well have been correct in attributing truthfulness to the original Gothic, but it struck others that neo-Gothic, no matter how honest in construction and materials, was intrinsically a sham in its imitation of a style alien to modern times. Lethaby referred to the "sham antiquity of our buildings," and W. Miles Barnes, a member of the S.P.A.B., commented that "to imitate old work is a forgery. . . ."[89] On the other hand, in their zeal for Gothic some Revivalists forsook the principle of truthfulness and justifiably drew the charge of committing shams. Had Pugin lived to see the iron structure of Tower Bridge disguised by stone in a medieval style (and perhaps he did see Pope's Oscillating Engine decorated with Gothic tracery at the Great Exhibition), he would have lamented along with Ruskin "the accursed Frankenstein monsters of, indirectly, my own making."[90] "Shade of Pugin," says Hardy's George Somerset on viewing a red-brick chapel, "what a monstrosity!" Unfortunately, some of these monsters were creatures of Pugin's own inadvertent making.

In this chapter a consideration of the aesthetic origins of the Gothic Revival has led to some of the reasons for its ultimate failure, since, like Frankenstein's monster, the seeds of destruction were implanted with those of conception. With the waning of the classical ideal in architecture and the dissolution of the general cultural ideal of which it was a part, a hodgepodge of different styles rushed in to fill the artistic vacuum. As a way of restoring order and at the same time breaking whatever last grasp the classic held on public taste, the revivers of Gothic sought to return to that style of architecture whose development had been so unnaturally interrupted by the introduction of an alien style at the time of the Renaissance. Their avowed purpose was not to restore Gothic in its medieval form but to use Gothic as a point of departure, by drawing upon its principles and by adapting its forms to modern purposes, for a continued development toward a style that would bring stability and order to architectural chaos. This is the aesthetic motive of the Revival. However, to bring this about it was first necessary to learn about that art which their predecessors had neglected so long as to allow for its lapse into obscurity, and so they set about their antiquarian searches, busily making notes and drawing sketches of the wealth of medieval buildings across their land. But, paradoxically, as they accumulated the information necessary to provide a foundation upon which to erect their new buildings after the old style, they found that the greater the amount of facts they had available, the more difficult it was to break with the old in pursuit of the new. Too much knowledge became a dangerous thing. Their return to Gothic created problems without their ranks as well in the modernist opposition to revivalism in any form, even that which meant ultimately to go forward.

There is, however, another aspect to the aesthetic motives of the Gothic Revival, and one that, in the end, is more completely satisfying as an explanation for its popularity. It is that, despite so many avowals that the purpose of the Revival was not to bring back Gothic specifically but art generally and that the Gothic style was only a means to this greater end, at bottom the Revivalists were devoted to Gothic for what it was in itself. To say this is not to impute hypocrisy, for the two motives are not really contradictory and the architects themselves would have admitted as much; but it is to say that they combined a calculated mission to save art with an impulsive love of Gothic. This taste for Gothic is the more satisfying explanation because it alone accounts for the widespread acceptance of the style. It is all very well for a few to take upon themselves the high purpose of rescuing art from the depths to which it had fallen, but how many ordinary people would be concerned enough with art in the abstract to rally to such a standard? It is safe to say that those who worshiped in Gothic churches, lived in Gothic houses, sat on Gothic furniture, and who, in short, responded so enthusiastically to Gothic designs of all sorts as to ensure the popularity of the style, did so not because they shared the expressed goals of the Revival's leaders but because, to put it quite plainly, they liked the way it looked. They liked it because their tastes were determined by the radical changes in aesthetics wrought under the name of Romanticism. To these changes, then, the popular acceptance of the Gothic Revival is largely due, and to these changes and their part in what Eastlake called "one of the most interesting and remarkable phases in the history of art"[91] we now turn.

II. ARCHITECTURE AS MUSIC, PAINTING, AND POETRY

1. LAOCOÖN AND ANALOGIES AMONG THE ARTS

> True Poetry the Painter's power displays;
> True Painting emulates the Poet's lays;
> The rival sisters, fond of equal fame,
> Alternate change their office and their name.
> William Mason, "Fresnoy's Art of Painting"

All art constantly aspires towards the condition of music. (Walter Pater, "The School of Giorgione")

To jumble up one art with another, to lose sight of the peculiar functions and special advantages of each, to talk of music as if it were painting, and painting as if it were music, cannot but lead to hopeless confusion. (Arthur Tilley, "Two Theories of Poetry")

In 1776 Gotthold Ephraim Lessing, in a book called *Laocoön: An Essay on the Limits of Painting and Poetry*, objected to the contemporary practice of transferring aesthetic principles from one art form to another. Lessing's title derives from the famous Greek statue of Laocoön, which Johann Joachim Winckelmann had used to illustrate a point about classical art. Although the figure of Laocoön is entwined by the constricting coils of serpents, his face betrays not horror but a restraint and composure that caused Byron later to speak of "Laocoön's torture dignifying pain" when he recorded his impression of the work in the fourth canto of *Childe Harold*. Winckelmann assumed that the artist had refrained from depicting the contortion of an agonized scream on the principle, characteristic of Greek culture, that crying aloud when in pain is ignoble. Lessing refuted this assumption by citing numerous incidents in classical literature where heroes do cry out, and he proposed as an alternate explanation that the rules of sculpture or painting were different from those of poetry and that what could be done in one could not be done in the other. The poet may describe the cry in words, as Virgil in fact did in the *Aeneid*, but the sculptor may not portray it in stone. The gist of Lessing's argument is that painting is spatial and deals with coexistent elements, whereas poetry is temporal and deals with consecutive elements. In other words, painting represents concrete things, and poetry represents actions. Therefore, as Lessing's subtitle makes clear, painting and poetry are distinctive art forms with inherent limitations. The significance of this idea is not in its revelation of an obscure pedantic squabble between Winckelmann and Lessing but in its protest against the widespread eighteenth-century tendency to equate poetry with painting, frequently by relying upon the authority of Horace's phrase, taken out of context, "*ut pictura poesis*"—"as is painting, so is poetry."[1]

That Lessing failed in his attempt to stay the identification of art forms generally and of poetry with painting specifically is apparent from the continuation of descriptive poetry well into the nineteenth century, not only in the works of the Romantics, where the tendency is widely acknowledged, but later on in the works of Tennyson, whose reviewers almost invariably commented on the excellence of his "word-painting." Further evidence is that almost exactly one hundred years after Lessing's protest, Matthew Arnold felt it necessary to redefine the boundaries of the arts in his "Epilogue to Lessing's Laocoön." Arnold follows Lessing very closely in attributing to painting the depiction of the moment and to poetry the task of representing action. The narrator of the poem tells his friend that since the painter has but a moment to work with, he must make his choice with care:

> In outward semblance he must give
> A moment's life of things that live;
> Then let him choose his moment well,
> With power divine its story tell.

Despite Arnold's effort to follow Lessing in separating the arts, there is in this passage a subtle but significant variation when the speaker says that the painting should tell a story, a function of painting forbidden by Lessing. Perhaps the two arts had become so assimilated into each other by this time, especially in the popular genre of narrative paintings, that it was impossible to maintain rigid boundaries despite one's best efforts. The line reveals, further, that poetry is gaining the upper hand in the partnership by imposing its values upon painting rather than the other way around. Whatever the case, the poet, on the other hand, concentrates on action:

> he must life's movement tell!
> The thread which binds it all in one,
> And not its separate parts alone.
> The *movement* he must tell of life,
> Its pain and pleasure, rest and strife.

It is significant that Arnold should include music as the third major art form in the poem, for Lessing had not considered it, although he had proposed to do so; and the addition of it here indicates its growing ascendency and the need to delineate its separate principles. The musician's province is feeling:

> The inspired musician what a range,
> What power of passion, wealth of change!
> Some source of feeling he must choose
> And its locked fount of beauty use,
> And through the stream of music tell
> Its else unutterable spell;
> To choose it rightly is his part,
> And press into its inmost heart.

It is evident from this why the equation between music and poetry came to supersede that of painting and poetry: once Wordsworth's definition of poetry as "the spontaneous overflow of powerful feelings" became generally accepted in the nineteenth century, once, that is, poetry was no longer to imitate external phenomena but to express internal emotions, it was a short step to seeing poetry as music, the art form that is least imitative and most passionate. But Arnold was not among those who subscribed to Wordsworth's definition. In the "Preface" to the 1853 edition of *Poems*, he explains the deletion of "Empedocles on Etna" from the volume for the reason that the representation of thought and feeling provides no pleasure unless accompanied by an Aristotelian catharsis through action. Also, since Aristotle meant by *imitation* the imitation of action, it is not surprising that the classical bias of Arnold's mind should lead him to emphasize that art which most effectively portrays

action and to declare at the end of the "Epilogue" that "Beethoven, Raphael, cannot reach/The charm which Homer, Shakespeare teach."

The voices of Lessing and Arnold were crying in the wilderness; but at the beginning of our own century, at least one
person heard their plea and resumed their theme: Irving Babbitt in *The New Laokoon: An Essay on the Confusion of the Arts*. A
comparison of the subtitles—Lessing's *An Essay on the Limits of
Painting and Poetry*, Babbitt's *An Essay on the Confusion of the
Arts*—reveals an important change that had occurred during
the century and a half that separates the books: what was a
cause for concern to Lessing has become a cause for alarm to
Babbitt, who chooses to describe this artistic phenomenon with
the pejorative word *confusion*. In Babbitt's view the arts, forget-
ful of their proper limitations in a misguided search for correspondences one with the other, had arrived at an anarchic jumble; and if we trace the development of the tendency from the
time of Lessing up to that of Babbitt, we shall find that the
transposition of artistic values became more complete as well as
more frequent.

Sir Joshua Reynolds proposes as a common denominator for
the convergence of art the popular eighteenth-century idea
that the end of art is to please:

> All arts having the same general end, which is to please; and addressing
> themselves to the same faculties through the medium of the senses; it
> follows that their rules and principles must have as great affinity as the
> different materials and the different organs or vehicles by which they pass
> to the mind, will permit them to retain. ("Discourse VII")

In the typically neoclassic manner, Reynolds supports his contention with a classical authority, in this case Cicero: "Omnes
artes quae ad humanitatem pertinent, habent quoddam com-
mune vinculum, et quasi cognatione inter se continentur." Ten
years later in 1786, Reynolds reflects the increasing importance
of the imagination in contemporary aesthetics by singling out
that mental faculty as the common target toward which all art
aims:

To enlarge the boundaries of the Art of Painting, as well as to fix its principles, it will be necessary, that, *that* art, and *those* principles, should be considered in their correspondence with the principles of the other arts, which like this, address themselves primarily and principally to the imagination. ("Discourse XIII")

Only a few years after Reynolds made these statements in his addresses to the Royal Academy, A. W. Schlegel was to propose a unification of the arts as well, but at the same time he was to do so in a radically different way. Writing in the *Athenäum*, Schlegel suggests that

we should once more try to bring the arts closer together and seek for transitions from one to the other. Statues perhaps may quicken into pictures, pictures become poems, poems music, and (who knows?) in like manner stately church music may once more rise heavenward as a cathedral.

The difference between Schlegel and Reynolds is immediately apparent: although both assert the commonalty of the arts, Reynolds never goes so far as to identify one with another, maintaining only that they are as similar "as the different materials and the different organs or vehicles by which they pass to the mind, will permit them to retain." Schlegel, on the other hand, goes a step further, passing as it were from a simile to a metaphor, and suggests not simply parallels but complete and total identifications, ignoring altogether the differences that Reynolds is so careful to point out.

Finally, approaching the time of Babbitt, Oscar Wilde defended the notion that a nonpainter may properly criticize painting with the statement that "there are not many arts, but one art merely; poem, picture, and Parthenon, sonnet and statue—all are in their essence the same, and he who knows one, knows all" ("Mr. Whistler's Ten O'Clock," 1885). The statements of Reynolds, Schlegel, and Wilde pretty clearly indicate a development from comparisons among art forms to complete identifications among them.

It is not my purpose to agree or disagree with Babbitt's conclusion, and I leave the reader free to trace the continuation of this tendency in modern art and to determine for himself if it is responsible for the present state of things. My purpose in this chapter is only to show that during the years of the Gothic Revival the majority of artists, critics, and aestheticians regarded the interchangeability of principles between art forms as a matter of course and quite consciously drew parallels and sought correspondences between poetry, painting, sculpture, music, and architecture. This purpose serves two functions. The first is to justify the method of the following chapters where I discuss the aesthetic theory of Gothic Revival architecture by comparing it with the aesthetics of other art forms, especially literature. Again, it does not matter whether the theorists of the Revival were right in seeing architecture as painting, poetry, or music, whether all the fallacies Geoffrey Scott has attributed to them in *The Architecture of Humanism* are indeed fallacies; but what does matter is that these people did in fact look at architecture from the perspective of the other arts and that it is therefore proper to examine Gothic Revival architecture from their own point of view.[2]

The second function treats more of subject than of method and prepares more specifically for chapter 3, which deals with expressionism. There are several explanations for the mixing of art forms. It may be, as some have observed, that there is a correspondence between synesthesia and the transposition of the arts in that both involve a combining of sense impressions to the end of effecting a more intense aesthetic response. In other words, the impact of any work of art is increased by imbuing it with the features of other art forms just as a poetic image is more vivid when perceived by two senses. Possibly, therefore, both synesthesia and the mingling of artistic forms may be attempts to burn with a "hard, gemlike flame." A second explanation is that the breakdown of barriers between the arts proceeded from the same defiance of authority and restrictions that led to social freedoms beyond the arts and to poetic license within them, the best example of the latter being the dissolution of the traditional poetic genres. These genres were varied and blended with the same freedom from convention with which the Pre-Raphaelites approached painting and with which artists of one form borrowed the values of another.

A third explanation, quite probably intertwined with the other two in this difficult problem, is that each age has a dominant art form that determines, and is determined by, in a reciprocal causal relationship the dominant aesthetic theory of the time. This art form is the one that best translates the theory into practice. All the other arts adapt the principles of the dominant art in an attempt to conform to the theory. I propose this explanation tentatively, not as an inviolable law of aesthetics, but it does seem to account for the varying dominance of certain artistic analogies in the eighteenth and nineteenth centuries. For example, the most important aesthetic theory in the eighteenth century is imitation, and painting, as the most imitative art, is supreme. Poet and architect assume the role of painter in their attempts to imitate in words and stone what painters more naturally imitate in oil. When the aesthetic emphasis shifts during the Romantic age from imitation to the expression of ideas, poetry ascends the throne, and paintings and buildings become poems or stories to be read for meaning. And, finally, when the Aesthetic movement at the end of the century sought to extirpate meaning from art and to identify form with substance, music becomes the most common analogy, and writers and painters follow Pater's dictum—"*All art constantly aspires towards the condition of music*" ("The School of Giorgione," *The Renaissance*)—by naming their poems and paintings symphonies, etudes, and nocturnes. Architecture does not participate as fully in this last development as the other arts owing to its essential differences with music and to its increasing tendency at the end of the century away from art and toward science, but it does reflect the earlier shift from imitation to expression by turning more frequently to the analogy of poetry.

II. ARCHITECTURE AND PAINTING

The architecture of buildings in the country should be *architetto-pittore*. (Sir Uvedale Price, *On the Picturesque*)

As the primary modes of decoration, painting and sculpture traditionally have been regarded as the sister arts of architecture, and this age-old association continued unbroken through-

out the eighteenth and nineteenth centuries. Ruskin was to
contend, in fact, that decoration separates architecture from
mere building. Although function is the prerequisite, it is decoration that defines architecture: "The essential thing in a
building,—its *first* virtue,—is that it be strongly built, and fit for
its uses. The noblest thing in a building, and its highest virtue,
is that it be nobly sculptured or painted."[3] T. G. Jackson echoes
this opinion in *Modern Gothic Architecture* when he writes that
"architecture then cannot be perfect unless painting and sculpture are associated with it. . . ."[4] Furthermore, we find that decoration and architecture are mutually dependent and that if
architecture requires decoration, then decoration requires
architecture. The first proposition of thirty-seven in Owen Jones's "General Principles in Architecture and Decorative Arts"
is that "the Decorative Arts arise from, and should properly be
attendant upon, Architecture."[5]

These writers are in perfect accord with popular taste and
practice, for there is certainly no dearth of ornament in Victorian architecture. To the contrary, one of the chief characteristics of Victorian buildings is their profusion of ornament and
general effect of busyness. What the writers do object to in
contemporary practice is the division of labor that allocates the
decoration to separate hands without the close supervision and
master design of the architect. The modern world had brought
about a disunity in this, as well as in so many other areas of
Victorian art and life, and many architects called for a
reunification of the sister arts. T. G. Jackson, for example,
maintains that it is insufficient for a building to be ornamented
with painting and sculpture; all three arts must be molded into
a homogeneous unity by a single plan of design. Having stated
his belief in the necessity of painting and sculpture to architecture, he goes on to say that "mere juxtaposition of painting and
sculpture to architecture is not enough to produce that sort of
association that is wanted; they must be combined, united,
harmonized, and they must be all the essence of the design."[6]

As long as the architect, no less a victim of the division of
labor than the painter or sculptor or assembly-line worker, con-

tinued in his specialized education and interests, there could be no cure for the problem. What was needed was an artistically well-rounded architect with diverse interests and skills who could coordinate all the elements of architecture. Thus, George Edmund Street laments the "practical divorce of the arts" on the basis that "the first test of an artist is that he should feel a real and absolute, if not an almost equal, interest in all the arts. . . . The three arts [architecture, sculpture, and painting] are indeed all dependent on each other."[7] And like so many other Victorians, Street finds the solution to the problem in ideal models from the past:

> For myself, I hope that the time may come when we may again see that the great painter and sculptor may also be the great architect. Of old we know that this was so. Giotto was not only a painter but an architect. Niccola Pisano was in the same way both sculptor and architecture. Those were the palmy days of art upon which one looks back with a hope that in course of time they may be revived.[8]

This sort of complementary association between the sister arts is not, however, what Babbitt meant by "the confusion of the arts" nor what one finds in the adaptation of visual principles by poets. These statements argue for a traditionally close relationship but not a merger. Yet there is evidence of the transposition of values. Pater acknowledged so much when he wrote in *The Renaissance* that

> architecture, again, though it has its own laws—laws esoteric enough, as the true architect knows only too well—yet sometimes aims at fulfilling the conditions of a picture, as in the *Arena* chapel; or of sculpture, as in the flawless unity of Giotto's tower at Florence. . . . ("The School of Giorgione")

Pater is vague here in saying just how architecture is like painting and sculpture, but other writers are very specific in pointing out that a building should blend into its surroundings as harmoniously as if it were placed on canvas by a landscape artist. For Sir Joshua Reynolds, "What the back-ground is in Painting, in Architecture is the real ground on which the building is erected. . . ." He then proceeds to praise Vanbrugh, "an Architect who composed like a Painter," because his buildings "did not abruptly start out of the ground without expectation or preparation" ("Discourse XIII"). In attributing this virtue to Vanbrugh, Reynolds is applying the principle of insensible transitions, a principle that Edmund Burke, and Sir Uvedale Price after him, regarded as essential to beauty and in opposition to the abrupt contrasts of the picturesque.

Shortly after Reynolds delivered this discourse, Sir Uvedale Price was to write in much the same vein that

> the architect of buildings in the country should be *architetto-pittore*; for, indeed, he ought not only to have the mind, but the hand of the painter— not only to be acquainted with the principles, but, as far as design goes, with the practice of landscape painting.[9]

It is, of course, natural that people who were accustomed to gardens enhanced with fanes and ruins, to landscapes by Poussin and Claude decorated with such buildings, to the observation of nature, in fact, through a Claude Lorraine glass as if all creation were one gigantic painting, should come to view architecture from the perspective of the painter. On the other hand, one is altogether unprepared for the following remark, not so much because it was made in the late 1860s as because it refers to a design for the New Law Courts in the heart of London. George Edmund Street, wrote a journalist, by virtue of this design manifests his ability as "not only a great architect, but a consummate landscape artist."[10] Either the meaning of landscape has changed to include urban settings, or the tradition was extraordinarily potent.

The architect, then, is like the painter in that he should design the building and choose the site in order for the architecture to become an integral part of the landscape. Another similarity of the two is that both should stimulate the imagination of the viewer. This aesthetic branch of psychological associationism, common to the theories of Archibald Alison and the Romantic writers later on, occurs somewhat earlier in the lectures of Reynolds, who in "Discourse XIII" proposes:

> Architecture certainly possesses many principles in common with Poetry and Painting. Among those which may be reckoned as the first, is, that of affecting the imagination by means of association of ideas. Thus, for in-

> stance, as we have naturally a veneration for antiquity, whatever building brings to our remembrance ancient customs and manners, such as the Castles of the Barons of ancient Chivalry, is sure to give this delight. . . .

Gothic architecture, he concludes, is more successful in this respect than is Grecian.

A third attribute common to both painting and architecture is that they reveal the artist behind the work. The nineteenth century ordinarily used the poetical analogy to explain how the expressive theory applies to architecture, but Street chose a comparison with painting when he wrote, "On the canvas of a great painter you see not only the man who sat for his portrait, but almost equally the man who painted it. In a more subtle way the architect is revealed in his work."[11] The dominance of the expressive theory in the nineteenth century was to make the notion that art reflects the artist and the age in which he lived very much a commonplace. But by the end of the century, when John Sedding wrote *Art and Handicraft*, all three of these parallels between painting and architecture still survived. Sedding describes the architecture as "a pictorial artist on a large scale" and as "a picturesque manipulator of vast forms," whose work, like that of the painter and poet, is both expressive and imaginatively affective: "The singular attractiveness of a work of art—poem, building, painting—is borrowed from the personality of its creator. The artist strikes the imagination of others by pressing into his work his own imaginative qualities."[12]

Not everyone, of course, held to these aesthetic equations. Standing at the threshold of the Art-for-Art's-Sake movement, which was to strip from art all ulterior motive and most especially utility, George Gilbert Scott recognized that here was a portal through which architecture could never pass. Perhaps, too, the gap had been widened for him as much by architecture's increasing momentum toward functionalism as by the Aesthetes' insistence on the inutility of art. Whatever the reason, for Scott architecture was not an identical twin:

> Architecture differs from her sister arts of painting and sculpture in this, that while they directly originate from a feeling for beauty, and are either wholly independent of utility, or only accidentally connected with it, archi-

tecture results in the first instance from necessity, beauty being a *super-added* grace.[13]

Another difference had been proposed in the previous century by Reynolds. Although he conceded that all arts share the common aim of acting upon the imagination, he drew distinctions as to how they accomplish this goal by applying the principle of imitation, the central aesthetic standard of his age. Architecture is unlike painting because it is not an imitative art, because "it applies itself, like Musick (and I believe we may add Poetry), directly to the imagination, without the intervention of any kind of imitation" ("Discourse XIII"). Those who saw in Gothic architecture a reflection of German forests or an application of natural principles were to circumvent this barrier between the arts, but they would agree with the identification of architecture and music, as we shall now see.

III. ARCHITECTURE AND MUSIC

> I was trying to recollect a quotation (as *I* think) of Stael's, from some Teutonic sophist about architecture. "Architecture," says this Macoronico Tedescho, "reminds me of frozen music." It is somewhere—but where?—the demon of perplexity must know and won't tell. (Lord Byron, *Journals*)

> The sight of such a monument is like continual and stationary music. . . . (Madame de Staël, *Corinne*)

> "I have found a paper of mine among some others," said Goethe to-day, "in which I call architecture 'petrified music.' Really there is something in this; the tone of mind produced by architecture approaches the effect of music." (Johann Wolfgang von Goethe, *Conversations of Goethe with Eckermann and Soret*)

> Architecture in general is frozen music. (Friedrich von Schelling, *Philosophie der Kunst*)

The perception of architecture as "frozen music" draws upon a mythological tradition perhaps more ancient than the sisterhood with painting and sculpture. With the enchanting strains of his lyre, Amphion miraculously charmed stones to take their places in the walls of Thebes, and Apollo built the walls of Troy with music in much the same way. The secret of their constructional technique has been lost for all time, only to be partially recovered by poets, whose airy castles, unlike the earthbound edifices of practical builders, can defy the principles of Newtonian physics. In the first book of *Paradise Lost*, Mulciber raises Pandemonium to the accompaniment of music:

> Anon out of the earth a Fabric huge
> Rose like an Exhalation, with the sound
> Of Dulcet Symphonies, and voices sweet,
> Built like a Temple. . . .

Tennyson was seemingly taken with these myths, which are the subjects of two poems, "Amphion" and "Ilion, Ilion," and the source of Tithonus's reference to "that strange song I heard Apollo sing,/While Ilion like a mist rose into towers." Also, when Gareth first comes to Camelot, Merlin tells him:

> For an ye heard a music, like enow
> They are building still, seeing the city is built
> To music, therefore never built at all,
> And therefore built for ever.
>
> "Gareth and Lynette"

Gareth has no idea what Merlin is talking about, and the reader, even with the help of Tennyson's note, "By the Muses," has little more. However, we may speculate that Tennyson, writing before Schliemann had discovered the site of Troy and before later archaeologists tentatively confirmed the reality of Camelot, meant to say cryptically through Merlin that these cities existed only in legend and, therefore, lived forever in the music of poetry although never having literally been built at all.

But whatever Tennyson meant by it, the lines explain little about the basis of comparison between music and architecture. Probably the most traditional basis in the nineteenth century was that which had earlier been proposed by Saint Augustine involving mathematical proportions and the principles of harmony.[14] An article in the *Builder* points out that both music and architecture have rhythm, which it defines as "the recurrence of an accentuation at marked and equal periods." The only difference between the rhythm of the two arts is that "what regular division in *time* is to music, regular division in *space* is to architecture."[15] Street, too, believed in the rhythm of architecture, a value that he found difficult to express in words but that he nevertheless attempted to describe thus: "It is an art depending on numbers and proportions. Some expression caught up, repeated, balanced, emphasised in succeeding passages, at intervals which are either regular or regulated, constitutes usually the rhythmical beauty of a work of architecture."[16]

Since rhythm, defined as balance and regularity, is a far more obvious feature in the symmetrical design of a building constructed on classical principles than in the irregularity of the Gothic, one might expect the leaders of the Revival to forsake the musical analogy altogether. However, this was not the case, for they were able to avail themselves of the analogy not only by asserting a peculiar kind of symmetry for their preferred style but more convincingly by establishing the analogy on a different basis, that of expression. Architecture is like music, G. F. Bodley argued, in that "it expresses abstract ideas, such as power, simplicity, grandeur and beauty. For neither music nor architecture sets forth facts, they express ideas."[17] Similar comparisons by other writers indicate that the analogy was continued during the course of the century on this basis, but the notion was admittedly never very widespread. If music had been the art form most fluent in the expression of ideas, then architecture, despite fundamental differences, would no doubt have been perceived in musical terms more frequently than it was, so completely had expressionism swept the field and so eager were all the arts to embody the principles of the victor. Rather, it was poetry that proved most articulate in expressing ideas, and it was poetry, then, that architecture sought to become.

IV. ARCHITECTURE AND POETRY

Architects should make a point of incorporating Poetry in their architecture. . . . (Etienne-Louis Boullée, *Architecture, Essai sur l'art*)

[The] architect should possess certain mental qualifications, of which a sense of the poetry of his art is perhaps the most important. (G. F. Bodley, "Architectural Study and the Examination Test")

> Deprive art of its poetry, you kill its soul; enrich it by the co-operating powers of invention, the sphere in which it may act is immense, the progress it may make is illimitable. (Edward Chatfield, "Poetic Painting and Sculpture")

In a general way literature played a much greater role in the Gothic Revival than either painting or music by establishing a popular taste for the Middle Ages, and, above all writers, Walter Scott was most frequently credited with reversing the long-standing bias against this epoch with his sympathetic portrayals of medieval life. Of course, any number of names might be counted as contributors to the widespread appreciation of the Middle Ages before Scott—Gray, the Wartons, Walpole and other writers of Gothic novels, Bishops Hurd and Percy, Chatterton, Macpherson—the list can be multiplied; but it was pre-eminently Scott, through the immense popularity and influence of his poetry and novels, to whom people looked as the dominant figure in the Medieval Revival.[18]

A corollary of this belief is that literature was directly responsible for the Gothic Revial. William Morris, for example, wrote in 1888 that "the revival of the art of architecture in Great Britain may be said to have been a natural consequence of the rise of the romantic school in literature . . . ("The Revival of Architecture"). Perhaps, though, the strongest advocate of this theory is Kenneth Clark, who has written in *The Gothic Revival* that "more than any other movement in the plastic arts the Revival was a literary movement, every change in form being accompanied by a change in literature. . . ."[19]

However, literature did more than establish a congenial climate for the growth of Gothic architecture: it also provided analogies for the definition of certain principles common to both art forms. One of these, and a most important one to Romantic theory, is the principle of irregularity. At the end of his preface to *The Works of Shakespeare* (1725), Pope justifies the irregularity of the plays by comparing them to Gothic architecture:

> I will conclude by saying of Shakespeare that with all his faults, and with all the irregularity of his drama, one may look upon his works, in comparison

of those that are more finished and regular, as upon an ancient majestic piece of Gothic architecture compared with a neat modern building: the latter is more elegant and glaring, but the former is more strong and more solemn.

As we know from *The Essay on Criticism*, although Pope revered the rules, he was no narrow-minded stickler for them.

Another basis of comparison is the eclectic assimilation of pagan and Christian elements by both architecture and poetry. Browning's Bishop at St. Praxed's impartially selects subjects from both areas for the sculpture on his tomb, Pugin condemns on artistic and religious grounds the inconsistent juxtaposition of pagan and Christian subjects during the Renaissance, and James Fergusson finds Milton and Wren to be alike in adapting classical forms for Christian purposes. Fergusson maintains that *Paradise Lost* and St. Paul's Cathedral were designed on the same principles. By transforming biblical narrative into Greek epic, Milton used the *Iliad* and the *Aeneid* in the same way Wren used the Pantheon and the Temple of Peace.[20]

We are still not dealing with aesthetic transpositions, for these examples reveal similarities instead of identifications. It is only when we come to "the poetry or architecture," to use Ruskin's title, that we have the assumption by architecture of poetic principles. To understand how this came about, we must first recall that one of the crucial changes wrought by Romanticism was the investiture, or perhaps I should say more accurately the reinvestiture, of meaning into the universe. Like so much of Romantic doctrine, this was a reaction to the previous age, whose mechanistic philosophy and natural theology tended to separate the physical and spiritual. Furthermore, since reason could comprehend only what was empirically available to it, men should acknowledge their intellectual limits and content themselves with the investigation of material reality. "Presume not God to scan," Pope warns in his *Essay on Man*. Imitative aesthetics followed course by demanding that the artist represent the world in its material form, and the artist responded with landscape paintings and with the descriptive poetry against which Lessing protested. To be sure, the nature they followed was General Nature, or, as André Chénier puts it in *L'Invention*, the artist should portray "ce qu'elle [la nature mère] n'a point fait, mais ce qu'elle a pu faire," but still material nature for all that. The organic philosophy of Romanticism, on the other hand, infused the material with the spiritual, emphasized the spiritual half, and claimed as its proper sphere the apprehension of that spiritual essence, with, however, the imaginative rather than the rational faculty of mind. As Browning has Fra Lippo Lippi say, the world "means intensely, and means good. . . ." Aesthetics changed accordingly by calling upon artists not to imitate the outer, material form, but to express the inner, spiritual reality in an attempt to penetrate to the fundamental meaning of things, or, in religious terms, to God's very presence in the world.[21] Fra Lippo Lippi states his purpose, "To find its meaning is my meat and drink," thus fulfilling the role of the Romantic artist as seer, prophet, priest, who expounds to others mysteries vouchsafed his eyes alone. The artist interprets the meaning of the world through his art, and this is why Henry Taylor declares in his preface to *Philip Van Artevelde* that "no man can be a very great poet who is not also a great philosopher."[22]

Meaning, then, came to be not only the most important element in art but its *sine qua non*, its definitive essence. John Addington Symonds, for example, wrote that "art gives form to human consciousness; expresses or presents the feeling or the thought of man . . . there is no work of art without a theme, without a motive, without a subject. The presentation of that theme, that motive, that subject, is the final end of art. . . . Quite meaningless poetry . . . is a contradiction in terms" ("Cherubino at the Scala Theatre," *Italian Byways*). Early in the century Friedrich Schlegel had similarly made meaning a condition of the fine arts when he applied the principle to architecture: "Let a building be ever so beautiful, if it be destitute of *meaning*, it cannot belong to the fine arts" ("Lecture VIII," *Lectures on the History of Literature, Ancient and Modern*).

The second thing to keep in mind for an understanding of the comparison between poetry and architecture is that of the

various art forms poetry was thought to be the best suited for
expressing ideas. That is, to return to a point made earlier in
this chapter, poetry best fulfilled the dominant aesthetic theory
of time, which I have just briefly described. As Symonds points
out in another place, poetry is less sensuous than the other arts,
appealing less to hearing than music and not at all to sight.
"But," he goes on, "language being the storehouse of all human
experience, language being the medium whereby spirit com-
municates with spirit in affairs of life . . . it follows that, of all
the arts, poetry soars highest, flies widest, and is most at home
in the region of the spirit. What poetry lacks of sensuous ful-
ness, it more than balances by intellectual intensity. . . . It is the
metaphysic of the fine arts" ("The Provinces of the Several
Arts," *Essays: Speculative and Suggestive*).

The conclusion I have been working toward should now be
fairly clear: because poetry proved so successful in embodying
the new artistic theory, the other art forms sought to adapt
poetic principles, as painters, for example, attempted to introduce narration into their works, unmindful of Lessing's
strictures against such usurpation of prerogatives. More fundamentally importantly, however, so completely had poetry
come to be identified with the chief end of art that the name
"poetry" was given to the intellectual message art was intended
to convey. This development defined poetry in the broad sense
that was usually intended when writers referred to the poetry
of, say, architecture and painting as well as when they referred
to the poetry of such widely dissimilar things as life, science,
windmills, flowers, and even early rising.[23]

In the eighteenth century Blondel and Boullée had spoken
of the poetry of architecture, using "poetry" in the broader
sense of the word; but in England, at any rate, it was Ruskin
who popularized the concept by insisting over and again that a
building should be read. We should, he counsels, read "a building as we would read Milton or Dante" and treat buildings "as
books of history."[24] A person who studies the pieces of sculpture on a building should "set himself down to read them.
Thenceforward the criticism of the building is to be conducted

precisely on the same principles as that of a book. . . ."[25] Finally, in perhaps his best known statement on the subject, Ruskin writes of St. Mark's in Venice that

> the whole edifice is to be regarded less as a temple wherein to pray, than as itself a Book of Common Prayer, a vast illuminated missal, bound with alabaster instead of parchment, studded with porphyry pillars instead of jewels, and written within and without in letters of enamel and gold.[26]

Just what a builder should write in the book of architecture and just how he should translate the geometrical shapes of his alphabet into a comprehensible language we shall discover in the next chapter.

III. EXPRESSIONISM

I. SUBJECTIVE AND OBJECTIVE EXPRESSIONISM

> [Expression] may mean the expression which resides in the object itself, which the artist seeks to seize and to render as powerfully as he can—the expression which belongs to a good portrait. Or it may mean the expression of subjective thought and feeling, not inherent in the object, for which the forms of art are vehicles. (John Addington Symonds, "Beauty, Composition, Expression, Characterization")

In showing how the mimetic concept of art as mirror gave way during the Romantic age to the expressive concept of art as lamp, M. H. Abrams treats expressionism as a unified doctrine, but there were in fact two types of expressionism current during this time. The one with which Abrams is concerned focuses not upon external reality as with the mimetic approach, nor on the audience as with the pragmatic, but on the artist himself, whose purpose is to express his own thoughts and feelings. We shall look more carefully at the origin of this doctrine when we consider associative aesthetics in chapter 5; for the moment we need only recall that when associationism removed reality and beauty from the external world to the world of the mind, in order to portray reality and beauty the artist found that he must express his thoughts and feelings rather than imitate the somewhat insubstantial object that served merely to arouse those thoughts. This kind of expressionism is the subjective type and is best exemplified by Wordsworth, whose poetry Keats called the "egotistical sublime" because of the extent to which the elder poet impressed his personality upon his work.

The other form of expressionism is objective in that, rather than emphasizing the artist's associative reaction to an object and thereby diminishing the value of the object to a mere stimulus, it conversely emphasizes the object in its attempt to express the inherent and definitive essence of the object. Objective expressionism is obviously more in keeping with traditional

91

mimetic aesthetics since the focus in both is the object to be portrayed in art, but it differs from earlier artistic theory by requiring that the artist express the peculiar characteristic of the object from within as it were rather than that he imitate the general form of the object from without.[1] To express an object in this way, an artist needed above all things to be capable of sympathy—or better still, empathy—by means of which he could join imaginatively with the object and thus, having become a part of it, express from within its very nature. By emphasizing the independent identity of the object and by calling upon the artist to project his personality sympathetically into the object and so be absorbed by it, objective expressionism diminishes the artist's sense of selfhood and leads Keats to remark that the poet is a chameleon with no identity of his own. This form of the expressive theory was discussed by Hazlitt in his lectures, practiced by Keats, who was very likely influenced by Hazlitt, and later embodied in Hopkins's theory of inscape.

These two types of expressionism depend upon their own particular form of the imagination. Objective expressionism requires what Ruskin calls in *Modern Painters* the penetrative imagination and what a later writer defines as "the imagination which pierces right to the heart of things, seizes hold of their most characteristic and life-giving quality, and reveals it in language as simple as it is pregnant."[2] Subjective expressionism, on the other hand, occurs when "the poet plays round his subject rather than penetrates it, contemplates it rather than interprets it. Thus, sometimes his imagination, instead of remaining concentrated on the object which has inspired the poem, flies off to fresh images, and so becomes creative instead of penetrative."[3]

When applied to architecture, subjective expressionism means that buildings express the thoughts and feelings of those who erected them. This is the subject of the first part of the chapter. Objective expressionism in architecture means that a building expresses its purpose or function. This is the subject with which the chapter concludes.

II. ARCHITECTURE AS AN EXPRESSION OF THE AGE

The architect
Built his great heart into these sculptured stones.
Henry Wadsworth Longfellow,
"The Golden Legend"

Artists reveal themselves so vividly in their pictures . . . that scanning their life-work is like reading a confession or autobiography. (J. B. Atkinson, "Mr. Holman Hunt: His Work and Career")

Each country of the globe presents the record of its own history, its manners, wealth, and especially its religion, in the contemplation of its architecture. (A. F. Ashton, "Architectural Reflections")

The artist who abides by the doctrine of subjective expressionism and takes for his subject his own thoughts and feelings is in effect writing autobiography, and his audience is invited to regard his work as an extension of his personality and to so identify the man and work as to evaluate the worth of one according to the worth of the other. This had not formerly been so. In the middle of the eighteenth century, Lessing took Milton's remark about some fallen angels praising Pandemonium and some praising its architect to mean that "praise of one, then, does not always mean praise of the other. A work of art may deserve all possible esteem without bringing the artist any special renown. On the other hand, an artist may justly claim our admiration even when his work does not entirely satisfy us."[4] Less than a hundred years later, the artist and work had been so totally merged that such distinctions were no longer possible. Ruskin says that the most important principle to be derived from *The Stones of Venice* is, "Art is valuable or otherwise, only as it expresses the personality, activity, and living perception of a good and great human soul. . . ."[5] Buffon's axiom, "Le style c'est l'homme même," had been carried far beyond the intent of its author.

But the nineteenth century took the axiom further yet by contending that style is not only the man but the age and society to which he belongs, and that the work of art reflects these as much as the personality of the artist. The idea appears at the

beginning of the Romantic movement in André Chénier's
"L'Invention" (1787):

> Les coutumes d'alors, les sciences, les moeurs
> Respirent dans les vers des antiques auteurs.
> Leur siècle est en dépôt dans leurs nobles volumes.

By the middle of the next century, the notion of art revealing
the age from which it sprang had become something of a critical truism. In his *History of English Literature* (trans. 1873),
Hippolyte Taine writes that during the last hundred years in
Germany and the last sixty in France this idea had transformed
the study of history because people had come to realize that "a
literary work is not a mere individual play of imagination, the
isolated caprice of an excited brain, but a transcript of contemporary manners." Architectural critics as well as literary ones
applied the principle. In the last decade of the century, John
Sedding wrote, "English architecture quite as much as English
literature, expresses the imaginative thought of the English
people during a long series of successive generations, and in a
true sense has concentrated and imaged the dominant qualities
of our race."[6] Ruskin and others believed that architecture is a
truer index than literature since a building, unlike a poem, is
the work of many hands and therefore more accurately
represents the society at large.[7]

Once the principle of art reflecting society became established, the next step was to determine more precisely what
aspects of society should be embodied in works of art. Voltaire
had written in *Essay on the Manners and Spirit of the Nations*
(1756) that the three main factors in a society's character are
climate, government, and religion; and most nineteenth-
century writers agreed, with slight variations, that these three
qualities therefore should be expressed in art. Since climate
figures in architecture more as a functional determinant, it will
be considered later on. The other two generally fell under the
headings of nationality and religion, and were used by the Revivalists in their arguments against revived classical architecture, which they considered foreign and pagan. Pugin, in fact,

ordinarily spoke of classical architecture as pagan and of Gothic
as Christian. He did not object to the antique classical, because
it properly expressed the religion of a pagan age, but he was
intransigent in his opposition to the revival of ancient architecture during the Renaissance since it was inconsistent with the
religious beliefs of a Christian people. Classical architecture,
having developed naturally as the religious expression of
pagans, could not express the very different religious concepts
of Christians, and so was entirely wrong for modern churches.
Only Gothic, which evolved from the Catholic faith, was proper
for worship in churches where, as Pugin thought, that faith
survived. This, for him, was the strongest argument in its favor:
"Pointed or Christian architecture has far higher claims on our
admiration than mere beauty or antiquity; the former may be
regarded as a matter of opinion,—the latter, in the abstract, is
no proof of excellence, but in it alone we find *the faith of
Christianity embodied, and its practices illustrated.*"[8]

As long as cosmopolitanism prevailed in the eighteenth century, an Englishman could consider himself a "citizen of the
world" and regard his Palladian home as perfectly appropriate.
Until Strawberry Hill he would no more have thought of building a house in the "national" Gothic style than he would have
learned Old English instead of Latin. But when England was
carried along in the general movement toward nationalism,
which gained added impetus during the long war with France,
the Revivalists were able to appeal to patriotic sentiments in
arguing that Gothic was national but classical was foreign and
could no more express the English character than it could the
Christian religion. Pugin, who championed Catholic architecture with the unremitting zeal of a convert, made the
nationalistic appeal with the patriotic fervor of a first-
generation Englishman: "How painful is it to behold, in the
centre of a fine old English park and vast domain, a square
unsightly mass of bastard Italian, without one expression of the
faith, family, or country of the owner."[9] Ruskin would have
none of this. Generally credited with the popularity of Italian
architecture in Victorian England, he accused the English of

confusing vanity and patriotism in their failure to acknowledge
that the French originated the Gothic and brought it to its
highest perfection. Palmerston also refused to accept Gothic as
a national architecture. In the debate over which style to choose
for the Foreign Office, he denied the main argument of Scott
and his defenders that Gothic was the English style: "Now, I
take leave to say that it is anything but the national style: it is a
foreign style, which at a particular period was imported into
this country. . . ."[10] The Revivalists were on weaker ground
here than with the religious approach, and this may be one
reason they were more successful with ecclesiastical buildings
than with public, secular ones.

The logical extension of individual expressionism to collective expressionism involved aesthetics in the conflict between
two contradictory elements of Romanticism—heroic individualism and populism—both of which gained impetus as the century matured. On the one hand, the hero as artist, more or less
comparable to the "great man" of historical theory, stands apart
from society by virtue of his superiority to it and frequently
expresses in his art ideas inimical to the commonly held values
of his time.[11] If such an artist reflects society at all, he does so
only inversely, and we must hold the image up to a mirror to set
it aright. On the other hand, art as the collective expression of
the people denies the individuality of the artist, who acts as little
more than spokesman for the prevailing sentiments of his age.
For example, though admitting that to some extent the architecture reveals himself in his buildings, G. E. Street goes on to
add, "The man is dominated to a great extent by the age; so
that the spirit of the age is seen more or less in the architectural
works of all times."[12]

Collective expressionism was strengthened by two related developments in the latter half of the century. The first of these
was social Darwinism, which explained that art reflected society
because art was environmentally determined by society at large,
and the artist, himself a product of the milieu, exerted no more
control over art than the least organism exerted over the evolution of its species.[13] The second development was political

socialism, which was applied to art by such people as William Morris and William Richard Lethaby. It follows from Morris's ideal of "art made by the people and for the people" that "architecture cannot flourish unless it is the spontaneous expression of the pleasure and the will of the whole people" ("The Beauty of Life" and "The English Pre-Raphaelites"). Lethaby agreed with Webb that "building is a folk art." "No art," writes Lethaby at another time, "that is only one man deep is worth much; it should be a thousand men deep."[14]

Of the two types of expressionism, the Revivalists overwhelmingly preferred the collective over the individual. For one thing, a building is less an individual achievement than any other work of art since its design is often determined in varying degrees by those who are paying for it and since its execution is in the hands of many. For another, the Revivalists were quick to realize that collective expressionism was an effective argument in the debate over styles. Gothic, as the spontaneous expression of the people, was more national, more universal, and more natural than the classical style, which had been imposed upon England by an aristocratic minority who had acquired a taste for it at the universities and on Grand Tours, and which, therefore, was foreign, elitist, and artificial. There is a distinct egalitarian strain, all of it by no means as calculating as perhaps I have implied, running throughout Gothic Revival polemics.

In promoting the idea that art reflects society, the Revivalists also took advantage of the growing interest in history, particularly medieval history, by pointing out that no records of the past were so accurate as architecture. Before Ruskin said in "The Lamp of Memory" that architecture surpasses both poetry and historical writing as a conquerer of forgetfulness, Pugin had written in *An Apology* that "the history of architecture is the history of the world: as we inspect the edifices of antiquity, its nations, its dynasties, its religions, are all brought before us. . . . By architecture and ornament alone, learned men of the present time are enabled to make the most important discoveries, relative to the history of nations. . . ."[15]

This archaeological approach to architecture, whereby an-

cient buildings become evidence of past civilizations to be an-
alyzed by the historian, is parallel to the paleontological
approach, in which buildings are regarded as fossils of extinct
creatures to be reconstructed by the anatomist. Both are natural developments of the expressive theory, and both explain
why the Victorians were concerned with what their architecture
would reveal about themselves to the New Zealander of the
future. But both approaches were leading in a dangerous direction, which was that architecture was becoming a means to an
end, important less in its own right than in its use to the historian. We see something of this tendency in a remark made by
the historian Edward Augustus Freeman: "We look upon an
ancient church or castle not merely as a work of art, but as the
relic and witness of a former age, of creeds, sentiments, institutions, and states of society which have passed away."[16] It is
to be expected that a historian should consider a building "not
merely as a work of art," but it is fair to say that the public as a
whole, many architects included, shared the opinion. Geoffrey
Scott recognized this tendency some time ago in *The Architecture
of Humanism* when he identified the habit of regarding architecture as symbolic to be a Romantic fallacy whereby architecture
"ceases to be an immediate and direct source of enjoyment, and
becomes a mediate and indirect one."[17] Had his subject been
broader, Scott might well have included literature in this statement; for a natural consequence of expressionism in any art
form is to emphasize the artist against the work, or, collectively,
to elevate the society over the work. Hippolyte Taine, for example, argued for a historical approach to literature by comparing a fossil shell to a literary work: "Why do you study the
shell, except to bring before you the animal? So you study the
document only to know the man. The shell and the document
are lifeless wrecks, valuable only as a clue to the entire and
living existence. We must get hold of this existence, endeavor to
recreate it. It is a mistake to study the document, as if it were
isolated" (*History of English Literature*).

This attitude toward literature generated a school of historical and biographical criticism that led ultimately to a reaction

against itself by the New Critics, who attempted to refocus attention on the work of art by regarding it in isolation and ignoring the contexts of history and biography. Both they and Geoffrey Scott were part of a general cultural reaction, begun by the Aesthetic movement and continuing into the first decades of this century, against Romantic and Victorian values. Although the reaction did not succeed with either literature or architecture in eliminating the historical bias from criticism (and perhaps it was never meant to do so entirely), it did restore a more evenly balanced study by emphasizing the importance of the work of art in its own right. The task of those involved in the reaction was a particularly difficult one, for they were opposing not only the expressive function of art but the didactic function as well. We shall see in chapter 6 that the Victorians looked upon architecture and the other arts as a means for improving the moral climate of the age. This didactic approach, by which art becomes an educational tool for the amelioration of society, subordinates the work of art to an ulterior function as much as the historical aspect of expressionism. One reason that didacticism became so firmly entrenched in Victorian aesthetics was that only by means of it could the Gothic Revival be saved. As we shall now see, the expressive doctrine had led the Revivalists into a trap from which they could escape by no other means than using their art to reform society.

III. THE PROBLEM WITH COLLECTIVE EXPRESSIONISM

A style of architecture is simply that characteristic and collective material expression in which all the artists concerned in its production, working among a given people or in a given age, coincide. To be true, it must indicate the people's or age's collective type of character. This is an indispensable requisite. . . . (E. L. T., "Style in Architecture")

Men in those days had convictions. We moderns have opinions. It requires something more than an opinion to build a Gothic Cathedral. (Heinrich Heine, *Confidential Letters to August Lewald on the French Stage*)

In his famous statement of subjective expressionism, Wordsworth defined poetry as "the spontaneous overflow of powerful feelings," and this basic tenet found its architectural application in Morris's comment that "architecture cannot flourish unless it is the spontaneous expression of the pleasure and will of the whole people." The universality of architecture was important to the Revivalists not only because it bespoke the diversity of Gothic as a style appropriate for all types of buildings but also because it meant that architecture was an accurate record of the entire society. Spontaneity was important to them in establishing the historical accuracy of architecture as well, for an unpremeditated impulse was natural and therefore true instead of artificial and false. Pugin wrote that it was impossible for people "to have built consistently otherwise than they did"; and T. G. Jackson maintained that "all styles that have ever lived, lived because they came naturally of themselves, not by conscious choice; and . . . they fell into styles under the influence of the habits and needs and the predilections of contemporary society. . . ."[18] Spontaneity and universality became, therefore, mainstays in the argument that architecture is a true image of society.

When, in turn, the Revivalists rejected Renaissance and neoclassic architecture as shams, they did so largely on the basis of these two criteria. Instead of rising naturally and spontaneously from the requirements of society, the classical style of the Renaissance was imposed by men who, in Cram's words, "selfconfidently set to work to invent and popularize a new and perfectly artificial style."[19] Instead of being the expression of the entire people, the new style brought to England from Italy was, according to Lethaby, "a 'taste' imposed on the top as part of a subtle scheme for dividing off gentility from servility. In England, Italian art (so-called) became a badge of the superiority claimed by travelled people, especially those on the grand tour, over people at home. It was an Architecture of Aristocracy. . . ."[20] If one filters out the socialism by dismissing the motive, the statement represents typically enough the Gothicist charge of exclusivity against neoclassic architecture. Neither spontaneous nor universal, the revived classical was a sham that defied one of the true principles of architecture.

The Gothic style, on the other hand, abided by the principle since it arose naturally and since it was popular in the sense of being an expression of all levels of society. This line of thought worked well enough in establishing the superiority of Gothic architecture over revived classical, but could it be used to justify neo-Gothic? Here was the problem, for what was the difference between the Gothic Revival and the Classical Revival three hundred years before? The very weapon the Revivalists used against the architecture of the preceding era could be as lethally turned against them since it could be argued that no revival is spontaneous. T. G. Jackson recalled having doubts about the Revival early in his career when he wondered whether "modern Goths were not after all pseudo-Goths [who] . . . had got the old dead style on its legs and propped it up, but they could not make it walk."[21] Once dead, no style can be made to live again because all living styles must develop naturally and unconsciously. Furthermore, not only was modern Gothic imposed, but it was imposed by a small group every bit as elite as the aristocrats who introduced the classic into Renaissance England. Eastlake concluded his survey of the Gothic Revival by saying that the movement would not be complete until it ceases to be pedantic and becomes popular. That was in 1872. Sixteen years later Morris believed that it had failed to achieve this goal: "The architectural revival, though not a mere piece of artifical nonsense, is too limited in its scope, too much confined to an educated group, to be a vital growth capable of true development" ("The Revival of Architecture").

If spontaneity and universality are essential to the success of a style, then the absence of these prerequisites may account for the failure of the Gothic Revival. If these same two conditions are necessary for a style to reflect accurately a time in history, then the absence of them may suggest that modern Gothic architecture does not present a true picture of the Victorian age. Pugin believed, to the contrary, that the "Babel of confusion" in architecture falsely represented modern values and that only Gothic could correctly express the soul of a Christian and English nation. "Will the architecture of our times," he

writes in *An Apology,* "hand down to posterity any certain clue
or guide to the system under which it was erected? Surely not; it
is not the expression of existing opinions and circumstances,
but a confused jumble of styles and symbols borrowed from all
nations and periods."[22] Pugin's failure to recognize that the
confusion of architectural styles faithfully reflected the uncertainty of modern life according to his own inviolable law
was, I think, the great mistake of his life. I prefer to believe that
he would not see it, but why he did not matters less than that he
achieved what he did only through an unshakable conviction in
the truth of his perception. Had he lived beyond mid-century,
he may have come to realize that England was no longer the
insular and devout nation once so consistently expressed in its
Gothic architecture. Perhaps he would not have, but from the
perspective of the twentieth century, Cram saw it and found
reason for hope in the immutability of expressive law: "Chaos
then confronts us, in that there is no single architectural following but legion; and in that fact lies the honour of our art, for
neither is society one, or even at one with itself. Architecture is
nothing unless it is intimately expressive, and if utterly different things clamour for voicing, different also must be their
architectural manifestation."[23] Pugin's mistake, then, lay not in
holding to an incorrect law but in thinking that the law had
been suspended. The law was in effect, only it operated under
different conditions since spontaneity and universality would
no longer be possible for any style in a civilized and complex
modern nation.

Cram's insight came, as I say, from the advantage of looking
back after the Revival had run its course and at a time when
Gothic architects were content to work with churches and col-
leges alone. Pugin, Scott, and others, however, were more
ambitious in their belief that if Gothic were to become a living
and dominant style, it must be universally applicable to all types
of buildings. But here they became entrapped, for they believed that architecture reflected the age, and it was manifestly
clear to all that nineteenth-century England was very different
from the nation that had produced pointed architecture. How

could they revive Gothic and reconcile the aesthetic principle with the historical change? The answer lay in compromise: on the one hand, as we saw in chapter 1, they adapted the style to suit the times by relying on principles rather than exact precedents and by allowing for modern developments; on the other hand, as we shall see in chapter 6, they meant to reform society by restoring certain medieval values and bringing it more in line with the age that had created Gothic originally. The means by which this reformation would be effected was art, and so they came to set up a reciprocal relationship between art and society. Art is the product and reflection of society at the same time that art determines the values of society. In this way expressionism and didacticism merge, and in this way the Revivalists hoped to extract themselves from a pitfall of their own unintentional making.

IV. SUBJECTIVE EXPRESSIONISM AND SINCERITY

The greatest art represents everything with absolute sincerity, as far as it is able. (John Ruskin, *The Laws of Fésole*)

Sincerity is of the essence of good art, and the detection of insincerity is certain. (G. E. Street, *Memoir*)

"It's gude to be honest and true." This line from an old Scottish song appears on the title page of Anthony Trollope's *The New Zealander*, a jeremiad warning that unless society becomes honest and true the New Zealander will arrive to view the ruins of English civilization rather sooner than expected. Critics entertained the same fears for art that Trollope did for society and proclaimed truthfulness with such urgency that it may be fairly said to represent perhaps the most important aesthetic value of the age. In the arts there are several kinds of truth, depending on the different aesthetic theories. For example, the mimetic theory values truthfulness as the accurate correspondence between a work of art and the object it imitates. This is the kind of truth Johnson had in mind when he told Boswell, "The value of every story depends on its being true. A story is a picture of either an individual or of human nature in general: if it be false, it is a picture of nothing" (*Life*, 16 March 1776). The expressive theory, on the other hand, demands a truthful correspondence between the work of art and the soul of the artist. John Stuart Mill describes this variety of truth when he writes that "the truth of poetry is to paint the human soul truly . . ." ("Thoughts on Poetry and Its Varieties"). Critics were careful to distinguish between the two types of truthfulness, and Mill separated them in this way: "Poetry, when it is really such, is truth; and fiction also, if it is good for anything, is truth: but they are different truths. The truth of poetry is to paint the human soul truly: the truth of fiction is to give a true picture of life" ("Thoughts on Poetry and Its Varieties"). Mill apparently makes this distinction on the basis that poetry is expressive and that fiction is mimetic. Pater makes a similar distinction, but at the same time affirms the supremacy of expression over mimesis: "In the highest as in the lowest literature, then, the one indispensible beauty is, after all, truth:—truth to bare fact in the latter, as to some personal sense of fact, diverted somewhat from men's ordinary sense of it, in the former; truth there as accuracy, truth here as expression, that finest and most intimate form of truth, the vrai vérité" ("Style," *Appreciations*, 1889). In *Literature and Sincerity* Henri Peyre differentiates between the two types by designating expressive truth as sincerity, and, although the Victorians seem to have used truth and sincerity synonymously, I shall employ Peyre's helpful distinction in the present discussion of expressionism.

In order to understand the novelty of sincerity as an aesthetic value, the origin of which Peyre traces to Rousseau, we must remember that, ever since the revival of learning in Europe, writers had adopted the classical concept of literature as rhetoric. The significance of this attitude Herbert Read has explained in *The True Voice of Feeling*: "Rhetoric is literature conceived as a game, and to conform to the rules of the game a writer must use and elaborate certain fixed forms, with the object of exhibiting his skill. There was never any question of sincerity. Poetry was treated as a literary game. . . ."[24] To a large degree, rhetoric is didactic; for the skill exhibited by the orator or writer is designed to persuade the listener or reader, and the audience, therefore, becomes the focal point of art. When, however, Romantic expressionism shifts the focus to the artist, the importance of the audience diminishes in consequence. Mill says that the difference between eloquence and poetry is, "Eloquence is *heard*, poetry is *over*heard. Eloquence supposes an audience; the peculiarity of poetry appears to us to lie in the poet's utter unconsciousness of a listener" ("Thoughts on Poetry and Its Varieties"). The importance of this shift in artistic focus from the audience to the artist in terms of sincerity is obvious: when one stands before people to persuade them, one neither can nor cares to be sincere; but when one writes for oneself alone with no thought of others, one can sincerely express one's feelings. The orator creates an effect by calculation and design; the Romantic artist spontaneously expresses emotions. The thoughts Hamlet sincerely reveals in soliloquies are quite different from the remarks he makes to Ophelia for the benefit of Claudius and Polonius behind the screen, and, as Mill says, "All poetry is of the nature of soliloquy."

Sincerity worked both for and against the Victorian artist. It was detrimental because it led him to ignore his audience and so to isolate himself further from it. But it could be beneficial, too, for the audience had come to value sincerity in art and to esteem it above all else. Thackeray appealed to the readers of *Pendennis* to excuse the flaws in his artistry as less important than his sincerity. He may have committed mistakes in writing, but he has been honest with his readers, who will find that he meets such proper expectations as these: "Is he [the author] honest? Does he tell the truth in the main? Does he seem actuated by a desire to find out and speak it? Is he a quack, who shams sentiment, or mouths for effect? Does he seek popularity by claptrap or other arts?" ("Preface," 1850). Henry James wrote later in the century that sincerity was "the only condition that I can think of attaching to the composition of the novel" ("The Art of Fiction"), but the most remarkable statement about sincerity in literature was made by the architectural critic

James Fergusson. It is an extraordinary statement because it in effect denies insincerity by taking as a fundamental rule "that sordid minds cannot express elevation, the impure cannot express purity, or the vulgar mind elegance. . . ." This extreme form of expressionism, which asserts that an artist has no choice but to reveal his character in his work, is augmented by the notion that sincerity is more important than morality and that an audience will respond to truthfulness even when it is offensive. Here is what he says:

> Lord Brougham somewhere remarks, that it is a strange, but melancholy fact, that the three best works of three of the greatest poets of modern times—Voltaire, Burns, and Byron—should be their most impure and licentious productions, the "Pucelle," "The Jolly Beggar," and "Don Juan." Had he looked a little below the surface, he would have known, that it was because the men were themselves impure that they could only truthfully express the impurity in which they revelled. And truth will always find an echo in every human heart, while falsehood can only please a passing fashion, but can strike no truly responsive chord. . . .[25]

It is questionable that Victorians preferred sincerity to morality, but that Fergusson could even conceive of such an explanation testifies to the forcefulness of sincerity as an aesthetic value when he wrote this.

Since architecture was thought to be no less expressive than the other arts, sincerity was as much a criterion for the architect as for the writer or painter. Thomas Graham Jackson used the synonym "frank" in saying that architecture must be "the frank expression of the mind of the artist and of his age. . . ."[26] Ordinarily, when writers spoke of sincerity in architecture they meant one of two things. First, just as collectively a Christian society was required to produce a Christian architecture, that is to say Gothic, so individually a church architect must be a Christian if he is to express sincerely his faith in his work. John Mason Neale and Benjamin Webb would not go so far as to say that "none but monks ought to design churches," but they did think that "a religious *ethos* . . . is essential to a church architect."[27] Pugin had said much the same thing, and Street affirmed that "the church architect must thoroughly believe the doctrines of the church for which he builds. . . ."[28]

Second, the architect must not only be sincerely committed to the religion for which he builds but also to the style in which he builds. For the Revivalists this meant that the architect must be dedicated to the Gothic and that this dedication precluded his working in other styles. This demand was peculiar to architects, for painters and poets were free to choose classical or medieval subjects and could work in whatever genres they pleased, all of which suggests that the restriction to one style proceeded less as a natural development of sincerity than as a capitalization of sincerity by Goths who were eager to promote their cause. The demand was also peculiar to the age in that architects had formerly moved freely from one style to another. The mainly classical architects Adam and Flaxman worked in Gothic, and William Wilkins worked equally in both styles, using the classic for Downing College, Cambridge, and the portico of University College, London, and the Gothic for New Court at Trinity College, Cambridge, and for new buildings at King's College, Cambridge. Sir Charles Barry had made his reputation as a classicist with the Travellers' Club and the Reform Club before he won the competition for the New Houses of Parliament with a Perpendicular design; and even there his son tells us that had it not been for the Gothic remains of Westminster Hall, Sir Charles would have preferred Italian.[29] A good illustration of the stylistic versatility of architects early in the century is an advertisement following the title page of James Malton's *A Collection of Designs for Rural Retreats, as Villas, Principally in the Gothic and Castle Styles of Architecture* (London, 1802): "From his acquaintance with the various styles of architecture, Mr. Malton will alter any sound old building, to any particular style desired, that it may be capable of being converted to; or he will extend any structure, strictly keeping, if desired, to the original style of construction."[30] There is no dedication to a single style and no respect for the historical integrity of buildings in this, which is the sort of indifferent restoration practiced by "Wyatt the De-

structive" that would enrage Ruskin and Morris. It is also the
sort of thing satirized by Pugin in *Contrasts*, where he attacks
modern architectural practice with an illustration of advertise-
ments, one of which reads, "Buildings of Every Description
Altered Into GOTHIC or GRECIAN on Moderate Terms,
Terrace Fronts Designed."

As I have suggested, the Revivalists may have insisted upon
an architect's commitment to a single style as a practical means
of opposing the stylistic indifference of men who were produc-
ing such an incongruous mixture of buildings and as a means
of promoting their own cause; but they urged this on the ultimate basis of expressionism and sincerity, without which values they could not have done so. We see the expressive
rationale in Arthur Edmund Street's comment that for his
father the true architect could work in only one style because
"an artist must show himself in his work, and it would be impossible to do this in antagonistic things." The value of sincerity
appears in another statement from Street's *Memoir*: "To have
designed in any other style would have been impossible to him,
feeling, as he did, that no architect could conscientiously be a
man of many styles. . . ."[31] This rather narrow attitude was probably never very popular outside the most zealous members of
the Revival and of Ecclesiological circles, and certainly it was
expressly opposed by the Eclectics, who advocated an appreciation of different styles. Oscar Wilde identified sincerity with
prejudice that blinds one to the beauties of all art forms. In
"The Critic as Artist" (1891), Wilde's spokesman, Gilbert, says a
"a little sincerity is a dangerous thing, and a great deal of it is
absolutely fatal." He goes on to explain by saying that the true
critic should be unbiased, seeking "beauty in every age and in
each school. . . ." The Gothic Revival had gained a foothold in
the eighteenth century only by establishing eclectic aesthetic
values to allow for the appreciation of styles other than the
overwhelmingly dominant classical one. Ironically, the Revivalists now discovered that the zeal of some was tending toward
the same exclusivity against which they once rebelled and was,

consequently, incurring the same eclectic argument they had themselves once used so effectively.

V. SUBJECTIVE EXPRESSIONISM AND MORALITY

> The revival of Gothic Art was, in short, an assertion of moral principle.
> (E. I. B., "On the Ethical Value of the Gothic Revival")

The introduction of morality into art criticism, what Geoffrey Scott has called the ethical fallacy, came partly from expressionism and sincerity. It came from expressionism in that if a work of art reflects the character of the artist, then its value depends upon the quality of the artist, which came to mean, given the Victorian emphasis on morality, that the value of a work of art depends on the moral rectitude of the artist. In Ruskin's words, "A foolish person builds foolishly, and a wise one, sensibly; a virtuous one, beautifully; and a vicious one, basely."[32] Collectively, the principle operates by establishing a correspondence between the art of any age and the morality of the society that produces it. Ruskin extended the principle in this way by organizing *The Stones of Venice* around the theme that the architecture of Venice flourished and waned in accordance with the morality and immorality of the state. But the relationship between morality and art was well established before the publication of the first volume of the book in 1851, for Pugin had shown in *Contrasts* how a morally upright and Christian Middle Ages had created the glories of Gothic art and how the immorality and corruption of the Renaissance were accountable for the decayed art of paganism. Also, in 1850 Frederick George Stephens wrote in the *Germ*, "The Arts have always been most important moral guides. Their flourishing has always been coincident with the most wholesome period of a nation's . . ." ("The Purpose and Tendency of Early Italian Art").

Morality entered art criticism through sincerity, on the other hand, because truthfulness is, after all, a moral virtue; and once sincerity became an aesthetic value, it was naturally attended by

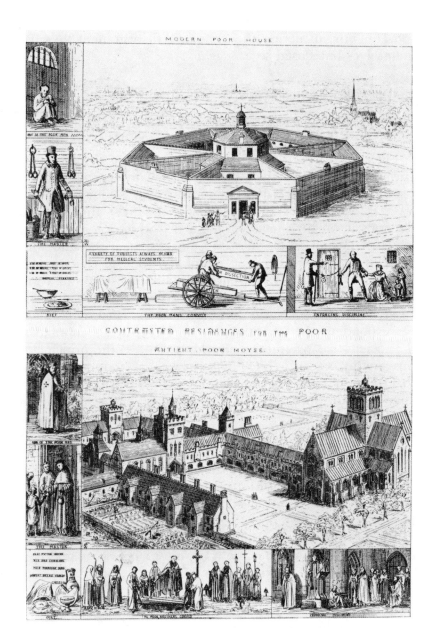

Fig. 8. An illustration showing the connection between morality and architecture. From A. W. N. Pugin's *Contrasts*, 2d ed. (1841; rpt. New York: Humanities Press, 1973), n.p.

moral implications. Christopher Dresser drew truth, morality, and art together in 1873 when he wrote, "There can be morality or immorality in art, the utterance of truth or of falsehood. . . ."[33]

If I am right in seeing these connections between aesthetics and morality, then Kenneth Clark's explanation for the nineteenth century's tendency to evaluate art according to the moral worth of the artist is misleading. In *The Gothic Revival* he writes, "Whenever esthetic standards are lost, ethical standards rush in to fill the vacuum; for the interest in esthetics dwindles and vanishes, but the interest in ethics is eternal."[34] I do not doubt that Victorian morality arose quite independently of aesthetics, but I do deny that ethical standards replaced absent aesthetic ones, for my point is that morality combined with art because of, not for lack of, the aesthetic values of expressionism, sincerity, and, as we shall see later, functionalism. Had these values not existed, there may have been morality and art but not morality in art.

In 1886 Henry Van Brunt described the Gothic Revival as "the only instance in history of a moral revolution in art."[35] Perhaps so, but Savanorola created a minor upheaval in the fifteenth century, and the association between morality and art extends as far back as the Platonic equation of the Beautiful and the Good. Christianity later affirmed the equation of the two through its teaching that goodness is beautiful and evil is ugly. When, therefore, the Victorians united ethics and aesthetics, they were calling upon the same Greek and Christian traditions as did Kant, who wrote in *The Critique of Judgment* (1790) that "the beautiful is the symbol of the morally good." And when they evaluated art according to the character of the artist, they were criticizing from the same point of view as Shelley, who had written in "A Defence of Poetry" that "the greatest poets have been men of the most spotless virtue. . . ." Finally, lest we believe that Robert Buchanan's notorious attack on Rossetti in "The Fleshly School of Poetry" was the simple consequence of Victorian morality, we should recall that Thomas Bowdler expurgated Shakespeare, Robert Southey accused

Byron of leading the "Satanic School of Poetry," and Lord Chancellor Eldon refused Shelley custody of his children because of "Queen Mab" long before the Victorian period ever began. The Gothic Revival, then, if it was "a moral revolution in art," was, like all revolutions, as much an evolution from certain elements in established authority as a rebellion against them.

If, furthermore, one chooses to regard the Revival in this way, one sees that it is like all revolutions in creating by reaction a counterrevolution. Referring to Ruskin, Charles Eastlake wrote in *A History of the Gothic Revival*, "To what extent morality and art were allied in the Middle Ages, or any other period of the world's history, may be doubtful. What we do know is, that in the nineteenth century a bad artist is not unfrequently a very good Christian, and that an indifferent Christian may be an excellent artist."[36] For the most part, though, opposition to moralistic art criticism came from the Art-for-Art's-Sake group, whose objective approach to art denied expressionism. For example, Théophile Gautier refuted the identification of author and work by writing in the preface to *Mademoiselle de Maupin* that the novelist maintains an objective distance between himself and his characters. In his "Ten O'Clock" lecture, Whistler argued that morality has nothing to do with art. "In no way," he says, "do our virtues minister to its [art's] worth, in no way do our vices impede its triumph!" He then goes on to prove his point by the example of worthy yet utterly uncreative Switzerland, whose liberty and righteousness have produced nothing more artistic than "the clock that turns the mill, and the sudden cuckoo, with difficulty restrained in its box."

The opposition to moral judgments of art was founded on other grounds than the objectivist denial of expressionism. One of these was realism, which stipulated that the accurate and unselective depiction of life in all its conditions, moral or immoral, was more important to art than its ethical value. Another of these arose in reaction to didacticism, whose chief point was that art should elevate the morals of the people through an overt and calculated design. Perhaps this was the stronger of the two, for artists perceived in didacticism a threat to the integrity of themselves and their art, and sought then more strenuously than they otherwise would have to wrest art from the dominance of morality by elevating art above all things. Instead of art serving religion, they made religion serve art, as when Rossetti uses Christian symbols for aesthetic effects rather than for the propagation of faith. The Aesthetes were to carry the tendency yet further by making a religion of their art.

VI. OBJECTIVE EXPRESSIONISM

Few monuments have a true character of their own and few architects appear to have concerned themselves with giving their architecture character; and yet this is the ideal, the Poetry of art, its most sublime aspect, and the one which makes it true art. (Etienne-Louis Boullée, *Architecture, Essai sur l'art*)

The style of a building should so correspond with its use that the spectator may at once perceive the purpose for which it was erected. (Welby Pugin, *Contrasts*)

Whereas subjective expressionism focuses upon the artist, whether individual or collective, by regarding art primarily as an expression of the artist's character, objective expressionism focuses on the object to be portrayed by regarding art primarily as an expression of the object's character; but in either case the presentation of this intangible quality is the key element in the creation of art, and without it the product, no matter how excellent technically, lacks life and therefore value. Objective expressionism requires, for example, that the portrait painter capture the personality of his model and somehow incarnate it in facial features on canvas. This, I take it, is where Fra Pandolf succeeds so well in painting the duke of Ferrara's last duchess and why the "depth and passion of her earnest glance" invests the portrait with its lifelike quality. The landscape painter or descriptive poet is similarly committed to embodying in his art the spiritual character of the scene.

Now what soul is to the person and what spirit is to the place, purpose is to the building; for just as surely as soul and spirit compose the inner and special character of people and places, so purpose defines the individual character of a building. The architect, then, for his part should try to express in his design the purpose for which the building is erected. Thus defined, his task was much easier than that of painter or poet since he needed little in the way of penetrative imagination to apprehend purpose; and once he grasped it, he had something rather more definite and substantial to work with than elusive abstractions like spirit and soul. Also, once he set about expressing purpose, although the materials with which he had to work were less tractable than paints and words, his task was easier than that of painting "earnest glances" since nothing could be simpler than designing for function by starting with the plan and allowing the elevation to develop more or less as it may. A building constructed on these principles must almost necessarily bespeak its purpose because its exterior is the natural outgrowth and visible manifestation of its functional purpose.[37]

The aesthetic principle of objective expressionism, then, lies behind Pugin's declaration in *Contrasts* that "the great test of Architectural beauty is the fitness of the design to the purpose for which it is intended, and . . . the style of a building should so correspond with its use that the spectator may at once perceive the purpose for which it was erected."[38] But, in addition, there was also the functional approach of eighteenth-century French rationalism, and there was further support for the notion that a building should reveal its purpose in the picturesque theorists Humphrey Repton and Richard Payne Knight as well as in the architectural writers John Britton and John Loudon. There was, therefore, a considerable weight of opinion behind Pugin when he satirized in the dedicatory illustration of *Contrasts* such execrable shams of contemporary architecture as "a moorish fish market," "a castelated turnpike gate," and "a gin temple in the baronial style." The same principle applied to smaller objects, and Pugin similarly objected to the disguise involved in designing a clock as "a Roman warrior in a flying chariot, round one of the wheels of which, on close inspection, the hours may be descried. . . ."[39]

If objective expressionism in architecture involved nothing more than the revelation of purpose, then the architect's task would have indeed been a simpler one than that of his fellow artists in poetry and painting, but the theory has a more complex aspect that draws architecture closer to the other arts both in the effect that it is supposed to create and in the difficulty with which the effect is achieved. To distinguish between these two kinds, we might borrow linguistic terms and call the simple variety denotative expressionsim and the complex variety connotative expressionism. Denotative expressionism means, carrying through the linguistic analogy, calling a house a house and not a temple, castle, or whatever. Connotative expressionism means calling the house a home, thereby going beyond the bare designation of the thing to summon up an aura of thought and feeling associated with the thing. This aura, it will be at once perceived, is more nearly akin than purpose to the soul or spirit of painting and poetry, its mode of expression is similar to the techniques in the other arts, and its usual name, consequently, is "poetry"—"the poetry of architecture." The expression of a building's abstract character, its connotative values, came to be regarded as the essential element in architecture as an art. George Gilbert Scott stressed the importance of this kind of expression while at the same time indicating appropriate qualities for various types of buildings, when he made this comment as president of the Royal Institute of Architects:

> That buildings should and may be noble, grand, beautiful,—should have an expression in accordance with their character and purpose . . . is what we properly understand by architecture, over and above the utilitarian purpose of building. Hence the *solemn* temple, the *sumptuous* palace, the *severe* court of justice, the *gloomy* prison, the *frowning* fortification, the *meditative* cloisters, the *seclusion* of the college, the *inviting, joyous rest* of home, are all expressions which have been sought and realised in building; and the true architect is he who perceives the possibilities of these vivid impressions of aesthetic pleasure, and is able to satisfy them. . . .[40]

Once the architect had perceived these possibilities, just how was he to satisfy them? Vitruvius had confronted a similar problem, although he conceived it in terms of propriety rather than of expression, and found an answer in the appropriate use of the orders. In building temples to the various deities, Doric should be used for the virile strength of Mars, Hercules, and

Minerva; Corinthian for the delicacy of Venus, Flora, and Pros-
erpine; and Ionic for the mediate divinities of Juno, Diana, and
Bacchus.[41] But the classic orders inadequately met the more
complex demands of expressionism, besides being altogether
useless for Gothic, and so new solutions had to be found. Boullée, who considered the poetry of architecture before anything
else in beginning a design, relied chiefly on symbolical arrangements. For example, he placed a prison underneath the Palace
of Justice to create "an impressive metaphorical image of Vice
overwhelmed by the weight of Justice." In designing the Municipal Palace, he "placed guard-houses at the four angles of the
foundation of the building to proclaim metaphorically that the
forces of public order are the basis of society."[42]

Boullée's method, although similar to the overt symbolism in
Victorian narrative paintings, is nevertheless somewhat crude
compared with later solutions. Samuel Huggins, for example,
explained that the expression of an institution's moral or mental qualities by the building's material qualities depends upon
analogies between the two kinds of qualities, by which he means
that certain ideas are associated with various shapes, volumes,
and textures in a way rather more vague and subtle than the
way ideas are evoked by symbols. "Thus," he says, "rough-hewn
and boldly rusticated masonry, harsh angular lines, lofty and
unpierced walls, will give the ideas of a prison; prison-like
strength, combined with palatial sumptuousness of decoration,
will characterise a bank; severity of outline and form, a character grave and solemn, of patriarchal simplicity, in which
nothing is hidden, intricate or but partially told, and the absence of all imaginativeness, will distinguish a justice court."[43]
Huggins does admit, however, that in some cases analogy alone
is insufficient and that the architect must then resort to allegorical sculpture.

In addition to the allegorical use of sculpture, though, the
degree to which ornament was used could be a means of expression and a fairly simple one, too. William Butterfield, for
example, used ornament to express social and religious
hierarchies at Baldersby village, where the laborers' cottages

Fig. 9. Allegorical sculpture—a moneky and a cat, representing litigants, carved over the judges' entrance to the Royal Courts of Justice, London.

are very plain, the schoolmaster's house is decorated Gothic, the vicarage is more ornate still, and the church is the most highly decorated of all.[44] Richard Norman Shaw kept ornament to a minimum in his design for New Scotland Yard, aiming, in the words of an interviewer from *Murray's Magazine*, "at solidity and sternness to give simplicity. . . . His view of the Metropolitan Police is that it is an essentially stern, and not at all frivolous body."[45]

VII. SUBSTANCE OVER FORM

> Expression is the soul of Art, without which it is inanimate and dead. ("On Invention and Expression")

> And in exactly measured and inevitable degree, as architecture is more ingenious, it is less passionate. (John Ruskin, "The Flamboyant Architecture of the Valley of the Somme")

What I have called subjective expressionism and objective expressionism, although at variance in some respects, are alike in exalting the poetry of art as the essential quality and in making it, consequently, the chief criterion in aesthetic judgments. Moreover, as feeling became the measure of all things, correctness, refinement, and technical expertise became devalued in a direct ratio, and Romantic primitivism drew support from yet another source.

This preference for feeling over skill was most frequently apparent in evaluations of painting, that art form which revealed the opposition of values most clearly. Ruskin, for example, criticized John Brett's landscape of the Val d'Aosta for being "wholly emotionless. I cannot find from it that the painter loved, or feared, anything in all that wonderful piece of the world. There seems to me no awe of the mountains there—no real love of the chestnuts or the vines. Keenness of eye and fineness of hand as much as you choose; but of emotion, or of intention, nothing traceable."[46] More than Brett, however, Browning's Andrea del Sarto is famous for making the mistake of gaining finish at the expense of substance. Andrea is the faultless painter who surpasses in technical expertise Raphael, Leonardo, and Michael Angelo, but in his faultlessness ironically lies his fault, for his paintings lack the soul and vital fire of his rivals' less perfect yet greater works.[47]

Although painting may be most suitable for illustrating this principle, other art forms, architecture among them, exemplify it as well. James Fergusson pointed out that although medieval churches lack technical perfection, they "must speak to the heart of man in all ages; whereas, in spite of all the perfection to which the mechanical processes of art have been carried in our days, there is an absence of mind in its productions that renders them vapid and powerless. . . ."[48] When applied to architecture, the principle was usually described with reference to the worker since it is he who actually executed the design, and surely the noblest statement is Ruskin's famous chapter in *The Stones of Venice*, "The Nature of Gothic." The theme of this chapter has been explained by its foremost exponent, William Morris, to be "that the art of any epoch must of necessity be the expression of its social life, and that the social life of the Middle Ages allowed the workman freedom of individual expression, which on the other hand our social life forbids him" ("The Revival of Architecture"). It is more important that the workman freely express himself than that his execution be perfect. Indeed, the two are incompatible, for, as Ruskin said, "*the demand for perfection is always a sign of a misunderstanding of the ends of art.*" With architecture none "can be truly noble which is *not* imperfect."[49] An indication of Ruskin's evolution from an art critic to a social critic is that he justifies these remarks by focusing on the welfare of the worker rather than the value of the artistic product. Of course, the emphasis on the artist over the work is part of subjective expressionism, but Ruskin carries the theory a step further by introducing religion and moral values with his concern for the happiness of the workman. Christian art accepts imperfection in workmanship since Christianity acknowledges the fallen condition of man. To demand perfection is immoral since it enslaves the worker by refusing him the free expression of ideas.

Others, with perhaps more of an artistic and less of a social interest, were not as sanguine about the creative expressiveness of workers as Ruskin and Morris. Butterfield, according to Swinfen Harris, "was opposed to the new cult of letting the workman think and act for himself"; and Pugin refused a request to support a school for laborers on the basis that "workmen are a singular class, and from my experience of them, which is rather extensive, are generally incapable of taking a high view on these subjects,—and ready at a moment to leave their instructors and benefactors for an extra sixpence a day for the first bidder that turns up. . . ."[50] Street's distrust extended even to his own draftsmen, whose work he directed and examined in every detail.

There is some evidence that these practicing architects were more accurate in their assessment of the workers' abilities than the theorists, Ruskin and Morris. One danger of granting workmen free rein and of glorifying imperfection was shoddy workmanship. For art and architecture in general, Fergusson advocated expression over form; but when it came to modern Gothic, he faulted the poor execution of it· "The carpentry must be as rude and as unmechanically put together as possible; the glazing as clumsy and the glass as bad as can be found."[51] These remarks might be attributed to his antipathy to Gothic Revival architecture were they not lent credence by Ralph Adams Cram's corroboration that architects are often dismayed to see their designs so imperfectly realized by poor craftsmanship.[52]

Another danger in allowing artisans freedom of execution was that their work was frequently at variance with, and sometimes in outright contradiction to, the architect's intent for the building, which could become a confused jumble of many minds rather than the unified product of a master design. Dr. Henry Acland's tribulations with the willful Irish sculptors O'Shea and the Oxford Museum provide a good illustration of the problems that might arise when a workman was determined to have his own way. The sometimes scandalous designs on the undersides of misereres were as independently carved by artisans in the Middle Ages as the figures condemned by Acland, and the Ecclesiologists found them just as unpardonable. On the other hand, the Ecclesiologists accepted the "disgusting forms" of gargoyles by justifying them as representative of demons driven from the church by the holy power of sanctification. But occasionally they are indefensible, as when some medieval O'Shea carved at St. Clement, Horsley, a wolf preaching in monk's attire.[54]

The Ecclesiologists' approval of gargoyles as symbolizing the power of Christianity over demons and Ruskin's justification of imperfect workmanship as a necessary feature of the thinking artist both proceed from the premise that expression in art, whether of a religious truth or of a craftman's soul, overrides beauty of form. There are, of course, other reasons for what some consider ugliness in Victorian art. Robert Kerr, C. F. A. Voysey, and, more recently, Peter Collins attribute ugliness in the useful arts to functionalism. John Summerson and Kenneth Clark, on the other hand, blame a deliberate preference for ugliness, which Summerson ascribes, in turn, to bourgeois Puritanism.[55] They are only partly right, for the ugliness to modern eyes of some Victorian art has multiple causes, and one of the most important is that expression as an aesthetic value came to have more weight than beauty of form.

In order to follow this change in taste, we must return to the starting point for Babbitt, Lessing's *Laocoön*. In explaining why the ancient sculptor portrayed Laocoön as sighing rather than screaming, Lessing said that for one thing Greek artists depicted only the beautiful and that a scream would distort the face into ugliness. In other words, for the ancient Greeks beauty of form was more important than expression of feeling. This is one reason, then, for the temperate sigh on Laocoön's face. The sculptor found that "the demands of beauty could not be reconciled with the pain in all its disfiguring violence, so it had to be reduced. The scream had to be softened to a sigh . . . because it distorts the features in a disgusting manner."[56] Lessing's contemporary, Sir Joshua Reynolds, applied the theory to modern painting in "Discourse V." "If you mean to preserve the most perfect beauty *in its most perfect state*," Reynolds counseled, "you cannot express the passions, all of which produce distortion and deformity, more or less, in the most beautiful faces." What was true for art was true for life. The earl of Chesterfield advised his son to refrain from laughter, which is the ill-bred and vulgar way "the mob express their silly joy at silly things; and they call it being merry" (9 March 1748). A gentleman should repress his low passions and allow expression only to wit and sense by means of a restrained cheerfulness of countenance, hence the serene and tranquil "smile of reason" in most eighteenth-century portraits. However, in addition to revealing the unruly passions of the vulgar, laughter is unbecoming according to Chesterfield because of "the disagreeable noise that it makes, and the shocking distortion of the face that it occasions." Laughter is as ugly to Chesterfield as the scream to the sculptor of Laocoön or the expression of any passion to Reynolds.

Charles Kingsley reaffirmed this idea in the next century when he spoke of the elevating influence of beauty on common workmen. A picture gallery, Kingsley wrote, is to the worker an oasis of beauty in a desert of ugliness, for "those noble faces on the wall are never disfigured by grief or passion" ("The National Gallery—No. I," 6 May 1848). But by the time he wrote this, most of his contemporaries had come to prefer expression over serene beauty. Much earlier, in fact, Blake had reacted to Reynolds's comment about the incompatibility of beauty and the expression of passion with this note in his copy of the *Discourses*: "What Nonsense! Passion & Expression is Beauty Itself. The Face that is Incapable of Passion & Expression is deformity Itself. Let it be Painted & Patch'd & Praised & Advertised for Ever, it will only be admired by Fools." Blake's own pictures support this change in attitude as do those, for example, of Fuseli and Goya. In poetry one might select the startling first line of the "Soliloquy of the Spanish Cloister"—"Gr-r-r—there go, my heart's abhorrence!"—as a further illustration of the change. Even keeping in mind Lessing's contention that writing is better able to describe violent feelings than sculpture or painting, we may take this line as indicating that Browning considered the expression of his speaker's malice to be more important than mellifluous verse. Whether a Victorian archtitect believed along with Blake that the expression of feeling is beautiful or with Browning that it is more important than beauty, in either case he would have chosen the irregular, even grotesque, forms of the Gothic over the placidly regular, but less expressive, forms of the classic.

PUBLIC BUILDINGS

Fig. 10. Midland Grand Hotel, St. Pancras Station, London, by Sir George Gilbert Scott, 1873.

Fig. 11. Victoria Tower and south side of the Houses of Parliament, London, by Sir Charles Barry and Welby Pugin, 1840–60.

Fig. 12. The Royal Courts of Justice, Strand, London, by George Edmund Street, 1874–82.

Fig. 13. Manchester Town Hall, by Alfred Waterhouse, 1868-77.

ACADEMIC BUILDINGS

Fig. 14. Charterhouse School, Surrey, by Philip Charles Hardwick, 1865–72.

Fig. 15. New Court, St. John's College, Cambridge, by Thomas Rickman and Henry Hutchinson, 1825–31.

Fig. 16. University Museum, Oxford, by Sir Thomas Deane and Benjamin Woodward, 1855–60.

CHURCHES

Fig. 17. All Saints', Denstone, Staffordshire, by George Edmund Street, 1860–62.

Fig. 18. Church of the Holy Angels, Hoar Cross, Staffordshire, by George Frederick Bodley and Thomas Garner, 1876.

Fig. 19. St. Philip and St. James's, Oxford, by George Edmund Street, 1860–66.

COUNTRY HOUSES

Fig. 20. Balmoral, Aberdeenshire, by Prince Albert and William Smith, 1853–55.

Fig. 21. The earl of Shrewsbury's Alton Towers, Staffordshire, by Welby Pugin, 1837–52.

HOUSES

Fig. 22. Tower House, Kensington, London, by William Burges for himself, 1875–81.

Fig. 23. The Grange, Ramsgate, by Welby Pugin for himself, 1843–44.

IV. MIMESIS

I. THE IMITATION OF NATURAL PRINCIPLE

> First follow Nature, and your judgment frame
> By her just standard, which is still the same:
> Unerring Nature! still divinely bright,
> One clear, unchang'd, and universal light,
> Life, force, and beauty, must to all impart,
> At once the source, and end, and test of art.
>
> Alexander Pope, *An Essay on Criticism*

> [Architecture] applies itself, like Musick (and I believe we may add Poetry),
> directly to the imagination, without the intervention of any kind of imita-
> tion. (Sir Joshua Reynolds, "Discourse XIII")

> [Architecture] does not consist, like the others, in the imitation of natural
> forms, but only of natural principles. (Edward Lacy Garbett, *Rudimentary
> Treatise*)

Just as Wordsworth's definition of poetry as "the spontaneous
overflow of powerful feelings" is the classical statement of the
expressive theory of art, so is Hamlet's instruction to the travel-
ing players that the end of drama is "to hold the mirror up to
nature" the corresponding summary of the mimetic approach.
M. H. Abrams has said that art as imitation—as a mirror, in
Shakespeare's words—is the oldest and most prevalent aesthetic doctrine in Western culture, extending back to Plato and
dominating classical and neoclassical art. One might add that
long before any formal criticism of art, imitation was the aim of
primitive art, guiding, for example, the hand of some prehistoric Iberian in the caves of Altamira. With so many centuries
of tradition behind it, mimesis was firmly enough established as
an aesthetic doctrine to maintain a powerful influence in the
nineteenth century, even though it was radically altered to
accommodate the new concepts of expressionism and organicism, and not until the end of the century did it cease to figure
importantly in artistic theory.

But can mimetic principles apply to architecture? Sir Joshua
Reynolds had said in "Discourse XIII" that architecture was not
an imitative art, and almost a hundred years later, T. G. Jackson admitted in *Modern Gothic Architecture* that nature was rarely

151

used as a principle in judging architecture since there is no
obvious connection between the forms of nature and of building. Painting and sculpture are preeminently mimetic, writing
can be vividly descriptive, and even music, as with Beethoven's
Pastoral Symphony, is able to represent nature, but architecture
seems to lie beyond the reach of this particular aesthetic doctrine.

Despite the apparent incompatibility of this art form and this
aesthetic doctrine, there were persistent attempts to make
architecture conform with mimesis and to show that buildings
could follow nature as readily as poems and paintings. In June
of 1860 the twenty-first annual meeting of the Ecclesiological
Society had as its topic for discussion "The Tendencies of
Praeraffaelitism, and its connection with the Gothic movement." The president, A. J. B. Beresford-Hope, argued that
the minute realism of the Pre-Raphaelites was at odds with the
Gothic Revival, which was essentially imaginative and spiritual.
It was commendable that the members of the Brotherhood
were interested in Arthurian legends, but they should not paint
Guinevere "with a face which they might see on the first passer-
by in Conduit Street." William Burges, on the other hand, said
that the two movements were parallel because both went back
to first elements, the Pre-Raphaelites to nature and the Cam-
dens to old churches. George Edmund Street agreed with
Burges and expanded on his remarks by saying the Pre-
Raphaelite school developed precisely as the Gothic Revival:
"Such a man as Pugin (though he might not be admired in all
things) taught them to think of nothing but truth in their art,
and that they should do in architecture what was true and
natural; and that was what seemed to be the object of the
Praeraffaelites."[1] Years later Lethaby made the same point in
comparing Philip Webb to Browning: "Webb was one of the
typical (and I believe great) Victorians; he did, or tried to do,
for building what Browning attempted for poetry: to revitalize
it by returning to contact with reality."[2]

Truth to nature, then, was as much a cardinal rule for architecture as it was for painting and literature. Garbett wrote that
"it is the highest possible aim of architecture, as of all the other

fine arts, to *imitate nature*"; and T. G. Jackson said that architecture is "based upon the recognition of certain forms or qualities in animate or inanimate nature."[3] There were several explanations of just how architecture imitated nature, one of the earliest and most popular being that the Gothic style was originally inspired by, and modeled on, the forests of northern Europe. R. C. Dallas mentions the explanation in *The Morlands* (1805) when he remarks that linden branches "it has been said, gave the first idea of those Gothic structures that are the pride of former days, and the admiration of the present"; and later in the century Richard Monckton Milnes described olive groves as "Sylvan cathedrals, such as in old times/Gave the first life to Gothic art, and led/Imagination so sublime a way" ("Corfu").[4]

Other writers, less interested in architectural origins, observed simple visual parallels between Gothic churches and trees. Goethe compared Strassburg Cathedral to a "lofty, far-spreading tree of God" (*Von deutscher Baukunst*, 1773), Friedrich Schlegel likened the interior pillars of Cologne Cathedral to an avenue of trees and the exterior to a forest (*Grundzuge der gothischen Baukunst*, 1805), and Chateaubriand saw similarities between the spires of a Gothic church and the tops of trees, between the music emanating from those towers and "the very winds and thunders that roar in the recesses of the woods" (*The Genius of Christianity*, 1802). Adelaide A. Procter, the eldest daughter of Barry Cornwall, provides an English and Victorian example of the comparison in "A Tomb in Ghent":

> Dim with dark shadows of the ages past,
> St. Bavon stands, solemn and rich and vast;
> The slender pillars, in long vistas spread,
> Like forest arches meet and close o'erhead.

The perception of Gothic architecture as being like northern forests, although persistent and popular in literary works, did not seem to gain much acceptance by architectural writers, who perhaps regarded it as too fanciful. Architectural writers did, however, believe that imitation of natural forms was possible by means of the mimetic sister arts of painting and sculpture; and by considering these arts to be of such integral importance to architecture, they were able to apply, indirectly at any rate, imitative standards to architecture. In some cases these writers agreed with the budding realistic tendencies of poets and painters to abandon artistic conventions and be true to nature. Ruskin wrote that "the greatest decorative art is wholly unconventional," and George Gilbert Scott recalled that at the outset of his career he copied the conventional foliage of early English work but that he later came to believe "it was inconsistent to revive bygone conventionalism in matters originally derived from nature; and that while we might imitate the architecture of another period, we must always go to nature direct . . . for objects of which nature was the professed origin. . . ."[5]

Both Ruskin and Scott stressed the importance of botanical knowledge for the architect, but there were far more who believed that such knowledge was as useless to an architect as to a Moslem artist, whose religion forbade direct representations of nature, and that nature should be conventionally treated in art. Christopher Dresser wrote in *Principles of Decorative Design* that *"if plants are employed as ornaments they must not be treated imitatively, but must be conventionally treated, or rendered into ornaments,"* and his attitude is in accord with what both Owen Jones in *The Grammar of Ornament* and Ralph Nicholson Wornum in "The Exhibition as a Lesson in Taste" had to say earlier on the same subject.[6] Architects as well as ornamentalists advocated conventional treatment of nature. Butterfield did, and so did Street, who gave several reasons for his choice. First, after pointing out that stained glass does not allow for accurate copying of nature, he goes on to say, in what amounts to the eighteenth-century concept of general nature, that "conventional representations of natural forms are usually the absolute forms which Nature has produced. . . ." Second, Street believes that the conventional is superior to the literal in beauty, for no "representation in oak or brass of a real eagle for a book-desk ever approached in real grandeur" conventional eagles. Finally, the conventional has been sanctified by time and custom, so that a conventional representation of Christ, though historically inaccurate, is more reverent than an attempt at realism. Consequently, "the religious conventions of many ages of often very devout artists are worth more than the latest conceit of the nineteenth century. . . ."[7]

There was, then, some disagreement among the proponents of the Revival about the proper way for architectural ornament to imitate nature, Street and Butterfield arguing for the conventional approach but Ruskin and Scott advocating the newer, realistic approach. In the end, the dispute was of little more consequence to architectural theory than the belief that Gothic arose in imitation of towering trees, for architects had by this time found a far more satisfactory link with nature through the imitation of principles instead of forms, discovering, in the words of Edward Lacy Garbett, that their art form "does not consist, like the others, in the imitation of natural forms, but only of natural principles."[8] This recognition is comparable to the reiterated advice of imitating the principles of artistic precedents rather than copying their forms and undoubtedly owes something to it, but no doubt the Romantic emphasis upon the abstract, spiritual quality of nature as the most important element and the one most worthy of representation in art contributed to architecture's reliance on principles. In "On Poesy or Art" (1808), Coleridge had written that the artist should imitate *natura naturans* rather than *natura naturata*; that is to say, he "must imitate that which is within the thing, that which is active through form and figure, and discourses to us by symbols—the *Natur-geist*, or spirit of nature. . . ." This interpretation of the artist's goal allowed for objective expressionism, but, more to the point, it also relieved the architect of the obligation to imitate outward forms and freed him to adapt abstract qualities, qualities that could, in turn, "discourse to us" in the special symbolical language of architecture.

II. THE PRINCIPLES TO BE IMITATED

> The Old Naturalism is at one, then, with the New in proposing conformity to nature as its great law. Where the two differ is in the meaning they set upon the words "conformity to nature." (W. S. Lilly, "The New Naturalism")

Accompanying the aesthetic shift reflected by Coleridge—or, perhaps more correctly, responsible for the aesthetic shift—was

the replacement of the old mechanistic concept of the universe
by the new organic concept of it. This new perception of the
world meant that when the artist sought out the principles of
nature, he would find not the inert, static, and regular properties of a world-machine that Newton had revealed to his predecessors but instead the vital, dynamic, and irregular elements
of an organic universe. Furthermore, when that artist was an
architect, he discovered that the principles inherent in the
organic view of the world accorded far more readily with the
Gothic than with the classic style. The time was ripe for a return
to pointed architecture.

One analogy between architecture and nature that was based
upon organic principles is rather general in its application and
was used to account for the development of architectural styles.
Sometimes this type of analogy was employed—by Samuel
Huggins, for example—to explain the environmental influence
on style: "As the geographical distribution of plants in the
vegetable world is influenced by conditions of soil, heat, mois-
ture, light, and many other causes, so the geographical
arrangement of architectural styles is ordered by conditions of
climate, scenery, &c.. . . ."[9] Revivalists were able to use this
point in arguing for the fitness of Gothic for English buildings
and for the unsuitability of classical, which had arisen in a totally different climate. At other times writers used the organic
analogy to justify stylistic evolution, as when M. H. Baillie Scott
wrote that "art, if it is alive, must always so change and develop;
for in the continual flux of human affairs, to stand still is to
fossilise and decay."[10] But most frequently, the organic analogy
was applied to the development of architectural styles to suggest their spontaneous origin. Just as the individual work of art
is the spontaneous expression of a single artist's mind, so is art
collectively the spontaneous and natural expression of the society out of which it organically grows. The "intertwined fibres"
of old English architecture, wrote John Sedding, "had grown
from one tree, from one root of national genius, in a leisurely,
unconscious way from first to last."[11] The Gothic Revivalists
were to turn this premise into an argument against both their

Greek enemies and those who were demanding a new style. To seek an entirely new style was absurd, Street said, because all styles must arise naturally and unconsciously: "Very cautiously must we use the word [*invention*], however, for no style has ever been invented; either it has come by growth or by decay, the process in either case being as gradual and as equal as it is in Nature itself."[12] It was no less wrong to build after classical models because they were of a style that had been artificially imported into England during the Renaissance and had not developed naturally. Art cannot survive transplantation, so dependent is it on the cultural soil from which it springs. In Cram's words, "You cannot sever art from society; you cannot make it grow in unfavorable soil, however zealously you may labour and lecture and subsidize. It follows from certain spiritual and social conditions, and without these it is a dead twig thrust in sand, and only a divine miracle can make such bloom, as blossomed the staff of St. Joseph of Arimathea at Glastonbury."[13] On the other hand, Gothic architecture, as Morris pointed out, "is the most completely organic form of the Art which the world has seen," in that it developed naturally and uninterruptedly in those countries where it is indigenous ("Gothic Architecture").

A second natural principle that was applied to architecture, as well as to the other arts, is organic form. In *On Dramatic Art and Literature*, A. W. Schlegel had defined organic form by contrasting it with mechanical form, and a few years later Coleridge repeated Schlegel's distinction in his lectures on Shakespeare. "The form is mechanic," Coleridge said,

> when on any given material we impress a predetermined form, not necessarily arising out of the properties of the material, as when to a mass of wet clay we give whatever shape we wish it to retain when hardened. The organic form, on the other hand, is innate; it shapes as it develops itself from within, and the fullness of its development is one and the same with the perfection of its outward form. Such is the life, such the form. Nature, the prime genial artist, inexhaustible in diverse powers, is equally inexhaustible in forms. Each exterior is the physiognomy of the being within, its true image reflected and thrown out from the concave mirror.

This belief in organic form is a part of other Romantic concepts and is of considerable use in explaining them. It clarifies, for example, the Romantic emphasis on particulars as means of access to the ideal; for if form is determined from within and is the true image of the internal, then the form of any object in nature, no matter how small or insignificant, reveals the life spirit inherent in it. When the life spirit is deified, nature becomes sacramental, revealing symbolically through form the divinity within. In other words, *natura naturata* reflects *natura naturans*.

Organic form also helps explain subjective expressionism, for the relationship between the artist and his work is similar to that between God and nature. Both artist and divinity create, both art and nature emanate from within, and, therefore, the artist reveals himself as completely in a work of art, whose form is an organic expression of the artist's soul, as God is revealed in nature. As we have seen, organic form in this sense was a popular architectural ideal; for the architect was supposed, either consciously or not, to express his character in a building just as society was to manifest its collective character in its buildings. One could, then, "read" the buildings and come to know the architect and his age.[14] In addition, organic form helps explain objective expressionism in architecture since the idea that a building's exterior should reveal the building's purpose is so closely akin to Coleridge's explanation of organic form as that in which the "exterior is the physiognomy of the being within."[15] These relationships explain in part why it was so important to Victorian architects, and Gothic Revival ones in particular, that a building accurately and honestly reflect its function and its social origins. Moreover, the analogy to organic form in architecture was a persuasive argument against neoclassic architects, who sometimes designed the elevation before the plan and who were, therefore, guilty of imposing a mechanical form from without rather than allowing the building to take an organic shape from within. In insisting that the plan should precede the elevation, that the interior requirements should determine the exterior form, and that the structure should not be disguised, Gothic Revival architects were arguing for organic form, although they came to understand the term in a somewhat different way from Coleridge; for the concept was being modified, and thereby brought more in line with architecture, by evolutionary doctrine that substituted function for a divine life force as the inner essence determining form. That is, Darwin and others showed that the shapes, sizes, and colors of animals and plants were all the results of functional determinants. While, therefore, the overlapping theories of expressionism and organic form continued throughout the century to support belief in architecture as revelatory of more or less spritual features of architect and society, the changing concept toward organic form led architecture in the direction of functional expressionism.

A very simple statement of this approach is Street's comment that "in good work the external form is always a translation of the internal structure, a building, if it is perfect, being as complete an organism as the human frame."[16] A more complex version of the same attitude, incorporating the values of truth and beauty, is the following passage from M. H. Baillie Scott's "Ideals in Building, False and True":

> If you look around you at the creations of nature, there is one striking fact in them which cannot be overlooked. It is that the forms of things are always the outcome of functions. The leaves and branches of the trees are all so shaped for certain definite practical purposes in the economy of the organism. . . . and if we apply this to art—to the building art in particular—we shall find that its products, if they are to be true like the creations of nature, must clothe themselves with forms which are the outcome of functions. . . . Let us try and remember, once for all, that the forms and features of building have no reason for existence at all apart from their uses. In the human frame the eye would be useless without sight, the arm useless without might. And so in a building, whenever the forms arrive naturally and obviously from the requirements of the structure, they achieve a kind of almost vital beauty.[17]

If one chooses to emphasize the word *vital* in the last sentence of Scott's comments, one is not far from a third natural principle assumed by architecture, which is that buildings are sometimes animated with a kind of living presence. Warren Hunting Smith has remarked that "the advent of the personified house

in literature coincided with the Oxford movement in England"
and surmises from this that Christian belief in the church building as God's dwelling place had something to do with the literary phenomenon.[18] But it is difficult to see how such a transference from church to house could occur, either in fiction or in
fact, and a better explanation is probably to be found in the
concept of organic form as applied to architecture. For example, it was usually a Gothic building, organically designed
and constructed, rather than a classic one with its mechanical
form, that was thought to be alive. In the following passage
Street contrasts the passivity of a Greek column with the activity
of a Gothic one:

> The Greek column, standing passively under a direct weight, is naturally
> very different in form from the column which supports an arch. The fixity
> of the one is shown by the way in which it spreads to its base; the other is
> only a part of one continuous growth: it carries and spreads itself into that
> arched form which is truly said never to sleep. Sometimes the arch mould-
> ings are gathered on to the cap and run down to the base in a different
> form; at other times they run down without, or almost without, a break.[19]

The comment that the Gothic column and arch are united in
"one continuous growth" suggests organic form, the active
verbs "carries" and "run down" imply vitality, and the arch that
never sleeps is outright personification. T. G. Jackson, too,
approaches personification when he refers to "the intense
struggling vitality that breathes in every stone of a Gothic
minster."[20]

On the other hand, it was possible for some to discern vitality
in Greek architecture. Charles Robert Cockerell, for instance,
wrote his father that the marble of the Parthenon seems to
breathe, just as Jackson said of the stones of a Gothic church:

> I have now concluded that the *vigorous, lifelike quality* of Ld Elgin's Mar-
> bles ... is the prime Beauty of Gk Arch[re] as well, for contrary to all we
> have been told, the whole Temple, far from being a collection of inert
> masonry, is *alive with movement* ... for the deviations which I have found in
> its construction provide an effect almost of breathing to the solid marble
> slabs.[21]

For that matter, pictures could seem alive, as with Browning's
"My Last Duchess" or Rossetti's "The Portrait"; but they did so

for other reasons than organic form, and I think it is fair to say
that generally Gothic was more amenable to personification
than was classic. It is somehow fitting that the House of Seven
Gables, whose exterior was decorated with "the grotesqueness
of a Gothic fancy," should be likened by Hawthorne to "a great
human heart, with a life of its own. . . ."

A fourth principle that provided a common denominator in
analogies between nature and architecture has been discussed
by Arthur O. Lovejoy in "The First Gothic Revival and the
Return to Nature," the most important article that has been
written on the subject of this present chapter. Lovejoy's point is
that architecture in the eighteenth century, like all the arts at
that time, was judged according to its truth to nature, the dominant aesthetic criterion of the age, and that the change in taste
from classical architecture to Gothic was brought about in part
by a change in the concept of nature. That is, as long as nature
was thought to be regular, symmetrical, and simple, classical
architecture with its corresponding features met the criterion
and maintained its popularity. When, however, nature came to
be seen as irregular, asymmetrical, and various, Gothic architecture with its corresponding features met the criterion and
gradually won acceptance. Lovejoy suggests, then, as a partial
explanation for the growing popularity of Gothic architecture
in the eighteenth century, that

> this new appreciation of Gothic—not merely in England in the 1740s and
> 50s but in its later eighteenth-century manifestations also—was made
> possible by the supposed discovery that this style in architecture was really
> more "natural," more "in conformity with Nature," than the classical—in
> other words, by certain changes in ideas which enabled the "Goths" to steal
> the classicists' catchword. For the sacred though happily equivocal formula
> remained unchanged throughout; if it had not been possible plausibly to
> regard Gothic as a true "imitation of Nature" it could hardly have gained
> any wide acceptance in the eighteenth century.[22]

This change in the concept of nature is likewise partially
responsible for the continued popularity of Gothic architecture
in the nineteenth century. Pugin, for example, praised ancient
mansions for "harmonizing in beautiful irregularity with the
face of nature."[23] One should recognize, however, that neither

Pugin nor his contemporaries regarded artistic imitation of irregular nature as the prime cause of irregularity in architecture, whether of the original Gothic or the neo-Gothic. They understood instead that medieval Gothic buildings were irregular because their designers were chiefly interested in function and because they had been added on to through the centuries and so did not conform to a master design. In adopting medieval principles, Victorian architects thought first of function and admitted irregularity as an inevitable and pleasing consequence. They did not, therefore, set out to design irregular buildings for the sake of irregularity; but because the irregularity of, Gothic happened to be in accord with the new concept of nature, those buildings fortuitously fulfilled the aesthetic criterion of truth to nature and so were more widely approved than had they failed to do so.

Not unexpectedly there were some who neither approved of Gothic nor accepted the Romantic version of nature. For example, Edward Lacy Garbett, no admirer of Gothic architecture, found symmetry to be the dominant principle in nature: "We need hardly observe that it [the uniformity of halves] is the most universal quality in nature, pervading all ranks of organic life, from the leaf and the flower, up to man; and all separate and distinct creatures, even when inorganic, from a crystal to a world."[24] But this attitude is a vestige of an earlier time and more in line with John Dennis's belief that "the universe is regular in all its parts" ("The Grounds of Criticism in Poetry," 1704) than with prevailing nineteenth-century opinion.

The Romantic concept of nature is epitomized in the ruggedness of mountain scenery, and a person's fondness for either the highlands or the lowlands is an almost infaillable index of his preference for Gothic or classical architecture. On the one hand, as his son tells us, Barry cared little for the mountains through which he passed during his European tour in 1817–20: "His admiration of it [mountain scenery] was blended with the notion of something strange and almost grotesque in it. He speaks of it as exhibiting 'the freaks and outrageous effects of Nature' in its wilder features.... He delighted more in the

Apennines, rising in mountains of equal height. . . ."[25] One sees very clearly in this passage the importance of irregularity and regularity in determining Barry's preferences. On the other hand, Viollet-le-Duc was a mountain climber who once fell into a crevasse, Street was so fond of mountain scenery that it was "almost a doubtful point whether or not he preferred it to the handiwork of men as exemplified in Gothic buildings," and Robert Louis Stevenson regarded great churches as "my favorite kind of mountain scenery."[26]

Closely akin to the values of regularity and irregularity, and similarly involved in the changing ideas about nature, are those of uniformity and variety.[27] Here the shift is one of relationship and emphasis, as it is with the other pair; for both ages believed that a combination of uniformity and variety was consonant with nature and essential to aesthetic pleasure, uniformity alone being monotonous and variety alone being frenetic. The difference between them, as Heinrich Wölfflin has pointed out, lies in "the relation of the part to the whole—namely, that classic art achieves its unity by making the parts independent as free members, and that the baroque abolishes the uniform independence of the parts in favour of a more unified total motive."[28] These different relationships in art correspond to the shifting relationship between objects in nature as the mechanistic universe gave way to the organic universe, and what Wölfflin is describing in baroque art is an early tendency toward the organic unity of nineteenth-century art. "Gothic architecture," Francis Palgrave wrote, "is an organic whole, bearing within it a living vegetating germ. Its parts and lines are linked and united, they spring and grow out of each other."[29] In very nearly the exact words, Owen Jones made the same point about ornament: "Beauty of form is produced by lines growing out one from the other in gradual undulations: there are no excrescences; nothing could be removed and leave the design equally good or better."[30]

These statements are artistic versions of Coleridge's principle of the One Life as illustrated, for example, in the Ancient Mariner's lesson that all parts of nature, from albatross to sea

snakes, are organically related through a universal participation in One Life. But for Coleridge and others, there is not only
a new organic relationship between the parts and the whole but
a new emphasis as well; for despite what Wölfflin says about
baroque art, there is a new importance placed on variety over
unity corresponding to the Romantic emphasis placed on particulars over the general. To illustrate this change, let us compare two statements, one by Lord Kames and the other by
Coleridge. In *Elements of Criticism* (1762) Lord Kames writes,
"Nothing can be more happily accommodated to the inward
constitution of man, than that mixture of uniformity with variety, which the eye discovers in natural objects." In "On the
Principles of Genial Criticism" (1814), Coleridge says, "The
BEAUTIFUL, contemplated in its essentials . . . is that in which
the *many*, still seen as many, becomes one. . . . The most general
definition of beauty, therefore, is . . . Multëity in Unity." These
statements are remarkably alike, but I should say that Lord
Kames emphasizes uniformity by placing it before variety,
whereas Coleridge emphasizes the many by placing it before
the one and by italicizing it, as well as emphasizing Multëity by
putting it before Unity. I do not wish to make too much of this
contrast, for I quite realize that the evidence is too slight to bear
the full weight of my argument and that Coleridge shares with
other Romantics a philosophical commitment to the overwhelming importance of the Ideal One. But I do believe that
the differences in the two passages indicate a shift of emphasis,
however slight, from unity to variety. When we later examine
this change in another context, we shall find more proof; but
for the moment I should like to quote a passage that comes
later in the century, after the change developed more fully and
is therefore more discernible. In *Our Old Home: A Series of English Sketches*, Nathaniel Hawthorne recalled his impressions of
the cathedral at Lichfield:

> The traces remaining in my memory represent it as airy rather than mas-
> sive. A multitude of beautiful shapes appeared to be comprehended within
> its single outline; it was a kind of kaleidoscopic mystery, so rich a variety of
> aspects did it assume from each altered point of view, through the presen-

tation of a different face, and the re-arrangement of its peaks and pinna-
cles and the three battlemented towers, with the spires that shot heavenward from all three, but one loftier than its fellows. . . . A Gothic Cathedral
is surely the most wonderful work which mortal man has yet achieved, so
vast, so intricate, and so profoundly simple, with such strange, delightful
recesses in its grand figure, so difficult to comprehend within one idea,
and yet all so consonant that it ultimately draws the beholder and his
universe into its harmony. It is the only thing in the world that is vast
enough and rich enough.

Although for Hawthorne the cathedral combines unity and
variety, surely here the emphasis is on variety, the subject of the
entire description except for a prepositional phrase in the
second sentence and dependent clause in the penultimate one.

A third aspect of the shift in taste that accompanied the
change in the concept of nature is the growing preference for
ornateness. Linked to variety and manifested in the baroque
and the rococo, the artistic quality of ornateness paralleled, and
owed something to, the recognition of nature's profuseness. In
his lectures on Shakespeare, Coleridge said that nature is "inexhaustible in forms." A few years earlier Friedrich Schlegel
had made the comparison to architecture when he wrote of
Cologne Cathedral that "the inconceivable abundance of its
decorations vie with the inexhaustible profusion of nature"
(*Grundzuge der gothischen Baukunst*, 1805). It is possible, then,
that as people came to view nature as profuse rather than as
simple, they grew to have a new appreciation for the ornateness
of Gothic architecture on the basis of its truth to nature and to
develop a *horror vacui* in all artistic matters.

III. THE RELATIONSHIP OF ARCHITECTURE TO NATURE

> Ye might think
> That it had sprung self-raised from earth, or grown
> Out of the living rock, to be adorned
> By nature only. . . .
> William Wordsworth, *The Excursion*

As the Romantic view of nature helped change taste in architecture, there arose a new and associated development in the
relationship between architecture and nature. The Renaissance
attitude toward the relationship, which continued into the

eighteenth century, was that a building and the surrounding countryside were essentially distinct—the one artificial, the other natural—but were linked by the garden, whose precise geometrical forms allied it with the building's design and whose substance was that of the countryside. The popular writer on the picturesque, William Gilpin, expresses the idea in this way:

> A house is an artificial object; and the scenery around it, must, in some degree, partake of art. Propriety requires it: convenience demands it. But if it partake of art, as allied to the mansion; it should also partake of nature, as allied to the country. It has therefore two characters to support; and may be considered as the connecting thread between the regularity of the house, and the freedom of the natural scene.[31]

By the time Gilpin wrote this in the latter part of the eighteenth century, the change in taste from a formal garden to a natural one was well under way, and the impact of the change was to eliminate the separate though linking element of the garden by fashioning it more on the wildness of the natural scene and so, in effect, to bring nature up to the very doorstep of the house.

For other types of buildings than country mansions, the assimilation of architecture into nature was more readily and completely achieved. Ruins, overgrown with weeds and ivy, were for Gilpin more natural than artificial: "A ruin is a sacred thing. Rooted for ages in the soil; assimilated to it; and become, as it were, a part of it; we consider it as a work of nature, rather than of art. Art cannot reach it."[32] Cottages, too, could easily be wrapped in the enfolding arms of nature, as Wordsworth declares in his *Guide to the Lakes*: "These humble dwellings remind the contemplative spectator of a production of Nature, and may (using a strong expression) rather be said to have grown than to have been erected;—to have risen, by an instinct of their own, out of the native rock—so little is there in them of formality, such is their wildness and beauty."[33]

The Victorians, not content with ivy creeping up the walls, enticed nature yet farther into their homes through their obsessive love for natural ornamentation of all kinds. Modern practice seems to have completed the process by introducing plants into the house and by designing arboretums in public build-

ings. Also, as Nikolaus Pevsner has pointed out, modern construction, which requires of walls no weight-bearing function,
allows for an extensive use of glass, and thereby breaks down
the separation of exterior and interior, resulting in what Frank
Lloyd Wright termed the etherealization of architecture.[34] In a
way, then, houses have come full circle from those first rude
shelters of primitive man, natural in fact and undeserving the
name of architecture, to sophisticated dwellings assimilated by
nature.

IV. THE BREAK BETWEEN NATURE AND ART

> A really well-made buttonhole is the only link between Art and Nature.
> (Oscar Wilde, "Phrases and Philosophies for the Use of the Young")

Through the mimetic capabilities of ornament and even
more through the adaptation of certain natural principles,
architecture remained as closely associated with nature as did,
in a somewhat different manner, the novels of realism and
naturalism. On the other hand, the art forms of painting, sculpture, and poetry had begun by the end of the century to re-
pudiate not only realism but imitative theories of any kind, and
in England the leaders of the revolt were the Aesthetes. The
artists and critics of this group rejected the principle of art as
imitation partially because the perspective of nature had
changed, and to represent nature faithfully was to represent
ugliness. A hundred years before, Cowper had written in *The
Task* that nature surpassed art in beauty: "Lovely indeed the
mimic work of art;/But Nature's work far lovelier." Now,
however, Whistler turned this truism upside down by asserting
that art is more beautiful than nature, which does nothing
more than furnish raw materials, the piano keys on which the
artist plays:

> That Nature is always right, is an assertion, artistically, as untrue, as it is
> one whose truth is universally taken for granted. Nature is very rarely
> right, to such an extent even, that it might almost be said that Nature is
> usually wrong: that is to say, the condition of things that shall bring about
> the perfection of harmony worthy a picture is rare, and not common at all.
> ("The Ten O'Clock")

Another of the Aesthetes' aims was to establish the supremacy of art, not only by declaring its superiority to nature and all else but also by averring the independence of art from nature, instruction, audience, morality, and so forth. For them art was sufficient unto itself, a sort of self-contained religion. Wilde, in his extravagant and categorical fashion, flouted the age-old theory of artistic mimesis by dissociating art from nature altogether. In "The Decay of Lying," Vivian disagrees with those who "call upon Shakespeare—they always do—and will quote that hackneyed passage forgetting that this unfortunate aphorism about Art holding the mirror up to Nature, is deliberately said by Hamlet in order to convince the bystanders of his absolute insanity in all art-matters." But Wilde is not content simply to dissociate art and nature—he must reverse the imitative principle by declaring that nature follows art. Startling at first, this reversal amounts to little more than a notion to which we have now grown accustomed, which is that we transfer fiction into fact by basing certain behavioral patterns on artistic models. Nowadays it is television that influences the outlook and behavior of the masses, but for Vivian it is art—Turner, for example:

> Yesterday evening Mrs. Arundel insisted on my going to the window and looking at the glorious sky, as she called it. Of course I had to look at it. She is one of those absurdly pretty Philistines to whom one can deny nothing. And what was it? It was simply a very second-rate Turner, a Turner of a bad period, with all the painter's worst faults exaggerated and over-emphasized. ("The Decay of Lying")

In *Modern Painters* Ruskin had praised Turner's paintings for being true to nature, and so had used the traditional method of judging art according to natural standards. When, however, Vivian looks from Mrs. Arundel's window and sees a second-rate Turner, he is using artistic standards to judge nature and is looking at nature through art rather than at art through nature. In the brief span of half a century separating *Modern Painters* and "The Decay of Lying," the mimetic tradition of ancient authority was overturned, and art was headed toward the nonrepresentational forms of modern times.

V. PRAGMATISM: PLEASURE

I. PLEASURE, INSTRUCTION, AND FUNCTION

The pragmatic theory of art, as defined by Abrams in *The Mirror and the Lamp*, is that which is directed primarily toward the audience and which regards "the work of art chiefly as a means to an end, an instrument for getting something done, and tends to judge its value according to its success in achieving that aim."[1] This theory seemingly works against expressionism, which emphasizes the role of the artist while depreciating that of the audience. As Shelley says in "A Defence of Poetry," the "Poet is a nightingale, who sits in darkness and sings to cheer its own solitude with sweet sounds. . . ." Though he may be overheard by others, his song is not sung mainly for them but for himself—a soliloquy, to use Mill's analogy. But, in truth, the audience derives a special delight in eavesdropping on the artist, who can reveal his innermost thoughts and feelings by being consciously unconscious of his public. Mimesis, on the other hand, is incorporated by pragmatism as one means of attaining a desired effect on the audience. For example, in Johnson's comment "Nothing can please many, and please long, but just representations of general nature" ("Preface to Shakespeare"), imitation is clearly subservient to the pragmatic end of pleasing the audience.

Pleasure, then, as one of the intended results of a work of art, is part of the pragmatic theory and is applicable to any art form. More particularly applicable to literature is the other half of pragmatism—instruction. The traditional association between rhetoric—the art of persuasion—and writing, as well as the inherent suitability of written discourse for instruction, has identified didacticism with literature more than with the other arts, but they, too, are quite capable of instruction. When, however, they truly rise to the level of art, beyond such purely practical forms as maps and mnemonic ditties, these other arts always blend instruction with pleasure, ordinarily with a primary emphasis on the latter. So it is, too, when writing becomes imaginative literature, although the emphasis is not as constant as with painting or music and vascillates from age to age. Thus, Johnson says, "The end of writing is to instruct; the end of poetry is to instruct by pleasing" ("Preface to Shakespeare"). A generation later the Romantics would reverse the emphasis by celebrating pleasure at the expense of instruction.

Architecture is usually more like painting, sculpture, and music in having as its chief pragmatic goal pleasure than it is like literature in sometimes being predominantly instructive. When, however, one is dealing with church architecture, as one necessarily does with the Gothic Revival, there may be the appearance of an unalloyed or predominant design for pleasure; but behind the multicolored glass and the richness of the ornaments lies the ulterior goal of salvation, and the building, like Johnson's poetry, instructs by pleasing. Architecture, though, is unlike all these fine arts together, for it is after all an applied or practical art and so has the additional pragmatic purpose of fulfilling a specific utilitarian requirement, the shelter of those who use it. How well a building performs its function is the third aesthetic criterion of architectural pragmatism and will serve as a fitting conclusion to our survey of architecture's participation in the other two—pleasure and instruction.

II. THE PICTURESQUE

> Picturesqueness is the very soul of Gothic architecture. (J. L. Petit, "Utilitarianism in Architecture")

> It was the study of the picturesque, the desire for the picturesque, which led to the study of Gothic architecture; and it has proceeded on picturesque ground step by step from the days of Carter and Britton till now, when the desire for the picturesque in Gothic architecture has become almost unlimited. (Robert Kerr, "On the Architecturesque")

Throughout the centuries beauty has generally been regarded as the chief source of pleasure in art, and the Romantics did not break with tradition in this matter; but it is true that they were inclined to admit more tolerantly than their predecessors other sources of pleasure than beauty. Horror was one of these, as we see in the "shudder" of Gothic novels, the tales of Poe, Fuseli's *The Nightmare*, Blake's *Ghost of a Flea*, and Goya's *Caprichos*. Perhaps there is some explanation for the exquisite pleasure derived from the macabre and grotesque in an inscription on the frontispiece to *Caprichos*: "El sueño de la razón produce monstruos." This, after all, is the subject of Fuseli's *The Nightmare* and suggests that the turn from reason to the imagination, which faculty of mind is quite as capable of envisioning a hell as a heaven, played some part in the attraction of dark and forbidding subjects. These subjects, moreover, doubtlessly contributed something to the growing taste for Gothic architecture since they were so often set in ancient castles and abbeys, since they shared rather tenuously with architecture the name of Gothic, and since they had in common with the Gothic style an element of the grotesque.

Another source of pleasure, and of far greater relevance to the revival of Gothic, was the picturesque, a kind of aesthetic halfway house between the concept of natural beauty as regular and pacific to that of natural beauty as irregular and tumultuous. Picturesque doctrine became popular at the end of the eighteenth century when the old concept of beauty was still firmly rooted in tradition but when new sensibilities found stimulation in wild and rough landscapes whose qualities were just the opposite of what had long been considered beautiful. The dilemma confronting aestheticians at this time was that if mountain scenery, say, consisted of features directly opposite those of a landscape traditionally regarded as beautiful, then logically the mountain scenery must be ugly. But this designation would not do because a subtle and gradual shift in taste caused many people to delight in the rugged terrain of Scotland, Wales, and Switzerland. What was needed was a new category to account for this delight and to solve the dilemma, and in Sir Uvedale Price's "A Dialogue on the Distinct Characters of the Picturesque and the Beautiful," we are provided with just the term—the picturesque. In the dialogue Mr. Seymour, a novice, asks in regard to a gypsy hovel if there is not some term to describe that class of objects that he is inclined to label ugly

but that others consider beautiful. Mr. Hamilton, the authority
who accompanies him, replies:

> The term you require . . . has already been invented, for, according to my
> ideas, the word Picturesque, has exactly the meaning you have just de-
> scribed. . . . The set of objects we have been looking at struck you with
> their singularity; but, instead of thinking them beautiful, you were dis-
> posed to call them ugly. Now, I should neither call them beautiful nor
> ugly, but picturesque; for they have qualities highly suited to the painter
> and his art, but which are, in general, less attractive to the bulk of man-
> kind; whereas the qualities of beauty are universally pleasing and alluring
> to all observers.[2]

The picturesque, therefore, was a compromise between an
old aesthetic bias that refused to release its hold on beauty and
a new sensibility whose popularity demanded official sanction.
Taste changes more slowly than politics: the Bastille might be
brought down in a day and the ancien régime in little longer,
but the artistic values of the old order persisted and required
the invention of a new aesthetic category before surrendering
altogether and leaving the field to the values of the new. As the
nineteenth century progressed, the lines of demarcation between these categories grew more indistinct and the picturesque was more frequently identified with beauty. As early as
1816 Francis Jeffrey equated the sublime, the beautiful, and
the picturesque in his "Essay on Beauty," and it would not be
long before the new taste was secure enough to render the old
distinctions unnecessary.

But at the end of the eighteenth century, those distinctions,
as well as the true definition of the picturesque, were vitally
important to such aestheticians as William Gilpin, Sir Uvedale
Price, Richard Payne Knight, and Humphrey Repton, who
wrote volumes on the subject and who engaged in sharp con-
troversies among themselves. Despite their many differences of
opinion about what constituted the picturesque, the one essential characteristic on which all agreed was irregularity. Price,
for example, wrote that the "qualities of roughness, and of
sudden variation, joined to that of irregularity, are the most
efficient causes of the picturesque."[3] In the next century
irregularity became practically the single feature of the pic-

turesque and was used synonymously with it. George Edmund Street described the Acropolis and the Forum as being "so picturesque, so irregular in their levels. . . ."[4] Alfred Barry used picturesque as an antonym of regularity when he wrote that his father seemed "often divided between an artistic love of the picturesque and a determined architectural preference for regularity."[5]

Street had found the Acropolis and the Forum to be picturesque, but he was talking about their arrangements rather than the irregular designs of the individual buildings, the Acropolis, for instance, adding "one building to another in an almost picturesque confusion,"[6] and it was generally conceded that Gothic architecture was more picturesque in its irregularity than was classic. Uvedale Price made this point when he said that the simplicity and symmetry of Grecian buildings make that style of architecture more beautiful than the Gothic but that the variety and irregularity of Gothic buildings make that style more picturesque than the Greek. He illustrates the point by contrasting the general outlines of the two types of buildings: the lines of the Grecian are straight and symmetrical, whereas with Gothic

> the outline of the summit presents such a variety of forms, of turrets and pinnacles, some open, some fretted and variously enriched, that even where there is an exact correspondence of parts, it is often disguised by an appearance of splendid confusion and irregularity.[7]

If, as Thomas Hardy told the S.P.A.B., "irregularity is the genius of Gothic architecture,"[8] then the defining characteristic of this architectural style and that of the picturesque were in fact the same, leading to an identification of the two. Robert Kerr asserted that the picturesque was "the essence of Gothic taste," and used the terms synonymously when he classified all architecture and art as either classical or picturesque.[9]

Naturally, the change from regularity to irregularity did not move from one extreme to the other, for neoclassic doctrine admitted variety and Romantic theory allowed symmetry. Wordsworth justified meter in poetry by saying that it provides regularity to temper passion, Burges felt that irregularity was permissible in the backs of large buildings but not the fronts, and Barry, more classically inclined than they, included variety only if it could be subordinated to the overall symmetry, as with the Houses of Parliament. Instead of moving from one pole to the other, taste changed by altering the balance, transferring aesthetic values from the scale of regularity to that of irregularity.

Combining with the picturesque on the common ground of irregularity, Gothic architecture gained respectability and acceptance through its association with the new aesthetic category. If Gothic could not be called beautiful, classical architecture still claiming exclusive rights to that aesthetic tribute, it had at least shaken off the contemptuous epithets to which it had for so long been subjected and established itself as an alternative source of pleasure by means of its designation as picturesque. As the nineteenth century progressed and the distinctions between the picturesque and the beautiful faded to join the two categories together and to make the picturesque a type of beauty, Gothic architecture emerged from its role as a stepchild and claimed in its own right the appellation of beautiful. By this time so firmly had irregularity implanted itself as an aesthetic virtue that the architects of the Queen Anne style attempted to satisfy their own and the public's taste for it through what Lethaby derisively called "the dilettante-picturesque by the so-called Queen Anne style."[10] The new style capitalized on the very principles that had made Gothic popular, assumed the term by which it became aesthetically respectable, and competed quite successfully with it in municipal buildings and private houses.

If the Gothic style was so consistently identified with the picturesque, it is puzzling how some writers, such as Henry-Russell Hitchcock and Robert Macleod, deny the influence of the picturesque on leaders of the Revival. After all, Alfred Barry declared that though his father favored symmetry, "many (and his friend Pugin especially) contended for irregularity, picturesqueness, and variety."[11] Yet Hitchcock has written that "Pugin and the Anglican ecclesiologists who soon echoed his principles verbally abjured the Picturesque. . . ."[12] The reasoning behind his claim, and Macleod's as well, is that the picturesque approach regards architecture from a predominantly visual point of view, whereas, in Macleod's words, "the progeny of the Gothic Revival can be most clearly identified by their primary commitment to non-visual criteria."[13] To be mainly concerned with non-visual criteria—that is, with function—does not mean, however, to be neglectful of the way buildings look, and we have already seen that the continuation of the painting-architecture analogy into the nineteenth century signifies the importance of visual criteria. One of the Revival's progeny, John Sedding, had in fact defined the architect as "a picturesque manipulator of vast forms."[14]

What perhaps both Hitchcock and Macleod are working toward, although they are not explicit, is that the Revivalists sacrificed visual principles, including those of the picturesque, when there was any chance of conflict with functional principles, and that the picturesque was admissible only when it proceeded naturally from the plan of the building. In other words, they did not object to the picturesque when it evolved spontaneously—indeed, they approved it wholeheartedly and welcomed its sanction—but only when it was contrived for its own sake and therefore militated against one of Pugin's true principles that everything should serve a purpose. Maybe this is what Hitchcock intends when he says that "the Victorians, when on their critical battle horses, almost consistently abjured the Picturesque as such,"[15] the key phrase being "as such." Therefore, we do find that Pugin condemns the picturesque when it is the primary concern in design: "An edifice which is arranged with the principal view of looking picturesque is sure to resemble an artificial waterfall or a made-up rock, which are generally so *unnaturally natural* as to appear ridiculous." What an architect should do, on the other hand, is to allow the picturesque to proceed naturally from the building's requirements "by turning the difficulties which occur in raising an elevation from *a convenient plan* into so many *picturesque beauties*. . . ."[16] This is what the builders of the original Gothic did and the

reason their buildings are naturally and beautifully picturesque. On this matter both Barry and Scott agreed. J. L. Wolfe
said this about his friend Barry: "That he had an artist's eye for
the picturesque was certain from the happy choice he was sure
to make of the best points of view for sketching. But actually to
plan irregularity, because it was picturesque, he thought unworthy of the dignity of art."[17] Similarly, Scott declared, "Especially have I spoken against all direct pursuit of the picturesque beyond what naturally results from skilful though simple
treatment. . . ."[18]

For the Revivalists, then, the picturesque was wrong if taken
as an end in itself but quite permissible, indeed very desirable,
if a natural consequence of a building's primary, functional
goal. As it happened, they could easily afford to be so haughty
in condemning a studied picturesque effect; for the picturesque was fortuitously an almost invariable result of functional
planning since a design based upon the principles of convenience and truthfulness, to use the Victorian terms, would
quite naturally have an irregular, picturesque elevation. "The
most picturesque objects I have seen," wrote J. L. Petit, "are
buildings of the most strictly utilitarian character . . . without
the slightest attention whatever to appearance."[19]

I have dwelt upon the intimate association of the picturesque
and the Gothic because I am convinced that the picturesque
was immensely important to the early rise and later popularity
of Gothic architecture in the eighteenth and nineteenth centuries. Because of its association with the picturesque, chiefly
through the common property of irregularity, the Gothic style
was enabled to emerge from centuries of disrepute and to gain
an aesthetic foothold, so to speak, which, if it did not allow
Gothic immediately to usurp the title of beautiful from the
classical antagonist, at least provided a measure of popular
acceptance secure enough to issue a challenge. By mid-
nineteenth century the picturesque had succeeded so spectacu-
larly in a brief span of time as to become a category of the
beautiful, thereby winning for itself and for Gothic the ultimate
artistic accolade. Finally, and perhaps in the end most im-

portantly, the association of Gothic with the picturesque provided a solution for an artistic problem that had long existed but that had become much more acute by the Revivalists' insistence upon designing for convenience—the problem of reconciling utility and beauty. Now, by reasoning that utility created irregularity, which was the chief quality of the picturesque, which was one type of beauty, architects could show that the ultimate cause of beauty—picturesque beauty, at any rate— was utility and thus satisfy at once the demands inherent in their ambivalent roles as practical builders and as artists.

III. UNITY AND VARIETY

> The fundamental and all-important principle of UNITY. (E. Trotman, "On the Comparative Value of Simplicity in Architecture")

> The human mind is adapted for viewing, as a whole, an indefinite number of parts. . . ." (J. C. Loudon, "On Those Principles of Composition, in Architecture, Which Are Common to All the Fine Arts")

Before the picturesque could be accounted beautiful, a change in the concept of beauty had to occur, and one of the elements in this change was a growing preference for variety in nature and in art. An early indication of this new development, discussed in a different context in the preceding chapter, is evident in Horace Walpole's comment to Sir Horace Mann about Grecian architecture: "The variety is little, and admits of no charming irregularities. I am almost as fond of the *Sharawaggi*, or Chinese want of symmetry in buildings, as in grounds and gardens" (1750).

But this change created an aesthetic problem because the newly emerging taste for variety was directly opposed to artistic unity, which had been an unquestioned aesthetic criterion from Aristotle's *Poetics* to Pope's version in *An Essay on Criticism*:

> In wit, as Nature, what affects our hearts
> Is not th' exactness of peculiar parts;
> 'Tis not a lip, or eye, we beauty call,
> But the joint force and full result of all.

Nor did the commitment to unity in art cease with the eighteenth century, for well into the nineteenth Walter Bagehot judged pure art, of which Wordsworth is the exemplar, to be superior to ornate art, as in the poetry of Tennyson, because the simplicity of pure art creates a unified effect whereas the multiplicity of ornate art distracts and fragments. "Such ever," he writes, "is the dividing test of pure art: if you catch yourself admiring its details, it is defective; you ought to think of it as a single whole . . ." ("Wordsworth, Tennyson, and Browning; or Pure, Ornate, and Grotesque Art in English Poetry,"1864). In his preface to the 1853 edition of *Poems*, Arnold took Greek poetry as his model for an art that subordinated the parts to the whole, and chose Keats as an example of one who was misled to reverse the order.

Here, then, was the predicament: on the one hand, unity in artistic form as an essential element of beauty was backed by centuries of tradition and seemed indomitably secure in aesthetic doctrine; but, on the other hand, variety, both as a characteristic of nature to be reflected in art and as a source of pleasure, arose as a contradictory principle. The way out of the predicament was similar to the aesthetic accommodation made for the principle of irregularity by the creation of a separate category, designated the picturesque, in that variety was reconciled with unity by adding to the old unity of form a new class: unity of expression or feeling. The reclassification of unity into two types allowed for the continuation of the traditional type, acknowledged the validity of variety, and avoided open conflict between the old aesthetic value and the new taste by a compromise between them that made it possible to invoke the one while approving the other. By the 1830s the two categories of unity were clearly defined, as one sees in E. Trotman's explanation:

> As to the principle of unity, it is necessary to premise, that it has, architecturally, a twofold reference; regarding, on the one hand, form and distribution, and, on the other, expression of style and purpose: the first embracing the symmetrical, the second the picturesque. Whatever praise such examples of Grecian art as the Parthenon and Theseum may have received on the ground of simplicity, it is rather for the merit of unity of form that we consider them admirable; and, though in our modern cruci-

form churches in the pointed style, that unity of form is not so entirely
acknowledged by the eye, the unity of expression and of character is
generally more than enough to satisfy the demands of taste.[20]

It is evident in this passage how much the new category is a
direct result of expressionism, with its emphasis upon substance and meaning. What has happened, it seems, is that
although the balance of artistic theory began to move from
imitation to expression, the principle of unity was retained, but
in its new application came to refer to inner substance rather
than outer form. Accordingly, it was less important that a work
of art achieve unity through simplicity, balance, repetition, and
so forth, than that the ideas and feelings it expresses be consonant and produce a single impression upon the audience.
There are signs that the redefinition of unity began at least as
early as Edmund Burke, who wrote that "when we consider the
power of an object upon our passions, we must know that when
any thing is intended to affect the mind by the force of some
predominant property, the affection produced is like to be the
more uniform and perfect, if all the other properties or qualities of the object be of the same nature, and tending to the same
design as the principal . . . " (A Philosophical Enquiry, 3).[21] The
new application of unity to feeling allows for variety and
irregularity since unity now depends upon consistency of details rather than, as was earlier the case with unity of form,
upon balance and simplification of details. In other words, as
long as the individual items in a composition are of a kind and
affect the audience in a uniform way, those items can be as
profuse and asymmetrical as one desires. But one should not,
for example, mix elements of the sublime, the beautiful, and
the picturesque (assuming them to be separate categories); and
one should not, as Pugin repeatedly argued, attempt to combine incongruous architectural styles in a single building.

That this redefinition of unity was crucial for an appreciation
of the Gothic style may be seen by briefly tracing the development of the artistic principle in its application to architecture.
As long as unity meant unity of form, Gothic always suffered in

comparison to classic, and so the diarist John Evelyn found that in looking upon Gothic buildings, "full of *Fret* and lamentable *Imagry* . . . a Judicious Spectator is rather Distracted and quite Confounded, than touch'd with that Admiration, which results from the true and just *Symmetrie*, regular Proportion, Union and Disposition [of classical buildings]. . . ." Not surprisingly, then, Evelyn found little to admire in Henry the Seventh's chapel at Westminster Abbey, with "its sharp *Angles, Jetties*, Narrow Lights, lame *Statues, Lace* and other *Cut-work* and *Crinkle Crankle*," since the abundance of Gothic ornament "rather Gluts the Eye, than Gratifies and Pleases it with any reasonable Satisfaction."[22]

A hundred years or so after Evelyn first made these observations, the concept of unity had begun to change, as we have seen in Burke's comments on the subject, and accompanying this change was a growing appreciation of Gothic. Hogarth stands at the crossroads of this new direction in the concept of unity. Writing in *The Analysis of Beauty*, he contrasts St. Paul's with Westminster Abbey, and though his preference for the former allies him with traditional taste, his appreciation for variety looks forward to things to come. Hogarth praises the moderation and subordination of ornament in St. Paul's where "you may see the utmost variety without confusion, simplicity without nakedness, richness without taudriness, distinctions without hardness, and quantity without excess." Westminster Abbey, on the other hand, lacks simplicity and distinctness, for "the great number of its filligrean ornaments, and small divided and subdivided parts appear confused when nigh, and are totally lost at a moderate distance. . . ." Yet, despite Westminster Abbey's inferiority, Hogarth admits, and in doing so anticipates the notion of unity of feeling, that the details are consistent and produce a uniform effect: "yet there is nevertheless such a consistency of parts altogether in a good gothic taste, and such propriety relative to the gloomy ideas, they were then calculated to convey, that they have at length acquir'd an established and distinct character in building" (chap. 8).

Although Hogarth is moving toward Coleridge's concept of multeity in unity, a preference for Westminster Abbey over St. Paul's would not be possible until people came to believe that unity of feeling was not only compatible with confusion and irregularity of details but as important as unity of form. By the second decade of the nineteenth century, they had come to believe so, as we see in Byron's description of an old abbey, perhaps modeled on Newstead:

> Huge halls, long galleries, spacious chambers, joined
>   By no quite lawful marriage of the arts,
> Might shock a connoisseur; but when combined
>   Formed a whole which, irregular in parts,
> Yet left a grand impression on the mind,
>   At least of those whose eyes are in their hearts.
>   *Don Juan*, canto 13

The change from unity of form to unity of feeling—from perception by the mind's eye to the heart's eye, as Byron has it—allowed Gothic to fulfill one of art's most firmly established standards; and it is just because of this change that E. Trotman could describe King's College Chapel, Cambridge, a building often compared with Henry the Seventh's Chapel, as "stand[ing] forth among human works in glorious pre-eminence . . . as an example of the supreme beauty of unity. . . ."[23] Unity of feeling did not, however, entirely displace unity of form, and some defenders of Gothic found that the new category was not an altogether satisfactory compromise. Ruskin, for example, although he believed that unity of feeling "is the first principle of good taste,"[24] nevertheless felt obliged to establish Gothic architecture as unified in form as well. Unity of form must have exerted a powerful influence at the time to force Ruskin not simply to reckon with it but to suggest such an extreme measure as viewing Westminster Abbey from Highgate Hill at five in the morning in order to satisfy it. Looking at the Abbey from a distance and in the greyness of dawn, Ruskin wrote, "You will receive an impression of a building enriched with multitudinous vertical lines. Try to distinguish one of those lines all the way down from the one next to it: You cannot. . . . Look at it generally, and it is all symmetry and arrangement. Look at it in its parts, and it is all inextricable confusion."[25]

Viewed under more normal circumstances, however—in daylight and at close range—Gothic architecture often upset the precarious balance of unity and variety with its irregular masses and profuse details. T. G. Jackson, for example, saw no such compromise when he made this contrast between classic and Gothic styles: "On the one side is clearness, on the other confusion; on the one hand simplicity, on the other complexity and turmoil; in the first, the calm and monotonous beauty of a classic temple, in the second the picturesque variety, and the intense struggling vitality that breathes in every stone of a Gothic minster."[26] Jackson's failure to assert the unity of a Gothic minster would not have been looked upon as an unfavorable reflection on the style at the time he wrote these words in 1873, for by then so well established had irregularity and variety become as aesthetic values that the catchword of "unity" was no longer necessary to sanction them and had, in fact, lost much of its influence as an evaluative standard. Gerard Manley Hopkins, like Byron and Ruskin, could perceive, and wish to perceive, unity in a Gothic building, but he makes it clear in the following letter to Butterfield that the majority of people had grown accustomed to associating the style with irregularity alone:

> I hope you will long continue to work out your beautiful and original style. I do not think this generation will ever much admire it. They do not understand how to look at a Pointed building as a whole having a single form governing it throughout, which they *would* perhaps see in a Greek temple: they like it to be a sort of farmyard and medley of ricks and roofs and dovecots.[27] (26 April 1877)

Perhaps in the end the compromise between unity and variety that Hopkins found in Butterfield's churches or that Ruskin discerned in Westminster Abbey was too subtle a combination for the ordinary Victorian to apprehend. Perhaps, too, its apprehension depended too heavily upon the mists of dawn or the imagination of a poet, and its incorporation in a building upon the genius of a Butterfield. At any rate, when C. F. A. Voysey surveyed the heritage bequeathed by the Revival and as revealed in private houses, he saw only confusion. These houses, Voysey wrote in 1909, are characterized by their

> angularity and infinite variety of shapes and proportions jutting out at you with surprising wildness as if they were waving their arms impatiently and angrily; and to add to their complexity they are composed of an infinite number of differently coloured materials and textures, just like the drawing-rooms inside, which I likened to drunken brawls. It is our mad rush for wealth and material things that feeds on advertisement, until our very houses shout at us for attention.[28]

What Voysey blames on a desire to advertise material wealth might also be attributable to the end result of the trend toward irregularity and variety, for what Voysey is describing here is what Bagehot had warned against when he said that art was defective when it drew one's attention to its details rather than to its single design. Also, the emphasis upon the individual features of these houses corresponds quite closely to the technique of Pre-Raphaelite painting, which distractingly highlights the minutest of details. In effect, the Pre-Raphaelites returned to the eighteenth-century principle of clarity and distinctness, although carrying that principle to an extreme, but adopted the new concept of particularity, and so contrived to make unity of composition very difficult if not impossible. One might achieve unity by drawing clearly and distinctly as long as the details were few and the object was general nature, or one could unify one's work using many details as long as they indistinctly blended together; but one could not combine unity and distinctiveness of profuse details. In this defense of Hunt's *The Awakening Conscience*, Ruskin addresses this problem by admitting that "to many persons the careful rendering of the inferior details in this picture cannot but be at first offensive, as calling their attention away from the principal subject."[29] Ruskin's answer is that since the distraught and excited mind fixes on trivial objects, the use of details accords with the mood of the picture, and so a kind of unity of feeling is achieved. This explanation answers very nicely for this particular picture, but what of the great majority of Pre-Raphaelite paintings whose subjects do not allow for so ingenious an interpretation? One is more likely to approach these pictures from the point of view of W. F. Axton, whose account of them is strikingly similar to Voysey's description of private houses. Axton points out that unlike traditional works in the Royal Academy, composed to create a unified impression, Pre-Raphaelite paintings made for a situation in which "the spectator's visual apprehension of such paintings is disturbed, if not confused, by their ambiguities and contradictions, and his comprehension is baffled by the plethora of glaring details, each and every one of which is crying out for narrow inspection."[30] "Our very houses," Voysey had written, "shout at us for attention." The compromise between unity and variety, even with the change from unity as form to unity as feeling, had collapsed, leaving variety the dominant aesthetic standard.

For some this development was not altogether undesirable. On the one hand, variety meant excitement, and, as we shall see shortly, Victorian art was calculated to stimulate thoughts and feelings by a restless, frenetic quality. On the other hand, whereas the unity of eighteenth-century works of art allowed the audience to comprehend them logically and instantly, the multiplicity and variety of Romantic art and Gothic architecture elicited in the audience a sense of wonder, which emotion was especially desirable in ecclesiastical buildings. Philip Webb wrote to Lethaby that "wonder *is*, I feel, an essential of Gothic. Indeed, I'm claiming it should be a primary essential; and only by the Gothic system of multiplication and disposition of parts can 'wonder' be gained. . . ."[31] Many years before, Pugin had recognized the same causal relationship between multiplicity and wonder. Like Hogarth, Pugin saw that an important difference between Gothic architecture and classic was that "in pointed architecture the different details of the edifice are *multiplied with the increased scale of the building*: in classic architecture they are *only magnified*."[32] Hogarth would not, of course, have said "only magnified," for he believed that this magnification made for clarity and that the multiplication of ornament led to confusion. Pugin, however, anticipated Webb in thinking that the multiplication of ornament in Gothic architecture accounts for the sense of wonder and awe produced by buildings in that style. "One of the great arts of architecture," Pugin wrote in *True Principles*, "is to render a building more vast and lofty in appearance than it is in reality."[33] The illusion of size and height, leading to wonderment, takes the place of a logical understanding of art and explains much about the aesthetic evolution from unity to variety. Why the illusion was more important than the fact we shall now see.

IV. ASSOCIATIONISM

The association of ideas is now generally asserted to be the only source of our perception of beauty. . . . ("On the Principles of Taste," 1821)

A second and more profound change in the concept of beauty was the transference of beauty from the object in nature or in art to the observer. The change had been set in motion by Locke and later exponents of the association of ideas, but it was not finally achieved until the end of the eighteenth century when Archibald Alison and others applied the associational theory directly to aesthetics. The basic premise of associational aesthetics is that beauty does not exist independently in objects of perception but only in the capability of those objects to excite the observer's imagination and to put in motion a train of thought, which, then, is responsible for the creation of beauty. It is significant that Alison refers to the "emotion of beauty," for the phrase suggests that beauty is subjective, dependent upon the observer's response, rather than objectively inherent in the object itself. The major emendations of Alison to Locke's theory are that the imagination is assigned the primary role in this perceptive process and that the ultimate effect is emotional. Alison's most succinct expression of the theory appeared in *Essays on the Nature and Principles of Taste* (1790):

When any object, either of sublimity or beauty, is presented to the mind, I believe every man is conscious of a train of thought being immediately awakened in his imagination, analogous to the character or expression of the original object. The simple perception of the object, we frequently find, is insufficient to excite these emotions, unless it is accompanied with this operation of mind; unless, according to common expression, our imagination is seized, and our fancy busied in the pursuit of all those trains of thought which are allied to this character of expression.

Thus, when we feel either the beauty or sublimity of natural scenery . . . we are conscious of a variety of images in our minds, very different from those which the objects themselves can present to the eye. Trains of pleasing or of solemn thought arise spontaneously within our minds; our hearts swell with emotions, of which the objects before us seem to afford no adequate cause. . . .[34]

In accordance with this theory, Coleridge refers in "Dejection: An Ode" to the imagination as "This beautiful and beauty-making power"; Wordsworth in the second book of *The Prelude* comments that "An auxiliar light/Came from my mind, which on the setting sun/Bestowed new splendour"; and Shelley writes "Hymn to Intellectual Beauty."

Of course, the transference of beauty from object to subject was not total, and most Romantic writers recognized that the quality of beauty was partially inherent in the object and partially created by the observer's imagination. Thus, Wordsworth writes in "Tintern Abbey" about "all the mighty world/Of eye, and ear,—both what they half create,/And what perceive"; in "Mont Blanc" Shelley describes the reciprocal relationship between the "everlasting universe of things" and the human mind; and later in the century, Alexander (Greek) Thomson explicitly states the idea when he writes, "The pleasures which we derive from objects of sight derive partly from the association which they suggest, and partly from their own inherent beauty."[35]

Expressionism naturally develops out of this new concept of beauty based upon the association of ideas, for if the artist is to portray beauty, as it is his primary goal to do, he cannot simply depict nature directly since beauty only partially resides there, but must instead express the effect of nature on him since his response, through an imaginative association of ideas, completes the act of perception and the creation of beauty. In other words, if "an auxiliar light," the imagination, bestows new splendor on the setting sun, then Wordsworth must describe the sun not simply and objectively, but express his own imaginative response to the sun, at least if the total beauty of sunset is to be conveyed to the reader. Therefore, Wordsworth writes that "the appropriate business of poetry . . . her appropriate employment, her privilege and her *duty*, is to treat things not as they *are*, but as they appear: not as they exist in themselves, but as they *seem* to exist to the *senses*, and to the passions" ("Essay Supplementary to the Preface of 1815"). As early as 1757 Edmund Burke had anticipated this expressive approach to art when he declared in his *Enquiry* that the purpose of poetry is "to display rather the effect of things on the mind of the speaker, or of others, than to present a clear idea of the things themselves" (5.5). In the Victorian era John Stuart Mill stated that "descriptive poetry consists, no doubt, in description, but in description of things as they appear, not as they are; and it paints them not in their bare and natural lineaments, but seen through the medium and arrayed in the colours of the imagination set in action by the feelings" ("Thoughts on Poetry and Its Varieties," 1833). Two years later Alexander Smith wrote an article for *Blackwood's Magazine* in which he made this distinction between poetry and prose: "Prose is the language of *intelligence*, poetry of *emotion*. In prose, we communicate our *knowledge* of the objects of sense or thought—in poetry, we express how these objects *affect* us" ("The Philosophy of Poetry").

What all of these writers have in mind when they speak of the effect of objects on the observer is the association of ideas stimulated by the object; that is to say, personal memories and feelings associated with the object and with each other. In Alexander Smith's words, "The mind [of the poet], anxious to convey not the truth or fact with regard to the object of its contemplation, but its own feelings as excited by the object, pours forth the stream of its associations as they rise from their source" ("The Philosophy of Poetry"). Moreover, not only does the poet present the ultimate feeling produced by the train of thought, but also the very process that creates the feeling.

Therefore, "Kubla Khan" and many other Romantic poems portray the creative act itself, and Wordsworth says that the object of the poems in *Lyrical Ballads* is to take common incidents and situations, and

> to throw over them a certain colouring of imagination, whereby ordinary things should be presented to the mind in an unusual aspect; and, further, and above all, to make these incidents and situations interesting by tracing in them, truly though not ostentatiously, the primary laws of our nature: chiefly, as far as regards the manner in which we associate ideas in a state of excitement. ("Preface," 2d ed., 1800)

This Romantic approach to art was directly opposed to objective realism, as indeed were eighteenth-century aesthetics, for the purpose of art was to present a subjective distortion of empirical reality rather than an objective, direct impression of it. At first there was no attempt to reconcile the artistic results of an imaginative association of ideas with truthfulness, pleasure being derived from sources admittedly magical and illusory. Bishop Hurd wrote, for example, that this type of poetry appeals "solely or principally to the Imagination; a young and credulous faculty, which loves to admire and to be deceived . . . " (*Letters on Chivalry and Romance*, 1762). Later, however, as expressive art became something more than a novel plaything and began to require the aesthetic sanction of truthfulness, so dominant a value in neoclassic art criticism, some compromise was necessary if the new art was to gain acceptance. Keats struggled with the problem and never did resolve it, but others did by dividing truth into perceptual and conceptual, phenomenal and noumenal, physical and spiritual, rational and imaginative. Referring perhaps to the Platonic concept of the poet, Macaulay declared that "truth, indeed, is essential to poetry; but it is the truth of madness" ("Milton," 1825). The Romantics went beyond this division, moreover, to assert that the truth of the imagination was superior to that of sensory cognition, and even so far, as with Shelley, to maintain that it was the only reality, this world being but a dream. Art based on visionary truth, therefore, grew to claim not merely acceptance but superiority over more earthbound works, and so it is that in his *Memoir* Hallam Tennyson recalls his father saying, "Poetry is truer than fact."

Because of its special nature, architecture has seemingly little to do with the subject we have just been discussing. In poetry Wordsworth can show how his imagination bestowed new splendor on the setting sun, and in *The Fighting Téméraire* Turner can do the same with paint. But how is the architect to do in stone what they accomplish in words and oil, and if he cannot, then how is the association of ideas pertinent to architecture at all? The answer is that the new mode of perceiving beauty was adopted by those who appreciated art as well as by those who created it, and that the same relationship as existed between nature and the artist obtained between the work of art and the audience. Consequently, although the architect does not build as the poet writes or as the painter draws, the beauty of his buildings depends upon the active, imaginative participation of the observer even as the beauty of poetry and painting depends on it and even as the beauty of nature requires the sensitive response of the artist.[36] We are, therefore, concerned here with the effect of buildings on those who see them, for our present subject is, after all, the relationship between art and the audience—pragmatism, that is, not the expressive theory dealing with the relationship between art and the artist.

A building can as successfully arouse the imagination to assemble thoughts and feelings leading to the emotion of beauty as any picture or poem or carving or song, and it is in this capability to affect the imagination that the beauty of architecture depends upon the association of ideas. Therefore, as a stimulus to the imagination, architecture shares in common the purpose of the other arts. Coleridge wrote in *Lectures on Shakespeare* that "the power of poetry is, by a single word, perhaps, to instill energy into the mind, which compels the imagination to produce the picture." Reynolds said in "Discourse IV" that the end of painting "is to strike the imagination," and later in "Discourse XIII" commented that one principle architecture shares with poetry and painting "is that of affecting the imagination by means of association of ideas."

This way of looking at architecture—regarding it and evaluating it not so much as what in itself it was but as how successfully it could arouse feelings by setting in motion a train of ideas—ran concurrently with Romanticism through the nineteenth century. One of the first things Ruskin ever said about architecture was that

> it is, or ought to be, a science of feeling more than of rule, a ministry to the mind, more than to the eye. If we consider how much less the beauty and majesty of a building depend upon its pleasing certain prejudices of the eye, than upon its rousing certain trains of meditation in the mind, it will show in a moment how many intricate questions of feeling are involved in the raising of an edifice. . . .[37]

Later Edward Burne-Jones provided an example of how the theory operated in practice when he described his impression of an ancient pile:

> I have just come in from my terminal pilgrimage to Godstowe ruins and the burial place of Fair Rosamond. . . . In my mind pictures of the old days, the abbey, and long processions of the faithful, banners of the cross, copes and crosiers, gay knights and ladies by the river bank, hawking-parties and all the pageantry of the golden age—it made me feel so wild and mad I had to throw stones into the water to break the dream. I never remember having such an unutterable ecstasy, it was quite painful with intensity, as if my forehead would burst. (Georgiana Burne-Jones, *Memorials of Edward Burne-Jones*)

There is not a word describing the abbey itself; instead Burne-Jones describes the associated images aroused in his mind by the building, and it is these, not the actual ruins, that produce the feeling of ecstasy.

The imaginative association of ideas described by Burne-Jones required certain things both on the part of the observer and on the part of the object. On the one hand, the observer's mind must be properly disposed to receive sense impressions and to allow the imagination free rein. But this state of mind is impossible when the observer attempts to analyze the object critically. Thus, Alison points out in *Essays on the Nature and Principles of Taste* that no feeling of beauty is possible when one analyzes the individual parts of a composition:

> When we sit down to appreciate the value of a poem or of a painting, and attend minutely to the language or composition of the one, or to the coloring or design of the other, we feel no longer the delight which they at first produce. Our imagination in this employment is restrained, and instead of yielding to its suggestions, we studiously endeavor to resist them, by fixing our attention upon minute and partial circumstances of the composition.[38]

Wordsworth had written in "The Tables Turned" that "Our meddling intellect/Mis-shapes the beauteous forms of things:—/We murder to dissect." Macaulay said in his essay on Milton that "analysis is not the business of the poet. His office is to portray, not to dissect." We have already seen how analytical reason stood opposed generally to art as a hindrance to its natural and spontaneous development. We now see that it was considered inimical to the appreciation of art by thwarting the imaginative association of ideas and thereby destroying beauty. Benjamin Robert Haydon recalled in his *Autobiography* the "Immortal Dinner" in December 1817 when Charles Lamb and Keats agreed that Newton "had destroyed all the poetry of the rainbow by reducing it to the prismatic colours." Keats later treated the subject poetically through the destruction of Lamia by the philosophic stare of Apollonius. Analysis and dissection could be just as destructive of architectural beauty, for, as John Sedding observed, to approach architecture scientifically as if one were an archaeologist or geologist is "ruthless or disastrous to the work upon its poetic side, for it strips it of wonder."[39]

A great deal of Romantic poetry describes the attempt to circumvent or somehow to render passive the analytic reason so that the imagination might be free to create beauty, and just as surely these poems record the ultimate failure to maintain that freedom because of the inevitable intrusion of reason. There exists in Nathaniel Hawthorne's *Our Old Home* an architectural parallel to the visions recounted in such poems as "Kubla Khan'" and "Ode to a Nightingale," and to the mood described by Alison. When first Hawthorne saw Lichfield Cathedral, the edifice appeared to be "the most wonderful work which mortal man has yet achieved," and he felt drawn "into is harmony"

while it "whispered deeply of immortality." This initial response of wonder, spiritual union, and immortality approaches
very near a mystical vision. However, just as Coleridge wakes
from his dream of Xanadu and is interrupted by the infamous
man from Porlock, so does Hawthorne's momentary vision
fade, giving way to a minute and unappreciative analysis of
individual features of the building:

> If the truth must be told, my ill-trained enthusiasm soon flagged, and I
> began to lose the vision of a spiritual or ideal edifice behind the time-worn
> and weather-stained front of the actual structure. Whenever that is the
> case, it is most reverential to look another way; but the mood disposes one
> to minute investigation. . . .

Now in a critical frame of mind, Hawthorne notices niches
empty of statues, statues corroded by time and climate, and a
disappointingly small interior, enveloped in "monkish gloom."
He learns from this experience

> the folly of looking at noble objects in the wrong mood, and the absurdity
> of a new visitant pretending to hold any opinion whatever on such sub-
> jects, instead of surrendering himself to the old builder's influence with
> childlike simplicity.

A similar incident occurs shortly afterward when Hawthorne
witnesses one of the services in the cathedral. Initially, his imagination conceives of the boy choristers as "a peculiar order of
beings, created on purpose to hover between the roof and
pavement of that dim, consecrated edifice, and illuminate it
with divine melodies, reposing themselves, meanwhile, on the
heavy grandeur of the organ-tones like cherubs on a golden
cloud." This glimpse into heaven, however, is curtailed when
one of the cherubs removes his surplice to reveal an ordinary
lad in frock coat and provincial trousers. This little shock,
Hawthorne confesses, "had a sinister effect in putting me at
odds with the proper influences of the Cathedral, nor could I
quite recover a suitable frame of mind during my stay there."
The change in perception recalls the difference between
Blake's "Holy Thursday" of Innocence and his "Holy Thursday" of Experience. The observer of architecture, like the percipient of anything, artistic or otherwise, must look through the

imaginative eyes of innocence, or "with childlike simplicity" to use Hawthorne's phrase, if he is to feel the emotion of beauty.

Granted, then, that the observer approaches the object in the proper frame of mind, the object for its part must fulfill certain requirements, too, in order that the imagination be adequately inspired. Although both Wordsworth and Coleridge maintained that sensitive minds needed very little from the object by way of stimulation, less poetic imaginations depended on particular features in the object for the apprehension of beauty, and it so happened that Gothic architecture possessed these features to a far greater extent than did classical. This ability of buildings in the Gothic style to arouse the imaginations of nineteenth-century people goes a long way in explaining the popularity of the Gothic Revival.

One requirement of the object is its ability to elicit the sympathy of the observer, whether he be artist or audience. For his part the artist attempts to merge sympathetically with his characters, as Wordsworth says when he declares that the poet should try "to bring his feelings near to those of the persons whose feelings he describes, nay, for short spaces of time, perhaps to let himself slip into an entire delusion, and even confound and identify his own feelings with theirs . . . " ("Preface," 2d ed. of *Lyrical Ballads*). It was Keats more than Wordsworth, though, who made this principle a cardinal rule of his poetic theory, and logically so since he was more dedicated to objective expressionism than the elder poet. Actually, Keats's concept is nearer to empathy and manifests itself in such familiar poems as "Ode to a Nightingale" and "Ode on a Grecian Urn," where in listening to the bird the poet grows "too happy in thine happiness" and in viewing the urn he participates in the happiness of its figures. But sympathy is the connecting link between art and the audience, too, as "Ode on a Grecian Urn" makes clear, and the reader was expected to react to a poem emotionally by means of a similar sympathetic identification and so join the poet in feeling the beautiful. After stating that the object of poetry is to affect the emotions, John Stuart Mill goes on to say that poetry "is interesting only to those to whom it recalls what they have felt, or whose imagination it stirs up to conceive what they could feel, or what they might have been able to feel had their outward circumstances been different" ("Thoughts on Poetry and Its Varieties").

J. C. Loudon made the same point about responding to architecture when he wrote that "the imagination sees only in other things what it has first made its own by observation and memory."[40] Loudon used this point to argue that a person should learn as much as possible about architecture in order to appreciate it fully, but other writers were to argue from the same premise that to respond properly to ecclesiastical architecture conscientious study was unnecessary since the Christian observer already possessed a storehouse of information, and, as importantly, of feeling, awaiting only the architectural inspiration to rise in the heart and mind. The end purpose of this line of reasoning in the hands of Gothic advocates should easily be foreseen: Gothic is the only possible style for churches since only Gothic can evoke thoughts and sentiments proper to Christian worship and crucial to the feeling of beauty. Greek architecture may please the eye, but it can never arouse feelings since people no longer believe in the doctrines it embodies. For this reason, writes a contributor to *Arnold's Magazine* in 1833, "If we were to erect a church upon the most perfect model of a Grecian temple, its architecture could never speak to our minds, that awe, that deep mystery, and overwhelming possession, which it spoke to the ancient Greek. . . . But in that which may with propriety be termed Christian architecture, how powerful and how sublime the association of thought. . . ."[41] The argument was not, however, restricted in its application to churches, for Gothic was superior to classic in secular buildings also through its ability to evoke historical and patriotic feelings, as, indeed, is clear in Burne-Jones's description of Godstowe ruins.

Another feature required of an object if the observer's imagination is to be allowed free play for the creation of beauty is the contrary of perfection—either imperfection or incompleteness. Formerly, of course, perfection had been an attribute of beauty. Uvedale Price adopts the neoclassic attitude when he says that organic beauty balances precariously on the cusp of immaturity and decay: *"Each production of nature is most beautiful in that particular state, before which her work would have appeared incomplete and unfinished, and after which it would seem to be tending, however gradually, towards decay."*[42] When applied to architecture, this principle means that buildings in good repair are more beautiful than ruins, although Price admits that ruins are more picturesque. The reason behind the principle lies in the effect of perfection on the viewer, whose mind delights in completeness. In Owen Jones's words, "True beauty results from that repose which the mind feels when the eye, the intellect, and the affections are satisfied from the absence of any want."[43]

By the time Jones wrote these words in 1856, however, most Victorians had come to demand of art incompleteness rather than perfection, unfulfillment rather than satiety, and excitement rather than repose. One can see the beginnings of this change of taste as early as Edmund Burke, who made infinity a necessary part of the sublime. Infinity, which is opposed to the finite completion of perfection, accounts for the pleasure one derives from the spring and from the young, since "the imagination is entertained with the promise of something more, and does not acquiesce in the present object of the sense." Similarly, Burke finds that with "unfinished sketches of drawing, I have often seen something which pleased me beyond the best finishing . . . " (*Philosophical Enquiry*, 2.11). About twenty years later, Sir Joshua Reynolds agreed with Burke that sketches give free scope to the imagination. Speaking generally and not in the context of the sublime, Reynolds writes in "Discourse VIII" that

> sketches, or such drawings as painters generally make for their works, give this pleasure of imagination to a high degree. From a slight undetermined drawing, where the ideas of the composition and character are, as I may say, only just touched upon, the imagination supplies more than the painter himself, probably, could produce; and we accordingly often find that the finished work disappoints the expectation that was raised from the sketch; and this power of the imagination is one of the causes of the great pleasure we have in viewing a collection of drawings by great painters.

In poetry a similar effect is achieved when the writer is suggestive rather than clearly explicit in his descriptions. Reynolds, in fact, draws an analogy between sketches and suggestive poetry when he attributes the beauty of Eve in *Paradise Lost* to Milton's use of "only general indistinct expressions, every reader making out the detail according to his own particular imagination,—his own idea of beauty, grace, expression, dignity, or loveliness . . . " ("Discourse VIII"). In the next century Macaulay, perhaps with Reynolds's words in mind, praised the suggestive quality of Milton's poetry as being the chief cause of its beauty. Also like Reynolds, Macaulay compares Milton's poetry with sketches:

> The most striking characteristic of the poetry of Milton is the extreme remoteness of the associations by means of which it acts on the reader. Its effect is produced, not so much by what it expresses, as by what it suggests: not so much by the ideas which it directly conveys, as by other ideas which are connected with them. . . . The works of Milton cannot be comprehended or enjoyed, unless the mind of the reader co-operate with that of the writer. He does not paint a finished picture, or play for a mere passive listener. He sketches, and leaves others to fill up the outline. He strikes the key-note, and expects his hearer to make out the melody. ("Milton")

In addition to liberating the imagination of the audience by the technique of suggestion, the artist could reach a similar goal through his choice of an incomplete action, which would compel the imagination to furnish its own resolution. In other words, if the artist portrays a completed incident with a clearly fixed ending, there is no opportunity of an imaginative participation by the audience since the climax is distinctly visible for all to see. As Dr. Johnson was in the habit of saying to ensure that his was the last word on a subject, "There's an end on't." If, on the other hand, the artist stops short of carrying an action through to completion, then the audience's imagination is stirred to furnish its own resolution; and so there is an active participation in the perception of art. Lessing applied this principle in explaining the sigh of Laocoön. Since the painter and sculptor have but one moment to work with and since they must choose the moment that gives freest rein to the imagination, they must never portray the moment of climax; for "there is nothing beyond this, and to present the utmost to the eye is to bind the wings of fancy and compel it, since it cannot soar above the impression made on the senses, to concern itself with weaker images, shunning the visible fullness already represented as a limit beyond which it cannot go."[44] The sculptor of Laocoön knew this and depicted only the sigh, allowing the viewer to imagine the cry for himself.

This principle explains why unheard melodies are sweeter than heard ones and why Keats's Cupid and Psyche, like the lovers on the urn, enjoy the divine bliss of anticipation, eternally and exquisitely poised on the verge of consummation:

> They lay calm-breathing on the bedded grass;
>   Their arms embraced, and their pinions too;
>   Their lips touch'd not, but had not bade adieu,
> As if disjoined by soft-handed slumber,
> And ready still past kisses to outnumber
>   At tender eye-dawn of aurorean love.
>
>   "Ode to Psyche"

Perhaps this principle accounts as well for so many of Tennyson's poems with unresolved endings, poems that Christopher Ricks has referred to as exercises in the "art of the penultimate."[45] Furthermore, if Owen Jones is right in saying that perfection in art leaves the audience satisfied, then incompleteness produces the opposite effect by arousing and stimulating, and thus the audience is made to share the delicious unfulfillment of Cupid and Psyche or of the countless other figures in nineteenth-century poetry who, "yearning in desire," embark on the Romantic quest. Thus does Tennyson's Ulysses, no more content than Achilles with the prospect of a long and easeful life of repose, call his mariners for one last exploit; and thus do readers of this and other poems, left with an indeterminate conclusion, imaginatively share the adventure with them.

The application of the principle of incompleteness to architecture is apparent with ruins, but perhaps less so with preserved buildings. In part the application is to the form of

Gothic, which, like Romantic organicism, is a matter of flux, always becoming and therefore always incomplete. "The Greek idea of perfection," according to Coventry Patmore, "demanded that its limits should everywhere be seen. Now, the perfection of modern art, as we find it in Gothic architecture . . . consists in its unlimited and illimitable character."[46] In other words, the illimitable character of Gothic suggests the kind of infinity Burke had in mind for sketches. Surely the great span of years required to build the large cathedrals, during which designs changed and portions were left undone, contributed to this characteristic of Gothic. Also, old houses in the Gothic style were added on to by successive generations and were, in fact, constantly changing, either away from original completion or toward future perfection, however one might view them. Neoclassic architecture, on the other hand, was not old enough for ruins or many additions and could not compete with Gothic on these grounds even if its principles of design were not based on symmetry.

In addition to form, Gothic architecture suited the new taste better than classic in execution, where the value of incompleteness is more fittingly described as imperfection. Ruskin had advocated imperfection of workmanship because of religion and morality. For these reasons he approved of Gothic architecture, disapproved of Egyptian and Renaissance, and opposed the use of machine-made ornaments. There was, however, a purely aesthetic reason for imperfect execution in that work which imperfectly realized an ideal concept, like work which incompletely realized it, suggests the infinite and allows the observer to participate imaginatively in the creation of beauty. This is the reasoning behind Baillie Scott's opposition to what he calls the "mechanical ideal" in buildings, which he defines as making "all surfaces smooth and all lines mathematically straight." The problem with mechanical perfection as an ideal, Scott says, "is that it is an 'ideal' which may be realised— the only goal worth striving for in art is that which can never be reached. In trying instead to express character, our work will become full of suggestions of the infinite rather than statements of the finite."[47]

In execution as in form, Gothic architecture is obviously less finished than classic and was therefore able to gain popularity on the strength of this curious and paradoxical change in taste whereby the incomplete and imperfect were more esteemed than the complete and polished. Browning's Andrea del Sarto, whose fault lies in his faultlessness, becomes entrapped in this paradox, as do the proponents of Grecian architecture, at least in the eyes of their Gothic antagonists. Ten years before Browning's poem, the *Ecclesiologist* provided the following architectural precedent of the "doctrine of the imperfect":

> It is clear that to satisfy the mind, any object presented to it ought to be infinite. It should stimulate the imagination; should give room for a play of thought and exercise of active reason; there should be scope for ranging into newly discovered fields of invention,—for achieving something ourselves, not merely observing what has been achieved by others. The spectator should be made to take part in the work of creation.

This is as neat a summary of the associative doctrine with which we are presently concerned as one is likely to find. But the writer goes on to tell why Grecian architecture furnishes less pleasure, according to the doctrine, than does Gothic. Grecian art is finite, exact, complete, allowing no imaginative play, whereas Gothic is infinite, inexact, incomplete, encouraging the active participation of the observer. The writer concludes with the paradox "Gothic architecture, therefore, to be perfect, must be imperfect; to be complete, it must have something to desiderate."[48]

Related to the change of aesthetic values from perfection to imperfection is the shift from clarity to obscurity. The relationship between the two is that the indeterminate, like the incomplete or the imperfect, is limitless, suggestive of infinity. Furthermore, the indefinite becomes a positive aesthetic value through its association with the sublime just as incompleteness had. Obscurity not only produces the terror necessary to the sublime, Burke says, but also is important because hardly any thing can strike the mind with its greatness, which does not make some sort of approach towards infinity; which nothing can do whilst we are able to perceive its bounds; but to see an object distinctly, and to perceive its bounds, is one and the same thing. A clear idea is therefore another name for a little idea. (*Philosophical Enquiry*, 2. 4).

As infinity ceased to be an exclusive property of sublimity and became a requisite of all art and all art subjects generally, obscurity similarly became a universal aesthetic value. Wordsworth comments in his preface to the 1815 edition of *Poems* that the imagination "recoils from everything but the plastic, the pliant, and the indefinite." Had, for example, Wordsworth understood Gaelic and been able to interpret the song of the Solitary Reaper, he could not have speculated imaginatively on the universality of the song. Because, however, the meaning of the song was obscure, he carries the music in his heart "long after it was heard no more." Reason feeds on clarity, imagination on uncertainty—such is the distinction Coleridge draws in an 1811 lecture entitled "The Grandest Efforts of Poetry": "As soon as it [the mind] is fixed on one image, it becomes understanding; but while it is unfixed and wavering between them, attaching itself permanently to none, it is imagination." Like Reynolds before him and Macaulay after him, Coleridge furnishes a quotation from Milton to illustrate his point about the value of suggestiveness.

In power of suggestiveness architecture and music rise above the other art forms, for, as J. M. Capes remarked in 1867, these two alone possess "no verbal language for expressing the definite emotions and actions of mankind, or the material phenomena of the universe." What might seem to be a handicap, however, is in fact an advantage since "it is through this very indefiniteness of the language of music and architecture that the two arts are able to kindle emotions and suggest currents of thought which are all their own. They ask more from those who are affected by them than is asked by the poet, the sculptor, and the painter; but in return they permit a far wider liberty of feeling and conception than is allowed by their rivals and sisters."[49] This suggestive power of architecture and music, Capes concludes, is their strength and peculiar charm.

A second application of the principle of obscurity to architecture is by means of interior light. Neoclassic windows are clear, admitting as much light as possible. The brightness of the rooms is further enhanced by the reflection of light on flat walls and ceilings that are generally whitewashed, or at least painted in light colors. Gothic windows, on the other hand, are stained, the walls are broken with niches and ornaments, and the dark stone and wood are left unpainted. I am thinking principally of churches, but the same distinction applies to domestic and public buildings. In fact, Palmerston turned the Gothicist argument against Scott in the debate over the style for the Foreign Office by saying that Gothic was not best suited for the English climate because it admitted so little light in a country that was dreary to begin with. What was needed instead was a style that would take advantage of what little light there was.

Palmerston, however, was taking a hardheaded, utilitarian approach to the matter and was not in the least concerned with the building's poetic side. But for those who were more interested in buildings for the effect they created than for their functional value, Gothic answered very nicely for the creation of a dim atmosphere so conducive to an active imagination. Burke had written that "all edifices calculated to produce an idea of the sublime, ought rather to be dark and gloomy . . . " (*Philosophical Enquiry*, 2. 15). William Beckford knew this and so arranged to show off Fonthill Abbey to his guests, Lord Nelson and the Hamiltons among them, in the darkness of night. Churchmen knew this, too, and so built Gothic and neo-Gothic churches to inculcate in the worshipers a sense of the mysterious and awesome sublimity of God. James Fergusson explained the connection between darkness, imagination, and religious awe in churches when he made these comments in reference to Butterfield's All Saints' in Margaret Street:

> It has to be observed that one of the primary principles in this extreme kind of ecclesiastical architecture seems to be the coercive production of the "dim religious light" of the poet. Internally, at least, the express exclusion of common worldly daylight—which has been a rule from the earliest ages to the latest whenever mystery had to be cultivated—contributes so greatly to the creation of a feeling of awe that it becomes a direct and

> leading historical element in Art. It may be suggested that one chief differ-
> ence between the forms of worship of the Romanists and those of the
> Protestants (until lately) is that in the one case the light of day is in-
> tentionally shut out, and in the other intentionally let in. In the one case,
> accordingly, the exercise of the imagination is encouraged, in the other it is
> restrained.

Although Fergusson acknowledges the effect of darkness in
churches, he is too fundamentally opposed to Gothic architecture to allow himself to praise Butterfield's church. He concludes, therefore, that the gloom of All Saints' is overdone and
that the church's merits "are generally voted to be, at the best,
needlessly lugubrious."[50]
Another change in taste relative to the principle of allowing
the imagination free play was the growing preference for distant objects over immediate ones. Ruskin advised viewing
Westminster Abbey from Highgate Hill, and in the preceding
century Arthur Young had recommended looking at ruins
from a distance because "the imagination has a free space to
range in, and sketches ruins in idea far beyond the broadest
strokes of reality" (*A Six Months Tour through the North of England*, 1770). William Hazlitt, who dealt with the subject directly
in the essay "Why Distant Objects Please," points up the similarity between obscurity and distance: "Whatever is placed beyond
the reach of sense and knowledge, whatever is imperfectly discerned, the fancy pieces out at its leisure. . . ." As Hazlitt goes
on to remark, distance of time has a similar effect as distance of
space; and when Thomas Campbell wrote his well-known line
"'tis distance lends enchantment to the view" (*The Pleasures of
Hope*, 1799), he was using a spatial analogy to describe a temporal phenomenon. Since it was a far easier matter to con-
template the antiquity of Westminster Abbey than to rise before dawn and view it from Highgate Hill, temporal distance
was the preferred mode of perception for buildings; and here
again the Gothic style held an advantage over the Grecian, for
the only examples of classical architecture in northern Europe
had been erected since the Renaissance and were far less old
than Gothic piles. In *The Genius of Christianity* (1802), Chateaubriand remarked how a Gothic church was capable of calling to

mind such vivid images of medieval life that "Ancient France seemed to revive altogether. . . ." The key ingredient is age, for "the more remote were these times the more magical they appeared. . . ." Revived Grecian temples, on the other hand, cannot stir these reveries because "there is nothing marvellous in a temple whose erection we have witnessed, whose echoes and whose domes were formed before our eyes." This release of the imagination affords yet another explanation of the nineteenth-century phenomenon that Tennyson called the "passion of the past."

Up till now we have been examining those features in an object of perception that allow the viewer to participate actively in the creation of beauty through an association of ideas. Whether the object is imperfect, incomplete, dark, or far off, its infinitude gives range for imaginative wanderings, unlike neo-classic art, where the contrary qualities clearly define boundaries and leave little scope for speculation. Neoclassic art attempts through its perfection to satisfy the reader or viewer and thereby bring forth a feeling of repose. Romantic art, and Gothic architecture, deliberately withhold the fullness of perfection so that the insatiate audience is enticed to complete the process on its own, and instead of creating a sense of repose, agitates the audience with desire. In "The Nature of Gothic," Ruskin listed "Changefulness" as the second most important characteristic of Gothic architecture, and described it thus:

> It is that strange *disquietude* of the Gothic spirit that is its greatness; that restlessness of the dreaming mind, that wanders hither and thither among the niches, and flickers feverishly around the pinnacles, and frets and fades in labyrinthine knots and shadows along wall and roof, and yet is not satisfied, nor shall be satisfied.[51]

Ruskin ascribes this characteristic of Gothic to variety, but certainly the infinitude of imperfection, incompletion, darkness, and distance are responsible as well. In addition, there are other features of Gothic architecture that produce an emotional reaction of restlessness rather than of repose and that, lacking the specific purpose of liberating the imagination, seem calculated simply to arouse. But these, too, have a part to play in the association of ideas, for they arouse feelings into a state of excitement conducive to imaginative activity. These features are angles, vertical lines, color, and profuse ornamentation.

The eighteenth century had a decided preference for curves over sharp angles as features of beauty, and Hogarth's "Line of Beauty" is the most famous example of this taste, although Thomas Jefferson's serpentine wall at the University of Virginia and John Nash's serpentine lake in St. James's Park are well known also. Burke acknowledged his indebtedness to Hogarth in proposing "gradual variation" as an element of beauty, and went on to add, "I do not find any natural object which is angular, and at the same time beautiful. Indeed few natural objects are entirely angular. But I think those which approach the most nearly to it, are the ugliest" (*Philosophical Enquiry*, 3. 15). Sir Uvedale Price and Archibald Alison agreed that "insensible transitions," as they called them, were essential to beauty; but, unlike Burke, they had a new and more acceptable category for angular objects—the picturesque. Just, then, as irregularity became a respectable aesthetic value by means of picturesque theory, so did angularity; and just as picturesque scenery excited rather than soothed the viewer, so did this particular feature of it have the same effect. Edward Lacy Garbett remarked that angles present contrasts, whereas curves owe their beauty to gradation. Furthermore, "Of these two qualities, contrast is certainly that calculated to excite; and gradation, that calculated to soothe."[52] Gothic architecture, which had risen to popularity along with the picturesque and which shares so many features with the theory, excited viewers with its sharp, acute angles and thus satisfied the growing taste for emotional stimulation.

Angles, along with the vertical lines necessary to their acuteness, were also opposed to horizontal lines, the trademark of classical architecture. As Garbett pointed out, with Gothic the vertical lines are continuous and the horizontal lines are broken, whereas with Greek buildings the pattern is reversed with continuous horizontal lines and broken vertical ones.[53] The horizontal character of classical architecture determined by these lines elicits a feeling of calm and repose, whereas the verticality of Gothic arouses and excites. Of all writers who made this distinction, Voysey best expressed it when he likened the effect of sharp angles to the movement of lightning and to crooked or cranky people who "show a want of stability that is disturbing." Horizontal lines, however, are prevalent in nature and express "the sweetest calm and repose." The difference between vertical angles and horizontal lines is the difference between a stormy sea and a tranquil one. Unfortunately, from Voysey's point of view, Victorian house-builders had ignored this principle, for "most of our houses resemble the forms of storms. Hardly anywhere do we see houses standing peacefully as if to stay and calm you by their reposefulness."[54]

This tumultuous effect is created, according to Voysey, not only by their angularity but also by the "infinite number of differently coloured materials and textures" of which the houses are composed. Neoclassic architects had neither painted buildings nor used constructional polychromy because they believed that the Greeks and Romans had not done so. But at the beginning of Victoria's reign, it was discovered that the ancients had in fact used paint, on statues as well as buildings, and neo-Gothic architects availed themselves of the classical precedent.[55] Butterfield is best known for his use of color, although unfortunately by the derisive remarks of journalists, who compared the walls of Balliol College Chapel to "slices of streaky bacon" and who described the style of Keble College as "holy zebra." Furthermore, writers pointed out that the effect of Butterfield's use of color, like that of angles and vertical lines, is restlessness, the R.I.B.A. *Journal* commenting, for example, that the interior of Keble College Chapel "is racked by restlessness. . . ."[56]

In discussing ornaments, Sir Joshua Reynolds had declared that "nothing will contribute more to destroy repose than profusion, of whatever kind, whether it consists in the multiplicity of objects, or the variety and brightness of colours" ("Discourse VIII"). By this standard there is nothing more destructive of repose than the Gothic style and Victorian art in general.

Fig. 24. The chapel, Keble College, Oxford, by William Butterfield, 1873–76.

Voysey believed that "lavish ornament is like a drug, the dose requires increasing as it loses its effect."[57] Ruskin, on the other hand, in defending the use of elaborate details in Hunt's *The Awakening Conscience*, had stated that attention to minute details is characteristic of a feverish and excited mind, a psychological proposition seemingly verified by the paintings of Richard Dadd. Whether the products of such minds or not, ornaments in abundance are the cause of similar mental states. As T. G. Jackson commented, a building with a profusion of ornaments and irregularities "has no repose. . . . Everything about it is 'busy'; it fidgets one to look at it; nothing seems at rest."[58] It may be, as Voysey said, that the Victorian public reacted less sensitively to abundant ornament because it had become inured to it, but I rather suspect that the Victorians had come to crave excitement from art and to value it above repose.

V. COOPERATIVE AESTHETICS

> You feel him to be a poet, inasmuch as, for a time, he has made you one—an active creative being. (S. T. Coleridge, *Shakespearean Criticism*)

It is no accident that these features of Gothic architecture should excite the viewer into a state approaching the creative passion of the artist, for the whole tendency of Romantic art is to draw the audience as an active participant into the act of artistic creation. The underlying principle of associative aesthetics—that beauty lies largely in the percipient's mind—requires that the artist work suggestively, indeterminately, for the very purpose of allowing his audience to complete imaginatively the building, or painting, or poem and so to become, as it were, collaborators in bringing forth artistic beauty. Macaulay had written that one cannot enjoy the works of Milton "unless the mind of the reader co-operate with that of the writer." The *Ecclesiologist* commented that in any work of art "the spectator should be made to take part in the work of creation." And George Wightwick, in *The Palace of Architecture*, elevated the observer to the level of the artist when he wrote,

> A spectator of this happy class, when contemplating a noble piece of Architecture, becomes *his own poet*; unites himself with it in the bond of a perfect

reciprocity; elevates it on the "vantage hill' of his own imagination; and there beholds it with all the rapture of an eager recipient.[59]

I remarked earlier that the relationship between an artist and nature is comparable to the relationship between the audience and a work of art in that nature inspires the artist's imaginative association of ideas even as his work of art inspires the audience's. We may now take the parallel further by saying that the relationship between an artist and God, the creator of nature, is similar to the relationship between the audience and the artist, the creator of art, in that the artist and God join imaginatively in the creation of natural beauty even as the audience and the artist join imaginatively in the creation of artistic beauty. Thus, the artist approaches divinity, since divine power, in Wordsworth's words, "is the express/Resemblance of that glorious faculty/That higher minds bear with them as their own" (*The Prelude*, bk. 14). In like manner the spectator of architecture "becomes his own poet," or, to use Wilde's phrase, the critic becomes an artist.

The chief prerequisite of impressionistic criticism is that the critic be able to respond sensitively to art, just as this is the main requirement of the artist, who must respond to nature. Pater wrote in his preface to *The Renaissance* that the critic should have "a certain kind of temperament, the power of being deeply moved by the presence of beautiful objects." Wilde repeated this in "The Critic as Artist" (1891), the most cogent statement of this theory of criticism, and proceeded to draw another parallel between artist and critic, which is that since both have sensitive temperaments they require very little stimulation. Gilbert, Wilde's spokesman in the dialogue, tells the naïve Ernest that "the critic occupies the same relation to the work of art that he criticises as the artist does to the visible world of form and colour, or the unseen world of passion and of thought. He does not even require for the perfection of his art the finest materials. Anything will serve his purpose." Wordsworth had indeed said that "the human mind is capable of being excited without the application of gross and violent stimulants" ("Preface," 2d ed. of *Lyrical Ballads*), and had shown in many poems how his own imagination had been aroused by the most trivial of things. The effect of Wilde's theory obviously is to lessen in value the work of art, which is important only insofar as it stimulates the imagination of the critic. The theory, furthermore, proceeds very naturally from associative aesthetics, which transfers beauty from the object to the observer, and we find an early version of it in Alexander Smith's remark that many imaginative readers "find any poetry exquisite, however destitute of meaning, which merely suggests ideas or images that may serve as the germs of fancy in their own minds" ("The Philosophy of Poetry," 1835). All poetry or any kind of art need do, then, is provide a "germ of fancy"—nothing more—and the audience supplies the rest. To return to Wilde, Gilbert says that criticism

> treats the work of art simply as a starting-point for a new creation. It does not confine itself . . . to discovering the real intention of the artist and accepting that as final. And in this it is right, for the meaning of any beautiful created thing is, at least, as much in the soul of him who looks at it, as it was in his soul who wrought it. Nay, it is rather the beholder who lends to the beautiful thing its myriad meanings, and makes it marvellous for us. . . .

A second result of Wilde's theory, implicit in the above passage, counteracts an effect of expressionism by diminishing the importance of the artist, whose role is usurped by the critic and whose intentions matter less than the artistic response of the critic. For Gilbert, therefore, Ruskin's response to Turner and Pater's response to Leonardo are as valuable and beautiful as the feelings and ideas of the painters themselves. The critic becomes an artist, Leonardo's *La Gioconda* becomes for Pater "older than the rocks among which she sits," Turner's *The Fighting Téméraire* becomes for Ruskin "that broad bow that struck the surf aside, enlarging silently in steadfast haste, full front to the shot—resistless and without reply," and St. Mark's in Venice becomes for all as once for Ruskin "a vision out of the earth . . . a multitude of pillars and white domes, clustered into a long low pyramid of coloured light. . . ."

Whistler, for one, recognized the dangers inherent in art

appreciation of the sort advocated by Wilde, rightfully fearing
the abolition of all values of aesthetic judgment. In its extreme
form the system asks only whether art stimulates the audience,
and because the sensitive critic requires so little stimulation,
even this question becomes unnecessary. Since all art capable
of providing the germ for imaginative associations, which is to
say practically all art, is worthwhile, there is no way of separating the good from the bad, and Beethoven's symphonies are on
a level with "Yankee Doodle." Whistler's opinion, as he states it
in "The Red Rag," is that "art should be independent of all
clap-trap—should stand alone, and appeal to the artistic sense
of eye and ear, without confounding this with emotions entirely
foreign to it, as devotion, pity, love, patriotism, and the like."

Some years later Irving Babbitt addressed the same problem
in *The New Laokoon*, where he quotes as an illustration of this
tendency toward leveling of the arts Gerard de Nerval's "Fan-
taisie":

> Il est un air pour qui je donnerais
> Tout Rossini, tout Mozart, tout Weber,
> Un air très vieux, languissant et funèbre,
> Qui pour moi seul a des charmes secrets.
>
> Or, chaque fois que je viens à l'entendre,
> De deux cents ans mon âme rajeunit;
> C'est sous Louis treize . . . et je crois voir s'étendre
> Un coteau vert que le couchant jaunit.

The poem continues on to describe other fanciful associations
inspired by the tune, which because of its associative power is
worth all the works of Rossini, Mozart, and Weber. One need
not agree wholly with Babbitt that this kind of attitude is
responsible for chaos in artistic judgments to admit that the
threat, at least, is there.

We are dealing here, however, with a tendency that develops
late in the Victorian era and that is not immediately applicable
to the contemporary appreciation of Gothic architecture. But if
the fully developed theory does not apply, the earlier form of it
does, and it is very important for an understanding of the
popularity of the Revival to remember the attitude with which

the Victorians approached architecture as well as the other arts. It is easy to forget in this analytical age of ours that the associations of a building or other work of art were perhaps more important to them as an element of beauty than any inherent properties in the work itself, and if one forgets this and insists on regarding Victorian art objectively, failing to participate imaginatively in the artistic process, he will fail to appreciate it and to understand the appeal it had as surely as, according to Macaulay, one fails to appreciate Milton who does not cooperate with the author.

There is a plate in Max Beerbohm's little book of pictures, *Rossetti and His Circle*, in which Benjamin Jowett is observing Rossetti paint a mural in the Oxford Union during the "Jovial Campaign." As he stands before the painting, rotund and professorial, Jowett asks the painter, "And what were they going to do with the Grail when they found it, Mr. Rossetti?" It is, of course, the wrong question, for not only did the Grail have no practical purpose but it was never really meant to be found. The quest was all—the reach that exceeded the grasp—for though the holy cup might never be discovered, heroic deeds, challenging boons, beautiful ladies were encountered along the way, all making the search worthwhile. So, too, with art. The imaginative quest for truth might never be realized as one struggled to apprehend the mysteries of nature or the wonder of a Gothic cathedral, but the fanciful images magically associated by the mind in its endeavor to do so brought joy to the beholder and made a beauty of their own. If we, like Jowett, ask the wrong, logical question, beauty will evaporate before us; but if, like Burne-Jones, we surrender to the spells of our imaginations, we too may glimpse "banners of the cross, copes and crosiers, gay knights and ladies by the river bank, hawking-parties and all the pageantry of the golden age," and come to understand what so many Victorians saw in Gothic art.

VI. PRAGMATISM: INSTRUCTION

I. THE DIDACTIC FUNCTION OF ART

> An Athenian Courtesan, we are told, forsook at once the habitual vices of
> her profession on seeing the decent dignities of a Philosopher, as repre-
> sented in a portrait; and the terrors of the day of judgment operated so
> forcibly, by means of a picture, on the imagination of a King of Bulgaria,
> that he instantly embraced the religion, which held out such punishments,
> and invited with rewards equally transcendant. (Viscount Sidmouth, "On
> the Affinity between Painting and Writing, in Point of Composition")

The pragmetic theory of art is so named because it regards art
as a means to an end, as having the practical function of creating certain responses in the audience. Further, since the audience represents, as it were, the goal of art, it becomes more
important than the individual artist, the universe he portays, or
the art object itself. One end of pragmatic art is pleasure and
the other is instruction, but ordinarily the two have been regarded throughout history as inseparable twins. For instance,
Horace wrote in *On the Art of Poetry* that "poets aim at giving
either profit or delight, or at combining the giving of pleasure
with some useful precepts for life." Sir Philip Sidney stated in
An Apologie for Poetrie that poetry was "a speaking picture"
whose aim is "to teach and delight"; and Samuel Johnson declared in the "Preface to Shakespeare" that "the end of poetry is
to instruct by pleasing." It is, then, perhaps artificial and misleading to treat pleasure and instruction separately, but at the
same time one might justifiably do so by recalling that although
pleasure is probably an inevitable adjunct to instruction in art
(though not necessarily in other types of communication), instruction is not required of pleasure, or so at least thought
those in the Art for Art's Sake group, who sought to banish
pleasure's ugly, didactic sister. Also, whether pleasure and instruction are inseparable or not, it is true that different ages
have chosen to emphasize one or the other, and there is implicit
in this fact a distinction of degree that allows for individual
analysis.

We see, for example, a shift in emphasis from instruction to
pleasure occurring during the eighteenth and nineteenth

centuries. In the middle of the eighteenth century, Joseph Warton complained that the art of his time was too much given over to instruction, and he expressed the hope in his preface to *Odes on Various Subjects* (1746) that his poems might return poetry to its proper middle course:

> The public has been so much accustomed of late to didactic poetry alone, and essays on moral subjects, that any work where the imagination is much indulged will perhaps not be relished or regarded. . . . But as he [the author] is convinced that the fashion of moralizing in verse has been carried too far, and as he looks upon invention and imagination to be the chief faculties of a poet, so he will be happy if the following odes may be looked upon as an attempt to bring back poetry into its right channel.

In the hands of the Romantics, poetry did indeed return to what Warton considered its right channel; for they, too, reacted against the excessive didacticism of the preceding age, and with a unanimity that made for success. Coleridge feared that the moral of *The Rime of the Ancient Mariner* was too explicit, and Keats unequivocally expressed his dislike of moralistic verse when he wrote his friend Reynolds, "We hate poetry that has a palpable design upon us . . . " (3 February 1818). In America, Poe spoke of "the heresy of *The Didactic*." The best poem, he argued, "is a poem and nothing more" and should be "written solely for the poem's sake" ("The Poetic Principle"). In time and in sentiment, Poe is not far from Théophile Gautier's declaration of Art for Art's Sake in the preface to *Mademoiselle de Maupin*. "Some one has said somewhere," Gautier wrote, "that literature and the arts influence morals. Whoever he was, he was undoubtedly a great fool."

From Gautier's point of view, there would have been very many great fools during the age of Victoria; for, even though these and other writers were calling for less didacticism in art if not its total elimination, probably the large majority of audience and artists alike retained the traditional faith in art as an instructional medium. As a matter of fact, that the outcries against didacticism continued throughout the nineteenth century and culminated in the Aesthetic movement clearly reveals the existence of an immediate and formidable danger, that is to say, of moralistic art. If, however, this minority did not succeed in expunging instruction from art altogether, it did partly win its goal by gaining for art the concept that instruction should be indirect instead of direct and that the didactic element should be subtle and subordinate. We shall investigate this change presently, but first we should consider what artists meant to achieve by means of art.

II. THE DIDACTIC SOLUTION TO THE EXPRESSIVE DILEMMA

> Revivals of old styles can never be a success, unless we reproduce the tone of thought of the age that gave them birth. (A Cambridge Graduate, "As to a New Style")

> Ancient feelings and sentiments . . . alone . . . can restore pointed architecture to its former glorious state; without it all that is done will be a tame and heartless copy, true as far as the mechanism of the style goes, but utterly wanting in that sentiment and feeling that distinguishes ancient design. (A. Welby Pugin, *Contrasts*)

One need not rely exclusively and indirectly upon reactions against didactic art to establish its existence in Victorian times, for there is ample direct evidence of it as an artistic goal. Frequently, writers speak of art as exerting a general, civilizing influence. John Tupper, for example, declared in the *Germ* that the function of art was to humanize and that art should become "a more powerful engine of civilization" ("The Subject in Art, No. II," March 1850). At other times art's didactic purpose is somewhat more specific, as when James Fergusson writes of moral improvement: the true object of art is "to win man to virtue and goodness, and to civilise and elevate him. . . ."[1] Or, there are religious overtones, as when Cram explains the title of his book, *The Ministry of Art*, to mean "that function which I think art has performed, and always can perform, as an agency working toward the redemption of human character. . . ."[2] Sometimes the motive is specifically artistic. In reviewing the Great Exhibition, Ralph Nicholson Wornum believed the chief question to be asked was, "How far our manufacturers may improve their taste through the present Great Exhibition of Works of Industry now established in Hyde Park?"[3] The entire purpose of the Exhibition to Wornum was to provide a lesson in taste whereby manufacturers may learn to improve the artistic aspect of their products.

One need not look far to discover why so many Victorians were ready to follow Prince Albert's lead in placing the arts in service to the public, for the march to democracy—or in Carlyle's phrase, the Niagara leap to it—required education of those who were rapidly rising in society and acquiring wealth and power for themselves. Under the old system an ignorant majority was no disadvantage—to the contrary, it was a real advantage in forestalling insurrection and such lesser evils as leveling. But under the new system, it was an absolute necessity that this new captain of industry, this new MP, this new buyer of pictures, and all those collectively rising up from the faceless masses of Disraeli's other England be properly equipped to discharge their responsibilities in a democratic nation. To leave them ignorant would be to court disaster, or, as Arnold put it, the alternative to culture is anarchy. Nor were the leaders of this age of awakening social consciousness unmindful of the poor, as we see in the establishment of the Working Men's College, where Rossetti and others taught, and of the Kyrle Society, founded in 1877 by Miranda Hill to introduce art to the lower classes. Both of these groups were formed on a principle set forth by Charles Kingsley earlier in the century, which was that art provided a refuge for those surrounded by ugliness and a subtle education for those standing in need of moral improvement:

> Picture-galleries should be the workman's paradise, and gardens of pleasure, to which he goes to refresh his eyes and heart with beautiful shapes and sweet colouring, when they are wearied with dull bricks and mortar, and the ugly colourless things which fill the workshop and the factory. For believe me, there is many a road into our hearts besides our ears and brains; many a sight, and sound, and scent, even, of which we have never *thought* at all, sinks into our memory, and helps to shape our characters. . . . ("The National Gallery.—No. I," 1848)

Architecture joined with the other arts generally in being considered an instructive instrument for social change and with a greater opportunity of providing culture to the masses than the other arts because of its public nature. Kingsley might be hard pressed to lure a single workman into the National Gallery, but thousands passed the building daily. And like the other arts, architecture's goal was broadly to elevate morally, religiously, artistically, in short, to be a civilizing influence in society. Yet, as we saw in chapter 3, the Revivalists had worked themselves into a corner by adopting the expressive theory that art reflects the society from which it springs. Now it was obvious that Victorian England with its materialism, religious doubt, and divided aims was a far different nation from the medieval England of idealism, faith, and unity. In fact, some of the leaders of the Revival, Pugin for instance, repeatedly drew contrasts between England's present, fallen state and its golden age. How, then, could the same style of architecture represent, according to the expressive theory, two vastly different societies? For one thing, contemporary England and medieval England were not, despite the contrasts so popular in the early part of the century, completely dissimilar. The nation was, after all, the same, the people were ethnically no different, and the climate was as ever. The Revivalists believed that all these things were important determinants of architectural style and that the continuance of them from the Middle Ages to the present made Gothic, which had arisen as a natural and spontaneous expression of these conditions, a far better candidate for revival than classical architecture, which was formed by foreign nations, alien people, and a happier clime. But only the blind would fail to see that changes had occurred between that age and this, and that reform was necessary for the successful revival of Gothic. Therefore, in addition to joining the other arts in an attempt to civilize society for the sake of society, neo-Gothic architecture took as its special didactic goal the reformation of society for the sake of the Gothic Revival; for only by creating a society similar in ideals to that which originally delivered Gothic could neo-Gothic, according to the principles of expressionism, flourish.

The architects of the Revival, then, took advantage of the didactic theory of art to save Gothic architecture from the predicament into which it had been led by the expressive theory;

and in bringing the two artistic approaches together, they postulated a reciprocal causal relationship between art and society in which art is both product and creator of the society in which it exists. Ralph Adams Cram best described the relationship when he wrote, "Every art is at the same time vocative and dynamic: it voices the highest and the best; it subtly urges to emulation; it is perhaps the greatest civilizing influence in the world."[4] Charles Eastlake, in saying that for Pugin and others architecture was only a means to an end, grasped only half the relationship—the didactic part—and was only half right.[5] He was right in saying that architecture was a means of reforming society, but wrong in failing to see that reformation was but a partial or immediate goal and that ultimately the Revivalists were attempting to restore Gothic by creating a society for which it would be the natural expression. On the other hand, Esmé Wingfield-Stratford went in the other direction by emphasizing the expressive aspect and neglecting the didactic. Here is his explanation for the Revival's failure:

> But after we have made every allowance, we shall find ourselves forced to the reluctant conclusion that the Gothic Revival was a failure, and not a very splendid failure at that. Its advocates founded their case on a simple fallacy of putting the cart before the horse. It was no doubt arguable that the original Gothic had expressed an ideal of civilisation saner and more spiritual than that of *laissez-faire* and devil-take-the-hindmost. But it did not follow that you could revive that civilisation by counterfeiting its effects, nor that such a counterfeit could be mistaken for anything else than what it was.[6]

This is a useful example since it comes from a nonspecialist and as such probably represents a more broadly typical attitude than Eastlake's. The problems in this argument, especially the last sentence of it, are mainly semantic.

First, the word *counterfeit* not only prejudices the case by its pejorative connotation but seriously misrepresents the intentions of the leaders of the Revival. As we have already seen, these men were not out even to copy, much less to counterfeit; for they repeatedly insisted that the architect should imitate— that is, follow principles—and not simply and slavishly copy forms. It was all right for the apprentice to copy old buildings in his sketchbook as a means of learning his craft, but the practicing architect should delve beneath forms to uncover principles when he conceives his designs. Pugin's primary message is that now that people are familiar with forms the time has come to understand the principles behind them and that these principles, which his books elucidate, should guide the Revival. He and others consistently derided the folly of trying to duplicate exactly, or counterfeit, old buildings. A Victorian building should obviously be Victorian, not deceptively medieval; it should be a modern building constructed on medieval principles.

Second, they were not attempting to "revive" medieval civilization but to reform modern society by appealing to certain medieval ideals, and there is a great difference between the two. To surrender to the spell of history and live out the past everyone recognized as delusion, and not even those who most adamantly believed in the superiority of the Middle Ages were so bemused as to think those days could be recaptured. The Eglinton Tournament was great fun, even in the mud and rain, yet no one made a habit of that sort of thing. What, in fact, the Revivalists were aiming for was compromise. On the one hand, the form—that is to say, Gothic architecture—should adapt to modern society, and could adapt if architects based their designs on general principles. On the other hand, through the agency of art, and architecture in particular, modern society might be reformed so that it shared more in common with medieval civilization and so that, therefore, it might not only be the better but also the more able to express itself naturally through the Gothic style.

With these two points made, I am prepared to argue that one can, theoretically at least, reform society according to an ideal by imitating the artistic manifestation of that ideal. In other words, it does follow from the notion that art expresses society that art can, in turn, change society; for if the two are as intimately and organically related as the expressive theory requires, then there should be a reciprocal action corresponding to that which exists between words and concepts. Words express concepts and, in the case of onomatopoetic or echo words, take their sound—that is, their form—directly from the concept. But the causal factor operates in the other direction, too, since the forms of words partly determine their meanings, that is, the concepts that they represent. Similarly, the Gothic Revivalists believed not only that architecture was the concrete expression (the form) of a time spirit (the concept) but that it could, in turn, shape that spirit just as their artistic colleagues believed that art in general could elevate and civilize. They of course did not succeed in restoring medieval ideals, and Victorian society succumbed to materialism as surely as Tennyson's knights, who found Arthur's ideals too stringent; but if Wingfield-Stratford's explanation is correct enough practically speaking, it still ignores the theoretical soundness of the Revival's approach.

Beginning, then, with the premise that the leaders of the Revival meant to introduce through their art medieval ideals that would reform society and create thereby a congenial climate for the growth of Gothic architecture, we may now ask what, specifically, they wanted most to change. Of the various social determinants of art—climate, nationality, customs— some, as I have said, remained constant and required no or little alteration. But the one determinant that everyone, both Goth and Greek, almost universally agreed to exert the most powerful influence on art and that all acknowledged to have suffered the most considerable transformation was religion. Tennyson's parson spoke for many in lamenting "the general decay of faith/Right through the world" ("The Epic"). For those, like Newman, who carried the restoration of faith to its ultimate end, this meant "going over" to Rome. Pugin, therefore, told his students at Oscott in 1838 that the Gothic Revival was part of the return to Catholicism:

> All I have to implore you is to study the subject of ecclesiastical architecture with true Catholic feeling. Do not consider the restoration of ancient art as a mere matter of taste, but remember that it is most closely connected with the revival of the faith itself, and which all important object must ever demand our most fervent prayers, and unwearied exertions.[7]

Others, like Street, stopped short of taking the final, extreme step and settle on High Church Anglicanism, but the aim to restore faith through architecture was the same. For Street the church building has a "power to promote and foster belief," and there should be in these buildings "such arrangements of the interior as would make it difficult, if not impossible, for people long to ignore those truths which the building is intended to teach."[8]

From regarding their mission as in part religious, it was but a short way for the leaders of the Revival to see themselves as divines. Cram wrote that those who promote Gothic architecture "do so less as artists than as missionaries,"[9] and Street went further to assert the superiority of the religious artist to the preacher: "Who among preachers can hope to preach as the gifted artist does? It is not only that the sermons are in stones or on walls or canvas, but that they are read and believed by generation after generation of the faithful. The greatest orator has no thought so comforting as this."[10]

III. THE DIDACTIC METHOD

> How rev'rend is the Face of this tall Pile,
> . . . .
>   It strikes an Awe
> And Terror on my aking Sight. . . .
>   William Congreve, *The Mourning Bride*

> Hail countless Temples! that so well befit
> Your ministry; that, as ye rise and take
> Form, spirit and character from holy writ,
> Give to devotion, wheresoe'er awake
> Pinions of high and higher sweep, and make
> The unconverted sould with awe submit.
>   William Wordsworth, *Ecclesiastical Sonnets*

> Then gazing up 'mid the dim pillars high,
> The foliaged marble forest where ye lie,
> *Hush*, ye will say, *it is eternity!*
> *This is the glimmering verge of Heaven, and these*
> *The columns of the heavenly palaces!*
>   Matthew Arnold, "The Church of Brou"

For the good of the church, for the good of the people, for the good of art, architects and churchmen sought to revive in England an age of faith, but how exactly was architecture to play its part? It is obvious how writing can be put to didactic use, but it is less apparent how the visual arts, and architecture in particular, can be instruments of instruction. The answer lies, I think, in the preface to *Prometheus Unbound*, where Shelley explains how the poet can reform society:

> I have, what a Scotch philosopher characteristically terms, "a passion for reforming the world." . . . But it is a mistake to suppose that I dedicate my poetical composition solely to the direct enforcement of reform, or that I consider them in any degree as containing a reasoned system on the theory of human life. Didactic poetry is my abhorrence; nothing can be equally well expressed in prose that is not tedious and supererogatory in verse. My purpose has hitherto been simply to familiarise the highly refined imagination of the more select classes of poetical readers with beautiful idealisms of moral excellence; aware that until the mind can love, and admire, and trust, and hope, and endure, reasoned principles of moral conduct are seeds cast upon the highway of life which the unconscious passenger tramples into dust, although they would bear the harvest of happiness

This statement embodies in part the lesson Shelley and others of his generation had learned from the betrayal of the French Revolution. Amidst the rubble of the old institutions, new "reasoned principles of moral conduct" had arisen; but since the fundamental nature of the people had not changed, these principles were trampled by a despotic reign more dangerously tyrannical than the one it replaced. Shelley's poem shows that as soon as the basic, essential change occurs in Prometheus, as soon as he turns from hate to love, his freedom follows inevitably and automatically. But more to the point, the statement also embodies the aesthetic shift of emphasis from didacticism toward pleasure to which I referred earlier. Shelley bans simple instruction to prose and reserves for poetry the portrayal of beauty, which, by appealing to the imagination, will touch the soul of the reader and elevate his moral character. The allotment of "reasoned principles of moral conduct" to prose and of "beautiful idealisms of moral excellence" to poetry is based, then, upon the Romantic distaste for too much morality and too little art. There is also here the Romantic notion that art should appeal to the imagination and the heart rather than to the reason. One should not forget, however, that all this is from a poet who admittedly has "a passion for reforming the world" and that his intention is ultimately practical, for not only is didactic writing out of place in poetry but also it is less effective in reforming society. Its precepts will be ignored and trampled until there is a fundamental change of heart, and the beautiful idealisms of poetry are what can touch the heart and move it to follow the model of Promethcus.

The change that comes about, therefore, in Romantic poetry and is later continued in Victorian poetry is not that writers are less interested in instructing their readers and in improving society but that they believed these ends could more appropriately and more effectively be gained by the indirect method of beauty and pleasure than the direct method of didacticism. Furthermore, these writers achieve indirection not only by demonstrating rather than by preaching but also by using symbolism. Thus, Shelley shows how the world might be reformed through the example of Prometheus, who represents mankind and who, once he renounces hatred, is reunited with Asia, the symbol of love.

Although poetry may choose between direct and indirect methods, architecture by its nature must follow the indirect course; but since the Romantics had steered poetry onto the course that architecture must necessarily take, the two forms converged in their approaches to the reformation of society. We shall find, therefore, that ecclesiastical architecture used beauty and symbolism to lead people to God. Had not poetry altered its direction and so established the literary precedent, it is unlikely that architecture would have been considered so powerfully instructive.

Beauty had been exiled from religious worship in Dissenters' chapels and Anglican churches alike at least from the time of Cromwell and the Puritan revolt, if not as far back as the break with Rome and the dissolution of the monasteries. In 1774 Sir Joshua Reynolds and James Barry offered to decorate St. Paul's free of charge, only to be refused by the bishop of London, who replied that he could never allow the cathedral to be so desecrated during his lifetime. In addition, behavior in church had degenerated so by the first decades of the nineteenth century that there are numerous accounts of sleeping, snacking, and chatting by inattentive and even boisterous members of the congregation. The restoration of beauty and decorum to Anglican churches and services came solely through the combined influence of the Gothic Revival and Ritualism.

In order for this change to come about, people had to be persuaded that instead of being inimical to religion art was, in Cram's words, "the handmaid of religion. . . . the God-given language of religion."[11] Browning's Fra Lippo Lippi argues against the Prior that earthly beauty is compatible with godliness, and Charles Kingsley earlier had said the same thing in prose:

> *Never lose an opportunity of seeing anything beautiful.* Beauty is God's handwriting—a way-side sacrament; welcome it in every fair face, every fair sky, every fair flower, and thank for it *Him*, the fountain of all loveliness, and drink it in, simply and earnestly, with all your eyes; it is a charmed draught, a cup of blessing. ("The National Gallery.—No. I")

There is in Kingsley's statement not simply a connection between beauty and God, but, more to the point, a view of beauty as a means of leading one to God, "the fountain of all loveliness." It is important to recognize this relationship between the two, for there has arisen what I consider to be a false distinction between the uses of ecclesiastical ritual (which very much involves church interiors and therefore includes architecture) as having either aesthetic or dogmatic motives. On the one hand, some have seen the Ritualistic movement as originating primarily from an aesthetic impulse in reaction to the bare churches and slovenly services of the preceding age. Furthermore, those who take this point of view sometimes draw parallels between the Ritualists and the Aesthetes, as J. W. Mackail, for example, does when he observes that when the movement spread into secular life it became "what was afterwards called Aestheticism."[12] The implication of this attitude, especially be-

Fig. 25. The University Museum, Oxford. Another kind of architectural didacticism: the capitals are examples of different types of foliage, and the columns are examples of different types of stone. The building is as instructive as the exhibits it houses. Iron-work by F. A. Skidmore, of Coventry.

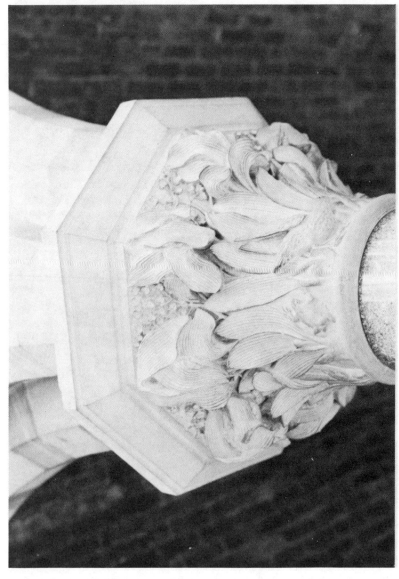

Fig. 26. Capital, University Museum, Oxford. Carving by James and John O'Shea, of Ballyhooly, Ireland.

cause of the link with aestheticism, is that ritual has little or no practical purpose. On the other hand, some have argued that ritual is basically dogmatic, being an attempt to set forth Tractarian doctrine (although they are careful to point out that the actual writers of the Tracts were indifferent to such matters). Thus, Vernon F. Storr was written that "the fundamental motive of the movement has been dogmatic, and is to be traced to Tractarian teaching"; and more recently James F. White has agreed that "the basic inclination of Ritualism was dogmatic and not artistic."[13] I say this is a false distinction, whichever of the two points of view one takes, because the Revivalists, Ecclesiologists, and Ritualists recognized no such differences, believing as they did that beauty as beauty, with no specific symbolic or dogmatic function, had the practical purpose of creating an atmosphere of worship conducive to religious meditation. Or, to consider the matter from Kingsley's perspective, all beauty is sacramental and therefore generally dogmatic. In this they naturally differed from the Puritans, who believed beauty distracted one's thoughts from God since it was the creation either of man or the devil.

I am led, therefore, to disagree especially with Peter Collins, who compounds the error of perpetuating the distinction between beauty and dogma by asserting that the preoccupation with the dogmatic function of ritual resulted in ugliness. I am loath to argue with any of Collins's statements in *Changing Ideals in Modern Architecture*, by the far the best book we have on the subject, but it is impossible to agree with this interpretation:

> The architectural programme of the Oxford Movement was put into effect by the Cambridge Camden Society, founded in 1839, and by its magazine, *The Ecclesiologist*, founded in 1841. Both were inspired by the ideal of what we would now call "functionalism"; that is to say, they were not primarily concerned with promoting beautiful churches, but with creating churches which would effectively serve the Anglo-Catholic requirements regarding ritual. Indeed, it can be convincingly argued that the Camden Society (or Ecclesiological Society, as it was later called) preferred a certain brutal ugliness to the more traditional notions of beauty, as may be seen in the most famous church of their most famous protégé, William Butterfield. "There is here to be observed the germ of the same dread of beauty, not to say the same deliberate preference of ugliness,

which so characterizes in fuller development the later paintings of Mr.
Millais and his followers," *The Ecclesiologist* noted with satisfaction in a
laudatory article published when All Saints', Margaret Street, London, was
finally completed.

   The fact is that, of the philosophical Trinity: the True, the Beautiful and
the Good, it was only with truth and goodness that these reformers were
really concerned.[14]

Professor Collins misinterprets his evidence, for though it is
true that the entire article in the *Ecclesiologist* is laudatory, the
particular passage he quotes occurs in a paragraph citing faults
with Butterfield's style and showing dissatisfaction rather than
the contrary. The sentence in this paragraph immediately
following the one Collins quotes is, "But these abatements do
not in any way diminish our general admiration for the manly
and austere design which is embodied in this church."[15] Far,
then, from approving the ugliness of Butterfield's church, the
Ecclesiologist disapproved its ugliness, calling it an "abatement";
and without more convincing evidence, I should be reluctant to
believe that those associated with the magazine did not think of
beauty as inseparable from truth and goodness. As a matter of
fact, I should go so far as to say that for them intentionally ugly
ritual was a contradiction in terms. We shall find in the next
chapter that functionalism did sometimes lead toward ugliness,
but there the functional motive has nothing to do with ritualistic requirements.

   It is wrong to distinguish between the aesthetic and dogmatic
ends of ritual, but it is true that the architectural features auxil-
iary to ritual operated in two, indirect ways for the ultimate
religious purpose: beauty and symbolism. These modes, in
turn, reveal some radical differences between eighteenth- and
nineteenth-century attitudes toward worship, and, beginning
with beauty, there are at least three changes. First, as the
church passed from the Age of Reason through the Romantic
age of imagination, its services forsook the rational approach to
God for the mysterious, and the church architect, correspondingly, sought through various means to reinforce this
approach. For example, in the words of John Sedding, "By his
divine craft the priest of form [the architect] can give to the

temple of God such an air of mystery and stillness, that you get a strange thrill of expectancy as you enter, and say, involuntarily, 'Surely the Lord is in this place.'"[16] Second, and following from the rationalistic approach, in the eighteenth century the chief vehicle for the transmission of religion was the sermon, whose importance was signified not only by its length but, architecturally, by the dominating three-decker pulpits and the general interior design of auditory churches, which were made principally for hearing. When, however, churchmen came to see that the essence of Christianity was mysterious rather than rational, church interiors were rearranged accordingly to diminish the size of the pulpit, remove it to one side, and make the focal point the altar, whereon was enacted the chief mystery, the sacrament of Holy Communion. So diminished had the sermon become in relation to the architectural component of ritual that Robert Louis Stevenson placed the church building far above the sermon as the means of salvation and spoke of the sermon almost as if it were a profanation in so sacred a place. After describing the beauties of Noyon Cathedral, Stevenson comments.

> I could never fathom how a man dares to lift up his voice to preach in a cathedral. What is he to say that will not be an anticlimax? For though I have heard a considerable variety of sermons, I never yet heard one that was so expressive as a cathedral. 'T is the best preacher itself, and preaches day and night; not only telling you of man's art and aspirations in the past, but convicting your own soul of ardent sympathies; or rather, like all good preachers, it sets you preaching to yourself,—and every man is his own doctor of divinity in the last resort. (*An Inland Voyage*)

This passage recalls Shelley's comments in the preface of *Prometheus Unbound*, for Stevenson seems to agree with Shelley that art's indirect message is more efficacious than the direct and overt instruction of prose.

Third, the Romantic concept of nature as sacramental, evident for example in the quoted remarks of Kingsley, controverted the Manichean dualism of Puritan theology. Since the body and its senses were no longer considered evil, one might piously appeal to the soul through the senses. Therefore, Isaac Williams explains that the church

> Breathes life in ancient worship—from their graves
> Summons the slumbering Arts to wait on her,
> Music and Architecture, varied forms
> Of Painting, Sculpture, and of Poetry;
> These are allied to sense, but soul and sense
> Must both alike find wing and rise to Heaven;
> Both soul and body took the Son of man,
> Both soul and body must in Him serve God.
>
> *The Baptistery*, 1842–44

The success of the aesthetic road to salvation is illustrated by Pugin, who freely admitted that "the study of ancient ecclisiastical architecture was the primary cause of the change in my sentiments," although he denied that his love of Gothic buildings was the sole cause for his conversion to Catholicism.[17] In Pugin's case architecture fulfilled its role quite properly and successfully, but what of such men as Burne-Jones and Pater who were drawn to church for the beauty of the ceremony and the building alone, with no thought of proceeding to the spiritual essence behind it? These liked ceremony for the sake of ceremony, not for the religious principles it expressed, and justified Anthony Trollope's warning about ritualism: "Forms and ceremonies are undoubtedly good, as long as they are made the vehicles and appendages of true doings. But alas, for a man, or a people, when he or they mistake forms for things, and ceremonies for deeds" (*The New Zealander*). Most Victorian social critics were apprehensive about the materialistic tendencies in general of the age, and the fascination with ritual for its own sake is in a way the religious form of the overall trend. Pater attended the High Church services at St. Austin's, London, conducted by his friend, the Reverend George Nugée. Nugée, like Trollope, was fearful lest forms be confounded with substance and once told Pater that "you quite misunderstand us. These ceremonies are but an outward expression of what is in our hearts. We don't want mere sight-seers—or, rather, we want them only because we are in hopes that they may be led to become sincere Christians." Pater responded to this argument by saying, "I can assure you, Mr. Nugée, I am interested in the Christian religion only from the fact of my being Page-in-Waiting upon your Professor of Church History. The Church of England is nothing to me apart from its ornate services" (Thomas Wright, *The Life of Walter Pater*, vol. 2). For Pater and an increasing number of his contemporaries, the substance within the form had vanished, leaving only the shell of the chrysalis behind.

But on the whole these "sight-seers" were of a small enough number to pose no true threat. Instead, the real danger as perceived by most was that ritualism was leading the Anglican church ever more perilously in the direction of Rome, and some powerful voices were orchestrated against this movement: the queen was against it, Ruskin was against it, Disraeli was against it, Carlyle was against it, and Parliament, by passing the Public Worship Regulation Bill in 1874, sought to put an end to it. Still, all their efforts together did not prevail, and the present state of worship and of church interiors testifies to the ultimate victory of art in reestablishing its place in the church.

The second way in which architecture works for religious ends is symbolism, and here again one remarks an association with Romanticism. I have already said that symbolism is a mode of indirection, but beyond that it is also a means of expressing things that are ineffable in direct and literal discourse. When, therefore, the Romantics took as their task the description of mysterious and spiritual elements in the universe or of equally indefinable emotions within their own hearts, they were more or less compelled to have recourse to symbols. Coleridge wrote in the *Biographia Literaria* that "An IDEA, in the *highest* sense of the word, cannot be conveyed but by a *symbol*." When the Oxford movement followed the lead of Romantic artists and reinstated mystery to its proper place in religion after the lapse of rationalism, churchmen, like poets and painters, found that literal, direct discourse (i.e., the sermon) was inadequate for the expression of mystery, and they too turned to symbols, be they in the form of sacraments or of art. Ralph Adams Cram has explained this need for symbolical expression by saying that "the theological peculiarities of Geneva and Edinburgh can adequately be communicated by the spoken and unadorned word: the marvelous mysteries of the Catholic Faith breathe themselves into the spiritual consciousness through the mediumship of art."[18] In another comment Cram anticipates my argument in this chapter by declaring that art achieves this goal of communicating the mysteries of religion through beauty and symbolism. Each art, he writes, "is but a dialect of a normal language that reveals, in symbolical form and through the unsolvable mystery of beauty, all that men may achieve of the mystical knowledge of that Absolute Truth and Absolute Beauty that transcend material experience and intellectual expression, since they are of the essential being of God."[19]

In their introduction to William Durandus's *The Symbolism of Churches and Church Ornaments*, John Mason Neale and Benjamin Webb wrote from the same perspective Cram later adopted: "Architecture is an emblem of the invisible abstract, no less than Holy Baptism and the Lord's Supper."[20] It is interesting that they should choose these two sacraments, for architecture was involved in both of them through the rearrangement of church interiors. Early in the Reformation the altar had been transformed into a table and moved out of the sanctuary and into the nave so that all could see. By the eighteenth century Communion was ordinarily celebrated only four times a year, and, since they were no longer used anyway, chancels were neglected or treated as storage areas. When, however, Communion was revived through frequent celebrations as the sacramental expression of the mysteries of Incarnation and Sacrifice, the table became once again an altar, it was restored to the holier environs of the sanctuary, high box pews obstructing sight of the altar were removed, and a center aisle made the altar the focal point upon entering the church. As for the baptismal font, it had been placed in the front of the church so that all could witness the sacrament; but when symbolism became so important, it was transferred to the rear of the church to show symbolically that it is by baptism that one enters the church.

In the end, perhaps it is not surprising that architecture should be involved in these two particular sacraments since

practically every architectural feature, from the smallest ornament to the general design, was thought to have religious significance. The ideal plan of neo-Gothic churches was cruciform
to represent the cross, the apex of which should point eastward.
The church interior was divided into the nave (the Church
Militant), the chancel (the Church Expectant), and the sanctuary (the Church Triumphant). The chancel screen separated
the laity from the clergy, and the crucifix atop it symbolized
death as the separation between worldly life without the chancel and spiritual life within. In short, Gothic Revival architects
were mindful of Neale's and Webb's statement "*Sacramentality* is
that characteristic which so strikingly distinguishes ancient
ecclesiastical architecture from our own,"[21] and were attempting to recover that essential element. In doing so they were not
copying mere forms but following fundamental principles, for
they thought that religious motives lay behind the forms and
that the forms were designed specifically to express religious
truths. Pugin believed that the great argument for Gothic
architecture was that "in it alone we find *the faith of Christianity
embodied, and its practices illustrated.*" This faith, moreover, by
expression through architectural forms is the very origin of the
Gothic style, which he significantly was in the habit of designating as Christian: "The three great doctrines, of the redemption
of man by the sacrifice of our Lord on the cross; the three equal
persons united in one Godhead; and the resurrection of the
dead,—are the foundation of Christian Architecture."[22] Pugin
goes on to explain that the cross determines the general plan of
the church, the Trinity determines the tripartite division of the
interior and triangular shape of arches and tracery, and the
resurrection determines the height and vertical lines.

This symbolical account of the origin of Gothic roused the
Calvinistic ire of Ruskin, who attempted to show that the style
arose from functional responses to climate. Northern roofs,
Ruskin argued, have steep pitches to throw off snow, not to
symbolize the resurrection. His contempt for such a preposter-
ous theory, which he attributes to German critics, is everywhere
apparent in this passage from *The Stones of Venice*:

We may now, with ingenious pleasure, trace such symbolic characters in the form; but we only prevent ourselves from all right understanding of history, by attributing much influence to these poetical symbolisms in the formation of a national style. The human race are, for the most part, not to be moved by such silken cords; and the chances of damp in the cellar; or of loose tiles in the roof, have, unhappily, much more to do with the fashions of a man's house building than his ideas of celestial happiness or angelic virtue.[23]

In choosing a house rather than a church for his example, Ruskin misrepresents the symbolical theory, which depends upon the premise that the Gothic style is ecclesiastical in origin, but others accepted the premise and argued against the theory on its own terms. T. G. Jackson believed that Gothic features derived from structural requirements and that symbolic interpretations were imposed later.[24] Robert Kerr satirized the symbolical theory by a fictitious dialogue between two yokels who ignorantly believe that the purpose of posts in a church is to support the roof. "Well now," Kerr asks rhetorically, "are we seriously to suppose that the clodhoppers who fill a country church are really to see in those four piers the four evangelists?"[25]

Pugin would not have argued with the functional use of either the posts or the pitched roofs, for everyone concerned with the Revival was committed to the functionalism of Gothic architecture and used that aspect of the style as a mainstay in attacking architectural shams. But to admit the functional purpose is not to discount the symbolical one, and Pugin showed how a pinnacle atop a flying buttress performed both roles by adding weight and therefore strength to the supporting member while at the same time symbolizing the resurrection by adding to the height. Furthermore, in believing that Gothic sprang from religious origins and that its distinctive forms were expressive of Christian principles they were right, as modern scholars have convincingly shown. Otto von Simson has explained in *The Gothic Cathedral* how the abby church of St.-Denis, built in the twelfth century and the prototype of all subsequent Gothic churches, was designed by Abbot Suger as a symbol of heaven. He concludes that both the origin and popularity of Gothic derive from its symbolical nature:

In other words, the technical achievements that distinguish the first Gothic from Romanesque seem to have obeyed rather than preceded Suger's symbolic demands upon architecture, and it was his overriding desire to align the system of an ecclesiastical building with a transcendental vision that ultimately accounted for the transformation of Romanesque into Gothic. The instant and irresistable success of the new style in France was owing to its power as a symbol. In a language too lucid and too moving to be misunderstood, Suger's Gothic evoked an ideological message that was of passionate concern to every educated Frenchman.[26]

Although we are ready to agree with the findings of von Simson, in condemning the Gothic Revival for mixing morality with architecture and in disdaining the religious enthusiasm of its leaders we are perhaps too apt to forget that these men perceived first what we have only recently been able to prove and that they were as committed to the sacramentality of church architecture as their medieval forebears. Only by remembering this can we hope to understand why they believed Gothic architecture, and Gothic architecture alone, was suitable for Christian churches. For them the style was not an accident or even a sign of the religion but in the truest sense of the word a symbol of Christianity. That is, a sign arbitrarily represents something else but has no essential connection with it, which is why one could as easily choose any Greek letter as π to represent 3.14 if all would agree to the equation. But, as Coleridge says in *The Statesman's Manual*, a symbol "always partakes of the reality which it renders intelligible; and while it enunciates the whole, abides itself as a living part in that unity of which it is the representative." Because symbols are intimately associated with what they represent, they cannot be interchanged as signs can. One cannot, for example, arbitrarily choose a color other than white to symbolize purity. Neither, since architecture is symbolical and shares with all symbols a participation in the reality that it represents, can one employ any style but Gothic to express Christianity. To attempt to employ Greek or Roman architectures, which are themselves symbolical expressions of pagan religions, to represent Christian doctrine is just as senseless as having the color green stand for purity and the color white stand for life. By extension, because architecture also expresses symbolically national character, though not with the instructional intent of religion, secular buildings should be Gothic as well.

The leaders of the Gothic Revival, then, could not acquiesce to Carlyle's retailoring of metaphysical clothes, for the basic concept of Christianity, unlike that of nature, had remained constant, and the symbolical architectural dress which expressed that concept fit as well in the nineteenth century as it had when Abbot Suger designed it in the twelfth century. To be sure, a minor alteration here or there might be made to accommodate new building materials and techniques, but the essence of the style was still perfectly suitable, especially for the purposes of High Church Anglicans and Roman Catholics. Unless we recognize the importance these men placed upon architectural symbolism, both as a mode of instruction and as a means of expression, we can never hope to understand their single-minded and uncompromising devotion to the Gothic style.

VII. PRAGMATISM: FUNCTION

I. ARCHITECTURAL TRUTHFULNESS

> There is however one grand principle at the foundation of all art, which must ever be far more than any other really obeyed and recognised when she does her work successfully and well. And this principle, or law, is that of truth. (George Edmund Street, "The True Principles of Architecture, and the Possibility of Developement")

"There are only two modern styles of architecture, one in which the chimneys smoke, and the other in which they do not."[1] Thus did W. R. Lethaby remark upon observing that all the flues of Butterfield's Keble College draw well, and if the opinion is somewhat reductive, it nonetheless accurately reflects the importance of efficiency in nineteenth-century architecture. This is not to say, of course, that efficiency as an architectural value was original in the Victorian age, for Vitruvius had spoken of fitness, and eighteenth-century French architects recommended a rational architecture. Furthermore, this aspect of architecture, what we are in the habit of calling functionalism nowadays, has always been an essential part of architecture as a practical art and will always separate it from the fine arts of writing, painting, sculpture, and music, whose ends can never be as pragmatically useful. It is to say, however, that the value of efficiency in architecture has fluctuated in emphasis from time to time and that its worth appreciated steadily throughout the nineteenth century until it came to be the principle criterion in modern architecture. To understand how the practical side of architecture rose to such dominance, we should begin with the term by which Victorians chose to call it—truthfulness.

We have already considered the different applications of truthfulness to art: how with expressionism it means the truthful correspondence between an artist's feelings and the work of art, and how with mimesis it means the truthful correspondence between the object and its depiction in art; how the Romantic shift from mimetic art to expressive art is indicated by the assertion that "poetic" truth is higher than literal truth;

and how, within the mimetic theory, there is a changing notion
of what constitutes truth to nature from Reynolds, to Wordsworth, to the Pre-Raphaelites, to George Eliot. Truth, then,
appears in many guises, but none so compelling to nineteenth-
century architecture as a building's truthfulness to its purpose
and function. That Victorian architects should regard this
aspect of building in terms of truthfulness may be largely explained by their contempt for neoclassical architecture, for of
the many sins committed by the Renaissance-Reformation
ogre, Revival architects considered none so heinous as the introduction of nonfunctional features, be they to achieve symmetry, to disguise structure, or to misrepresent material. Such
practices they thought of as architectural deceits, or more commonly, shams, and as deviations from the true principle established by the old builders of designing primarily for convenience. Their reasoning is clear: if nonfunctional architecture is false and deceitful, then functional architecture is honest
and true.

In condemning neoclassical architecture as false and advocating Gothic as true, the Revivalists share the concern of other
intellectual leaders about distinguishing between false appear-
ances and true reality. So dominant and recurrent a theme is
this that one could hardly overestimate its importance to Victorian artists and social critics. Carlyle had written in *Past and
Present* that "we have quietly closed our eyes to the eternal
Substance of things and opened them only to the Shows and
Shams of things." At the beginning of "Geraint and Enid,"
Tennyson wrote one of the strongest statements of the theme,
not only for this particular poem or for the *Idylls* as a whole, but
for the Victorian society that Camelot reflects:

> O purblind race of miserable men,
> How many among us at this very hour
> Do forge a life-long trouble for ourselves,
> By taking true for false, or false for true!

These are but a few of the innumerable expressions of the same
idea, an idea that the Revivalists translated into architectural
terms by attacking the nonfunctional duplicity of neoclassical

Fig. 27. "They are weighed in the balance and found wanting." From A. W. N. Pugin, *Contrasts*, 2d ed. (1841; rpt. New York: Humanities Press, 1973).

architecture and by extolling the functional honesty of Gothic architecture. It is no accident that Pugin should modify "Principles" with "True" in *The True Principles of Pointed or Christian Architecture,* nor that one of the plates in *Contrasts* should use *Veritas* as the standard of measure by which a fourteenth-century cathedral outweighs several nineteenth-century examples of neoclassicism. He was criticizing contemporary architecture on the same basis that Carlyle and Tennyson were

criticizing society at large, and thus places himself and those he
influenced in the mainstream of Victorian cultural thought.

There can be no denying that Pugin although perhaps not
the first to advocate truthfulness in this sense of the word for
architecture, nevertheless was responsible for making it the
dominant architectural criterion that it was to become. The
Times, for example, said this of Pugin not long after his death:

> He it was who first exposed the shams and concealments of modern archi-
> tecture, and contrasted it with the heartiness and sincerity of mediaeval
> work. . . . Let us remember to his honour that, if now there seems to be the
> dawn of a better architecture, if our edifices seem to be more correct in
> taste, more genuine in material, more honest in construction, and more
> sure to last, it was he who first showed us that our architecture offended
> not only against the laws of beauty, but also against the laws of morality.[2]

George Gilbert Scott also attributed the exposure of sham to
Pugin and recognized his influence by saying that for later
exponents of the Revival "the principle of strict truthfulness is
universally acknowledged as their guiding star. . . ."[3] Sometimes the enthusiasm for truthfulness could be taken to amusing extremes. T. G. Jackson recalled that when he first entered
Scott's office in 1858, one year after Scott made the remark
quoted above, one of his fellow students, Thomas Garner, fell
"into raptures over a hansom cab. It was 'so truthful,' he said,
'so-so-so mediaeval!'"[4] Fifteen years later truthfulness had become firmly established as something of an architectural catchword, and not only for neo-Gothic but other styles, too, as
illustrated by the *Building News* praising the New Zealand
Chambers for being "thoroughly truthful."[5]

The three specific areas in which the criterion of truthfulness
was most consistently applied by Victorian architects, and
correspondingly the three areas in which Renaissance and
neoclassical architects were most often thought to be guilty of
deceitfulness, were overall design, material, and structure. To
begin with design, we have already found in chapter 4 that the
leaders of the Revival believed in the concept of organic form,
which stipulated that the shape of organisms is determined
from within, and applied this concept to architecture by insist-

ing that both the overall design of a building and its individual features be the outcome of function. In addition, we have seen that this concept overlaps with expressionism, which theory requires that an object of practical art faithfully express its purpose and that, as Pugin pointed out, a home should not pretend to be a castle, domestic furniture should not attempt to pass for ecclesiastical, and a clock should not be disguised as a Roman chariot. A final impetus to the concept derived from the discovery that the original Gothic builders had designed primarily for convenience. As a result, these naturalistic, artistic, and historic justifications collaborated to form a very strong argument for designing the plan of a building before the elevation, and, indeed, of allowing the plan to determine the elevation.

Revivalist architects used the argument to attack the neoclassical emphasis on a building's façade and the simultaneous neglect of function. Joseph Gwilt tells the anecdote of a nobleman who boasted about his house's beautiful façade to a friend. The friend suggested that the peer take the house opposite so that he could look at it all the time.[6] The Revivalists also objected to the neglect of the sides and backs of buildings by those who attended only to façades, charging, as does Street in the following statement, such practice with deceit:

> There is no real respect for an art when it is treated, as it always has been by the Renaissance architects and their followers, as a mere affair of display; no good building was ever yet erected in which the architect designed the front and left the flanks or the internal courts to take care of themselves. So also no good building was ever seen in which the exterior only was thought of, and the internal decoration or design neglected. In such treatment of art as this there is an ingrained falseness which is as demoralising as it is ruinous.[7]

So successfully did they argue their point that later architects, not necessarily sympathetic to the Gothic cause, embraced the principle. Robert Kerr said that "a good house is like a good square of infantry: it looks you full in the face all round," and Richard Norman Shaw wrote, concerning New Scotland Yard, "The regulation modern building has generally a show front, or fronts, but round the corner or in any part supposed to be

Fig. 28. The True. According to his own precepts, George Edmund Street paid as much attention to the rear of the Royal Courts of Justice (above) as to the front (fig. 12). The polychromy is perhaps less formal than the monocromatic Strand front, but the rear is designed with no less care.

Fig. 29. The False. Sir John Wolfe Barry and Sir Horace Jones disguised the steel construction of Tower Bridge (1886–94) with stone facing.

not much seen it is made plain and common, if not hideous. I
dwell on New Scotland Yard being a genuine building, in which
we have no sham or shew fronts, all is of the same quality and in
the court it is the same."[8]

A second consequence of designing the plan before the
elevation was to deal yet another blow to the classical principle
of symmetry. Already weakened by the new concept of nature
as irregular and by the popularity of picturesque irregularity,
symmetry suffered further from the precept that convenience
should be the foremost concern of the architect, and here again
classical architecture proved inferior to Gothic. C. F. A. Voysey
made this distinction between the two styles:

> Renaissance is a process by which plans and requirements are more or
> less made to fit a conception of a more or less symmetrical elevation, or
> group of elevations. The design is conceived from the outside of the build-
> ing and worked inwards. Windows are made of a size necessary to the
> pleasant massing of the elevation, rather than to fit the size and shape of
> room.
> The Gothic process is the exact opposite. Outside appearances are
> evolved from internal fundamental conditions; staircases and windows
> come where most convenient for use. All openings are proportional to the
> various parts to which they apply, and the creation of a beautiful Gothic
> building instead of being a conception based on a temple made with hands,
> is based on the temple of a human soul.[9]

This statement should be compared with Sir Joshua
Reynolds's recommendation that since variety constitutes
beauty in other arts, the architect should design irregularity in
his buildings "if it does not too much interfere with convenience" ("Discourse XIII"). The great difference between
Reynolds and the Revivalists is that what for Reynolds is an end
is for the Revivalists a natural consequence. That is, the Revivalists, working on the principle explained by Voysey, built
first for convenience and admitted irregularity as the result,
whereas Reynolds is interested first in the aristic effect of the
building, in other words, the elevation. Pugin, to the contrary,
wrote his friend and client the earl of Shrewsbury, "I never
proposed anything for *mere effect*."[10] Whereas Reynolds sees a
possible conflict between irregularity and convenience, the Re-

vivalists believed that irregularity was the natural and inevitable outgrowth of convenience. For them it was symmetry that was opposed to convenience and that had long suppressed this most important true principle of Gothic architecture. One can sense the force of Pugin's wrath as he attacks "the mock-regularity system of modern builders":

> The senseless uniformity of modern design is one of its greatest defects. The idea of everything being exactly alike on both sides, has created an unreal style of building which was quite unknown to our ancestors, and it is most delightful to see the very soul of modern deformities thus ably attacked. When once the trammels and bondage of this regularity system are broken through, and people are taught not to consider a portico and two uniform wings the perfection of design, we may expect vast improvements. . . .

Those improvements, Pugin believed, would be attained by following the system of the old designers, who made their plans "essentially convenient and suitable to the required purpose. . . ."[11]

But symmetry had become so firmly entrenched through the centuries as a principle of taste that it was slow to relax its grip, even on those who agreed with Pugin that convenience should come first and that falsely symmetrical façades were shams. Barry's son tells us that his father was guided by two loves: foremost, the love of truth, which led him to abhor showy façades with such features as blank windows, and, second, a love of regularity, which caused him to subordinate all features to the general design.[12] Apparently he was able to reconcile the two loves, as was Street, who, in noting the symmetry of some Gothic cathedrals, commented, "It is not necessary to have uniformity to the sacrifice of convenience, but it is possible to have uniformity when it is desirable."[13] Burges believed that uniformity was desirable for the fronts of large building, although not necessarily for the backs or for small buildings; and, unlike Street, he was prepared to sacrifice convenience. With the fronts of large buildings, Burges wrote, "the architect must take more pains, and try to bring in his windows so as to balance in the general composition. Of course, this is much more difficult

to do than letting them crop out where they may be most convenient; but it can be done with care, and, in fact, it is simply an
affair of trouble and ingenuity."[14]

The second area in which the Revivalists insisted upon
truthfulness was in the use of materials, and here again they
were reacting to what they considered to be the fradulent practices of the preceding age. Robert Kerr believed that the Battle
of Styles arose in response to the falseness of architecture in the
latter part of the eighteenth century and the early part of the
nineteenth, when "not only was fictitious design, the bane of all
art, universally prevalent, but fictitious material came into
use,—cement, painted and sanded wood, and so forth,—to the
utter ruin of the art."[15] John Mason Neale brought the authority of the Camden Society to bear on the matter when he
avowed that "the first great canon to be observed in Church-
building is this: LET EVERY MATERIAL EMPLOYED BE
REAL."[16] Butterfield, who met the approval of the Ecclesiologists in most things, was scrupulous in abiding by Neale's
canon. When Butterfield's patron for the restoration of a little
church at Knook once objected to plans calling for a wooden
chancel arch instead of a stone one, the architect replied, "As
you are aware the gable at the East end of the nave at Knook is
only timber. There has never been a stone arch there. It is
timber at present and *disguised*. I make it of timber and *avow* it.
That is the difference."[17] Chiefly they objected to veneering,
whether of furniture or of walls. Christopher Dresser wrote
that veneering of furniture is "a practice which should be wholly abandoned. Simple honesty is preferable to false show in all
cases; truthfulness in utterance is always to be desired."[18] A
most flagrant example of dishonest use of material is provided
in Thomas Hardy's *The Hand of Ethelberta*, where Enckworth
Court is described as

> a house in which Pugin would have torn his hair. Those massive blocks of
> red-veined marble lining the hall—emulating in their surface-glitter the
> Escalier de Marbre at Versailles—were cunning imitations in paint and
> plaster by workmen brought from afar for the purpose, at a prodigious
> expense, by the present viscount's father, and recently repaired and re-

varnished. The dark green columns and pilasters corresponding were brick at the core. Nay, the external walls, apparently of massive and solid freestone, were only veneered with that material, being, like the pillars, of brick within.

The reason for the exterior veneer is that when the viscount showed off his house to King George, the king had said only, "Brick, brick, brick." And the crestfallen owner immediately covered the walls with stone veneer. It is easy to see how architects were appalled by such practices and by the vain and ignorant motives behind them.

The third, and probably most important, area where Revivalists were concerned with truthfulness was structure. One of the main faults Pugin found with "revived pagan buildings" was that they concealed structure, and to illustrate his point, he explained in *True Principles* how Wren designed a wall screen circumscribing St. Paul's to hide the flying buttresses. This, Pugin says, is a "Miserable expedient! worthy only of the debased style in which it has been resorted to."[19] On the same grounds he condemns the fictitious exterior dome of St. Paul's, which was designed only for effect, and considers St. Peter's, with its single dome, superior in this respect. In the next year (1842), Joseph Gwilt made the same evaluation.[20] Street put the principle upon which Pugin and Gwilt were basing their judgments in terms of truthfulness when he wrote sometime later, "The architect who attempts by concealed construction to imitate a wholly different sort of work must inevitably fail, for sincerity is of the essence of good art, and the detection of insincerity is certain."[21]

As with symmetry, however, all were not prepared to discard old practices so readily. Ruskin, for example, qualified his reproval of structural deceit by adding that "the architect is not *bound* to exhibit structure"; and George Gilbert Scott acknowledged that upon occasion, such as when two roofs form an uncouth intersection, nonfunctional features may be introduced for effect.[22] But neither Ruskin or Scott would have condoned Tower Bridge, where Sir John Barry and Sir Horace Jones concealed a steel structure with stone veneer, ironically to produce a medieval design consistent with the nearby Tower of London. The technical advances of the modern age make it capable of anything, Lethaby wrote, "anything that is, except the Tower Bridge as well."[23]

In addition to regarding the concealment of structure as a sham, the Revivalists thought it equally false to introduce exposed but nonfunctional structural features that exist only for effect. Pugin provides the premise behind this attitude in the first paragraph of *True Principles* when he declares that the first of the "two great rules for design" is, "*there should be no features about a building which are not necessary for convenience, construction or propriety.* . . ."[24] Ruskin agreed with this attitude in "The Lamp of Truth," and in *Principles of Decorative Design*, Christopher Dresser applied the rule to furniture. While examining wardrobes and cabinets at the 1862 International Exhibition, Dresser recalls that he

> was forcibly impressed with the structural truth of one or two of these works. One especially commended itself to me as a fine structural work of classic character. Just as I was expressing my admiration, the exhibitor threw open the doors of this well-formed wardrobe to show me its internal fittings, when, fancy my feelings at beholding the first door bearing with it, as it opened, the two pilasters that I conceived to be the supports of the somewhat heavy cornice above, and the other door bearing away the third support, and thus leaving the superincumbent mass resting on the thin sides of the structure only, while they appeared altogether unable to perform the duty imposed upon them. "Horrible! horrible!" was all I could exclaim.[25]

One can imagine the consternation of the proud exhibitor, who no doubt expected to receive further praise for the workmanship of the wardrobe. Obviously he had not read Pugin, but even those who had (Butterfield, for example) did not always consider the first of the "two great rules for design" as wholly inviolable and were quite capable of attaching sham half-timbers to brick walls and filling in with cement.[26]

II. TRUTH AND BEAUTY

Rudeness is better than a lie. (Edward Lacy Garbett, *Rudimentary Treatise*)

In *True Principles* Pugin maintained that an essential difference between classical and pointed architectures is that the former conceals structure whereas the latter reveals it. But pointed architecture does not simply and starkly reveal structure, for once this style reveals structure, it beautifies it by decoration. The second of the "two great rules for design" is, *"All ornament should consist of enrichment of the essential construction of the building."*[27] Implicit in this idea is that bare, unadorned structural features are unbecoming, if not ugly, and that beauty lies in ornamentation, which must be applied to those features in order to render them pleasing. If, however, the architect must decide between the extreme alternatives of sham decoration on the one hand and rude simplicity on the other, most Revivalists favored the second of the two choices, preferring the sacrifice of beauty to truth. Pugin expressed the idea, which overlaps generally with Romantic primitivism and more particularly with the "doctrine of the imperfect," in *True Principles* by saying that "the severity of Christian or Pointed Architecture is utterly opposed to all deception: better is it to do a little substantially and consistently with truth than to produce a great but false show."[28] Less than a decade later (1850), Garbett reiterated the notion in these direct terms: "If you cannot beautify without deceiving, do not beautify at all. Rudeness is better than a lie."[29] Because of the equation between fitness and truth, we seem to be witnessing here the triumph not only of function over beauty but of morality over beauty as well, and there is evidence to suggest that this triumph extended beyond the bounds either of the Gothic Revival specifically or of architecture more broadly. Carlyle, for example, who admired the Middle Ages but was impatient with any resuscitation of its forms, agreed in principle with Pugin when he wrote, "The Real, if you will stand by it, is respectable. The coarsest hobnailed pair of shoes, if honestly made according to the laws of fact and leather, are not ugly; they are honest, and fit for their object; the highest eye may look on them without displeasure, nay, with a kind of satisfaction" ("Hudson's Statue," *Latter-Day Pamphlets*). Although not perhaps "the highest eye," whatever Carlyle means by that, a discriminating eye, able to separate aesthetic from moral values, could in fact look with some displeasure upon the rude but honest. Robert Kerr, who had such an eye, saw the rude simplicity of neo-Gothic buildings as a reaction to the shams and to the feebleness of refinement in the preceding age of architecture. This reaction, Kerr asserted, sometimes led to ugliness:

> Hence the introduction of a love for undisguised honesty in the first place, however crude,—and in the second, for masculine simplicity, however unrefined; for unaffected construction, in other words, and unaffected form both in their extremes; for Gothic models, therefore, because, however rough-and-ready, they are truthful and sincere,—and for the Ugly, because, however odd, it has at least not the weakness of being feminine.[30]

But even as Barry and Jones disregarded the precept against concealing structure in the design of Tower Bridge, there were those, principally concerned with housewares, who were quite prepared to forfeit utility to beauty and who wanted no part of rude simplicity. Christopher Dresser ridiculed the absurdity of some households having two pokers—one, with a highly ornate and therefore uncomfortable handle, kept for show, and another, with a plain and therefore serviceable handle, kept out of sight for use.[31] More recently Nikolaus Pevsner has remarked on the uncomfortable handles of ornamental spoons, forks, and scissors, along with cut-glass drinking glasses and decanters, concluding that such items "remind us that there have been ages to which aesthetic considerations mattered more than utilitarian."[32] Although true in part, Pevsner's statement should be tempered with the skepticism one brings to all generalizations, for the work of William Morris in furnishings and that of the Gothic Revivalists in architecture tend to prove the contrary in this age of paradoxes.

III. UTILITY AND BEAUTY

> Who builds or plants, this rule should know,
> FROM TRUTH AND USE ALL BEAUTIES FLOW.
> > John Dalton, "Some Thoughts on
> > Building and Planting"

> In the universal acceptation of the inseparable nature of beauty and utility has ever been and must ever be, the true hope of all architecture. (William H. White, "On the Hope of English Architecture")

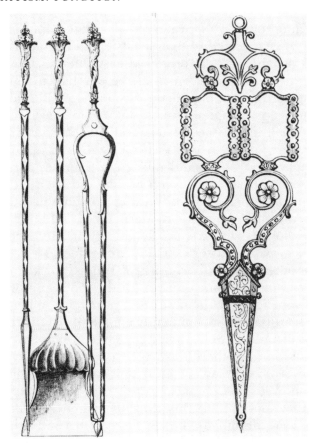

Fig. 30. Fire irons and scissors with ornate and uncomfortable handles. From *The Crystal Palace Exhibition Illustrated Catalogue* (1851; rpt. New York: Dover Publications, 1970), pp. 200, 43.

Alf Bøe has defined modern functionalism as a doctrine stipulating "that an object should be pre-eminently useful and practical; it implies the axiom that what is practical is also beautiful; and it excludes from the language of aesthetics the various kinds of associative ornament."[33] In order for this doctrine to take shape, the attitude that usefulness was frequently ugly and that ornament was required for beauty—an attitude, as we have just seen, shared both by those who recommended rude honesty and those who preferred decorated inutility—had somehow to be reversed so that beauty could be found in function, and ornament, now rendered aesthetically superfluous, could be dispensed with. In brief, beauty had to shift from ornament to function, or functionalism as we now know it, no matter how appealing pragmatically, could never have succeeded so well in the face of our aesthetic objections to it.

There were many in the Victorian age who opposed this reversal in values, and could muster in their support a long tradition of dissociation between beauty and usefulness. Longinus had contended that we consider homely those things of everyday use, and in more modern times, Edmund Burke, although allowing that frequently enough beauty is joined to usefulness in nature, asserted that the one does not necessarily entail the other. If beauty consists of fitness, Burke argues in his *Enquiry*, how does one account for the snout of a swine, the pouch of a pelican, or the quills of a porcupine, all eminently practical features and all eminently ugly (3.6)? In the following century William Whewell applied the same premise to building by pointing out that there was no architectural beauty in such utilitarian structures as a cotton mill or engine house (*The Architectural Notes on German Churches*, 1830), and twenty years later Garbett declared in his *Rudimentary Treatise* that when buildings were designed with no thought beyond utility they were invariably ugly. Surely, though, the foremost proponent of this attitude was Ruskin, who advised his readers over and again not to confuse beauty with fitness, urging them to keep in mind "that the most beautiful things in the world are the most useless. . . ."[34] This theory led Ruskin to separate building from architecture. Building, which he defined as the fulfillment of practical requirments, is the first and essential thing; but architecture, which he equated with ornamental painting and sculpture, is the highest and noblest thing. Building, then, by itself is unworthy the name of architecture and rises to the status of a fine art only by the addition of painting and sculpture. It follows from this distinction that *"a great architect must be a great sculptor or painter."*[35]

The uselessness of art became, of course, a principal tenet of aestheticism toward the end of the century. In the preface to *Mademoiselle de Maupin,* Gautier substituted a water-closet as an example of utilitarin ugliness for Burke's swine snout and Whewell's cotton mill; and in Wilde's "The Decay of Lying," Vivian observes that "as long as a thing is useful or necessary to us . . . it is outside the proper sphere of art."

Despite this opposition, however, there is a discernible and steady shift of opinion toward the belief that ornament, although conducive to beauty in architecture, is not essential to it, and that the true essence of beauty in architecture lies in form rather than in decoration. Such architects as Street, Jackson, Lethaby, and Sedding, all in one way or another participants in, or sympathetic to, the Gothic Revival, directly refuted Ruskin's distinction between building and architecture by insisting that architecture in its highest sense might exist quite independently of ornament. Though less well known than these architects, J. T. Micklethwaite disputed Ruskin's contention with an argument typical of the group when he reversed Ruskin's values by referring to decoration as a "less noble art" than building. "So far is true architecture from being a matter of ornament," Micklethwaite continues, "that it may exist entirely without ornament. Ornament is one of an architect's means, and he will seldom altogether neglect to use it: but a building of much grandeur and dignity may be obtained by the right management of the forms of construction only, without ornament of any kind."[36] But by the time Micklethwaite wrote these words in 1892, the next step toward modern functionalism had been taken by Edward William Godwin, who, in designing Whistler's "White House" in Chelsea in 1877, had perhaps neglected ornament to a greater degree than Micklethwaite had in mind. Also, in the very year of Micklethwaite's essay, Louis Sullivan wrote in "Ornament in Architecture" that "it would be greatly for our esthetic good, if we should refrain entirely from the use of ornament for a period of years, in order that our thought might concentrate acutely upon the production of buildings well formed and comely in the nude."[37]

These statements by Micklethwaite and Sullivan, along with

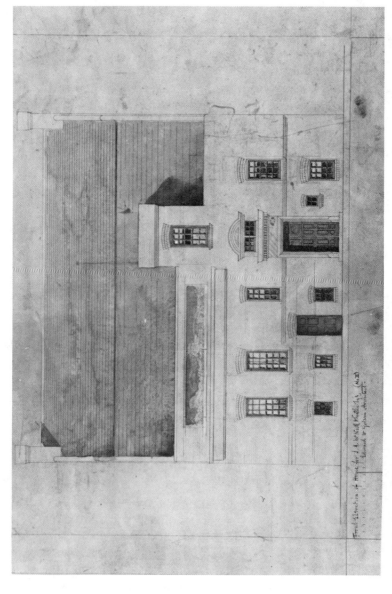

Fig. 31. Architecture without ornament—Goodwin's design (front elevation) for Whistler's White House, Tite Street, London (1877–79). Hunterian Art Gallery, University of Glasgow, Birnie Philip Gift; reproduced by permission.

similar ones made by other architects in the last part of the century, mark not only the beginnings of victory over the ornamentalists but an advance beyond the early stages of functionalism some decades before when simple and honest form, albeit infinitely preferable to purposeless decoration, was thought to be rude. True, the germ of this development was embedded in the ideas of the earlier architects, for Pugin had written that *"every building that is treated naturally, without disguise or concealment, cannot fail to look well,"*[38] and he had found that picturesque beauty proceeds naturally from a convenient plan; but if there was any question of conflict between honest utility and sham beauty, he and his contemporaries chose the moral and pragmatic alternative. They were somewhat of a mind with Thackeray, who declared in the preface to *Pendennis*, "If truth is not always pleasant; at any rate truth is best. . . ." The later architects, however, in believing that it was possible to have at once both honesty and beauty, were able to have their cake and eat it, too. What complicated set of ideas and events combined to effect this radical shift of beauty from ornament to functional form I cannot say, but I do suggest as a partial explanation that a special application of the traditional equation of truth and beauty was in some way responsible.

In 1864 Richard Norman Shaw submitted a competition entry for the Bradford Exchange bearing the motto "Rien n'est beau que le vrai." He could as well have sought authority in Platonism or Christianity as in an artistic treatise by Boileau since the idea has ancient and deep roots in Western culture. But in saying that only the true is beautiful, Shaw did not mean precisely what Plato or the church fathers or Boileau meant by it, there being as many meanings as there are definitions of truth; however, he could, just as the early Revivalists had appropriated the neoclassic principle of "truth to nature" and used it for their own ends to sanction irregularity, capitalize on the authority of the idea while applying it to his own particular, architectural purpose. Indeed, others had been doing the same thing. After commenting that rough simplcity is better than elegant sham, Garbett adds, in a literal translation of Boileau,

"Nothing is beautiful which is not TRUE. . . ."[39] The fifth general principle in Owen Jones's *The Grammar of Ornament* is, "Construction should be decorated. Decoration should never be purposely constructed." Although this part of the proposition comes directly from Pugin's *True Principles*, the rest of it echoes Keats's "Grecian Urn": "That which is beautiful is true; that which is true must be beautiful."[40] Although there is no consensus as to what Keats meant by the line, none would suppose he shared Jones's intention; and the quotation provides, therefore, a very good example of how this truism, with all the weight of authority such things have, could be adapted to particular ends befitting a revolt against the practices of an age that had itself embraced the same principle.

The equation of truth and beauty is the major premise of the syllogism toward which I have been working. The minor premise, that truth equals convenience (or function, to use the modern term), the Revivalists established by asserting that the nonfunctional features of neoclassical architecture were deceits and shams. By removing the common term, truth, one arrives at the conclusion, which is that beauty equals convenience. As the early Victorians approached this conclusion and as the later Victorians reached it, they established the basis of modern architecture, whose chief aim Bruno Taut has described as *"the creation of the perfect, and therefore also beautiful, efficiency."*[41]

Georg Germann has remarked that from early times all architectural theorists have regarded utility as the most important feature of architecture, but the nineteenth-century theorists were the first to equate utility with beauty.[42] This may be true of architecture in particular, but for aesthetics in general the idea is quite ancient. In *Memorabilia* Xenophon wrote that a dung-basket is beautiful if suited to its purpose and that a golden shield is ugly if it is not useful. Happily, the wonderfully wrought shield of Achilles combines beauty and utility; but had it not deflected the spear of Hector, no doubt Homer would have agreed with Xenophon. In more recent times the equation appears in prominent writers of the eighteenth century. David Hume wrote in *A Treatise of Human Nature* (1738) that "a great part of the beauty which we admire either in animals or in other objects is derived from the idea of convenience and utility," and a few years later illustrated this idea in *An Enquiry Concerning the Principles of Morals* (1751) by pointing out that a ship built to be seaworthy is more beautiful than one designed to be geometrically regular and that the windows and doors of a building are more beautiful when in proportion to human needs than when formed as perfect squares. Only two years later Hogarth used similar examples in *The Analysis of Beauty* to support his theory that fitness is an essential part of beauty. The steps of stairs and the seats in windows must be of heights suitable to human requirements, no matter the largeness of the building and the corresponding disproportion of these features to the overall bulk, else "they would lose their beauty with their fitness. . . ." With ships "the dimensions of every part are confin'd and regulated by fitness for sailing. When a vessel sails well, the sailors always call her a beauty; the two ideas have such a connexion!" (chap. 1). Both Hume and Hogarth would seem to agree with William Mason, who summarized the equation of utility and beauty poetically in his *English Garden*: "beauty scorns to dwell/Where use is exiled" (bk. 2, 1777).

There was, then, both ancient and modern authority for finding beauty in usefulness upon which the Revivalists could rely in justifying aesthetically the convenience of Gothic architecture. In *Contrasts* Pugin writes that "the great test of Architectural beauty is the fitness of the design to the purpose for which it is intended," and in *True Principles* he repeats the contention by saying that "all really beautiful forms in architecture are based on the soundest principles of utility."[43] The equilateral triangle, Pugin proposes as illustration, is because of its proportions the most beautiful of triangular shapes and is also the most functional design for the pitch of a roof since a roof with an obtuse angle at the apex does not throw off snow adequately and one with a severely acute angle creates too great a vertical strain. Implicit in these statements by Pugin, and in those of others writing in the earlier stages of the Revival, is the concept of utility as being not so much beautiful in itself, or an actual source of beauty, as coincidental with beauty. Ruskin, for example, argues for the pointed arch on the basis of its strength and beauty; but the beauty of the arch derives from its similarity in shape to a leaf, which "by its frequent occurrence in the work of Nature around us, has been appointed by the Deity to be an everlasting source of pleasure to the human mind."[44] For Ruskin it is only a happy accident that this pleasing form should be the strongest as well. So, too, argues Professor George Wilson, of Edinburgh, whom Dresser quotes approvingly in *Principles of Decorative Design*: "If there be one truth which the Author of all has taught us in his works more clearly than another, it is the perfect compatibility of the highest utility with the greatest beauty."[45] The nautilus, Professor Wilson points out, is both beautiful and utilitarian at once; but, like Ruskin, he believes that the combination of the two results from divine beneficence rather than from any innate beauty of usefulness. The word he uses to describe the relationship of the two elements—"compatible"—suggests the distinctness of them.

For those, however, who were less convinced of such fortuitous or divine combinations, these arguments would not serve to justify aesthetically the principle of functionalism in architecture; and a sounder, more integral relationship between beauty and use had to be found. By the end of the century, the premise that efficiency in itself is beautiful provided the solution and allowed for functionalism as we know it today. In 1892 Lethaby proposed "high functional *beauty*" as the ideal of modern architecture, and in his biography of Philip Webb, he quotes Webb as saying, in a latter-day version of Xenophon's dung-basket, that a new building's drainage system "is so beautiful I don't like it to be covered up."[46]

To see beauty in the efficiency of drainage pipes is to take a rational, mechanistic approach to aesthetics, and it is significant that such viewpoints occur either before the advent of Romantic emotionalism or after its full effect had waned. When Newton, for example, spoke of the "most beautiful system" of the universe, he was referring to the wonderful mathematical and physical laws by which the sun, planets, and comets mechanically operated. In 1785, before the Pre-Romantic doctrines of

Edmund Burke had come to dominate aesthetic judgments,
Thomas Reid found a correspondence between fitness and
beauty, remarking that when "an expert mechanic views a well
constructed machine. . . . he pronounces it to be a beautiful
machine" (*Essays on the Intellectual Powers*). Burke, on the other
hand, held that though one may admire the workings of a
watch, one could not find them beautiful since beauty depended on the emotional responses of love or passion (*Enquiry*,
3. 7). This doctrine, as we have seen, became the basis of associational aesthetics and was to control artistic evaluations for
the better part of the nineteenth century. But at the same time
that Romantic sensibility dominated the field of art, the rationalism of science and industry produced biologists, geologists,
mechanics, and builders who saw beauty in a different, functional light; and when this rationalism entered architecture
through its technical aspect, architects, too, especially those
preoccupied with the truthful efficiency of their craft, could
come to se the beauty of mechanical function. When Lethaby
wrote that houses should be "as efficient as a bicycle,"[47] his
attitude was a long way indeed from Ruskin's denunciation of
machine-work in architecture, but it approached very closely
Le Corbusier's famous statement in *Vers une architecture* that a
house should be a machine for living in. From this time forward architects would no longer have to justify convenience in
building by resorting to the appeal for rude but honest simplicity, for although the Dynamo had succeeded the Virgin, the
Dynamo had assumed a special beauty of its own.

IV. DURABILITY

> Build to-day, then, strong and sure
>   With a firm and ample base;
> And ascending and secure
>   Shall to-morrow find its place.
> > Henry Wadsworth Longfellow,
> > "The Builders"

Therefore, when we build, let us think that we build for ever. Let it not be
for present delight, nor for present use alone; let it be such work as our
descendants will thank us for, and let us think, as we lay stone on stone,
that a time is to come when those stones will be held sacred because our

hands have touched them, and that men will say as they look upon the
labour and wrought substance of them, "See! this our fathers did for us."
(John Ruskin, "The Lamp of Memory")

It would be a mistake, and one that I hope I have not fostered, to think of the Revivalists as utilitarians in a strict sense of
the word, because they looked with no more favor upon those
buildings erected in the name of inexpensive usefulness than
their friends in the church regarded the social and theological
implications of Benthamism. Pugin treated with contempt
modern churches "built on exactly the same principle as thea-
tres, to hold the greatest number of persons in the smallest
possible space," and Baillie Scott termed utilitarianism a false
ideal in architecture.[48] Yet, even while scorning stark utility and
thinking of themselves preeminently as artists, they time and
again refuted Ruskin's distinction between architecture and
building by consistently defining architecture not as
ornamental sculpture and painting but as the art of building
well. This belief that architecture's definitive essence lay in
sound building rather than in superadded ornamentation or
structural shams is reflected in a distrust of eye-catching competition designs. Hardy's Mr. Havil says bitterly that "nowadays
'tis the men who can draw pretty pictures who get recommended, not the practical men. Young prigs win Institute med-
als for a pretty design or two which, if anybody tried to build
them, would fall down like a house of cards . . . " (A Laodicean).
Mr. Havill, whose architectural apprenticeship had been in
gardening and road construction, might be dismissed as a
biased observer, but others with more traditional backgrounds
were of much the same opinion. Butterfield had little use for
these academic designs, and Lethaby, in saying that architecture may be divided into "sound, honest human building, or
brilliant drawings of exhibition designs,"[49] leaves no doubt
which of the two is preferable.

Beckford's Fonthill Abbey, which, like the competition designs, was planned more with an eye to effect than to use, had
indeed collapsed like a house of cards; but there were other
threats to durability, the aspect of function with which I shall

conclude, than the precedence of art over building, and all of
these participate in the general flux and instability of the age.
Ruskin attributed bad modern architecture to the attitude, created by the habit of constantly moving from one dwelling to the
next, of regarding houses as no more than temporary
lodgings.[50] To this habit was added the law of leasehold, for, as
Burges argued, "who will build in a substantial manner when
he knows that all his outlay will go to his landlord after a certain
time?"[51] Although both of these threats to durability in building remain with us today, perhaps the plea against temporality
that strikes the most responsive chord in a modern reader is
that of Street's against planned obsolescence. "I have myself
been told by a high Government official," Street lamented,
"that the best building is not that which will last longest, but
rather that which will last a limited time, and may then be
rebuilt with all the latest improvements."[52] Thus did progress
lay its snare. On the one hand, it made the Victorians mindful
of the future and urged them to build for tomorrow against the
arrival of some traveler from New Zealand, who would sketch
the ruins of St. Paul's from London Bridge. But on the other, it
militated against the durability of buildings by rendering them
obsolete, thereby ensuring that when this traveler from a far-
off land eventually came, what few architectural remnants survived as monuments to the achievements of the age would bespeak only the victory of time. Thus also did functionalism set a
paradoxical trap, for the same pragmatic principle that had
called for durability as an element of usefulness now disallowed
durability on the grounds of nonfunctional obsolescence.

CONCLUSION

I will not cease from mental fight,
Nor shall my sword sleep in my hand,
Till we have built Jerusalem,
In England's green and pleasant land.

"Would to God that all the Lord's people were Prophets." Numbers 11:29
William Blake, "Preface" to *Milton*

While I have life left, I will protest against the caricatures of ancient temples which are daily erected.... (A. Welby Pugin, "A Reply to Observations")

A problem that one encounters in a book such as this one,
dealing as it does almost exclusively with the theory of architecture and very little with actual buildings, is that the treatment is
partial at best, misleadingly incomplete at worst. The problem,
further, is made even more acute when the subject is architecture, where so many factors, unknown to the poet or painter or
musician, interpose themselves between concept and realization, increasing still more the distance between theory and
practice. This I cannot help; but to evaluate the Gothic Revival
from a theoretical point of view comes closer, perhaps, to judging it on its own terms than any other single approach might
do. "A perfect Judge will read each work of Wit / With the same
spirit that its author writ," Pope advised critics; and though I
make no claim to perfection, I do believe it a commendable goal
toward which to strive.

I am thinking not so much of Pugin's well-known comment
that his writing had been much more influential than his building when I assert a case for theory, although basis for an argument is there. What I have in mind rather is that to judge a man
and his work by what he intended more than by what he accomplished, by, that is to say, his theory more than his practice, is
the Romantic way of making judgments and is sharply different from both what went before and what came after. In the
eighteenth century a work of art was judged according to both
the intention and the execution. The critic should first assess
the purpose of the artist and then determine with what success
or failure the work of art realized that purpose. Thus, Pope

263

recommends in *An Essay on Criticism* that one first "regard the writer's End," and, having done so, "if the means be just, the conduct true," one should account the writer successful and approve the effort. There is a good, sensible balance between plan and execution in this advice, as one would expect from the author and from the age. Nowadays, however, we have a tendency to discount the intention and consider only the accomplishment. In *Huis Clos* Garcin pathetically attempts to win the respect of Inez by maintaining that although he fled Brazil in a most cowardly way, he was not actually a coward because he really meant to continue the fight with a pacifist newspaper in Mexico. But Inez scornfully rejects his appeal with the existential argument that intentions count for nothing; only actions matter. The same type of reasoning has been applied to the evaluation of art in recent times, or at least to that of literature, where the doctrine of the intentional fallacy has led so many to evaluate a poem by and in itself with no regard for the writer's intent.

The Romantic view, on the other hand, upsets the neoclassical balance in the other direction by elevating intention over accomplishment. Thus it is that Browning's Rabbi Ben Ezra says, "Not on the vulgar mass/Called 'work,' must sentence pass," but instead a person should be judged by his "Thoughts hardly to be packed/Into a narrow act . . . All I could never be." Limitless aspirations that distinguish man from animal and that resist incorporation in material form tell in the final reckoning, not the imperfect and incomplete realization of these ideals.

If these propositions are true enough (and I fully realize that each is an oversimplification, but true *enough*, I say), then it seems obvious that to judge the proponents of the Gothic Revival according to their avowed goals as stated in their writings is to judge them on the prevailing terms of their own time. I do not mean to suggest that the other critical standards are without value or inappropriate, for they do yield insights, which, moreover, the Revival is quite capable of withstanding. If, for example, one measures the accomplishment against the dream as a neoclassicist would have one do, is there such a falling off in the actual buildings as to make the Revival the colossal failure it has often been thought to be? It is true that Pugin himself, regarding his own work from this perspective, considered his life's work a failure. "I have passed my life," he lamented shortly before his death, "in thinking of fine things, studying fine things, designing fine things, and realising very poor ones."[1] It is also true that if one takes their primary goal to be the establishment of Gothic as the dominant architectural style for all buildings, ecclesiastical and secular, then one must conclude that they failed. And if, finally, one sees the Revival chiefly as a moral revolution, then again one is confronted with defeat. But, on the other hand, if one takes them at their word and views their primary aim as leading architecture out of a wilderness choked with the decaying remnants of classicism and overgrown with alien weeds of every imaginable stylistic extraction, then perhaps one finds that they did not fail so utterly after all. They sought a style distinctive of their own age, and they realized this end in buildings that, for all their historical echoes, are unmistakably Victorian. And who is to say that they did not make considerable contributions to the formation of modern architecture, the new style so much debated in their own time, just as surely as their contemporaries in other fields prepared for the arrival of the twentieth century?

If, secondly, one views the Revival from the modern perspective that attends little to goals in its concentration upon accomplishment, one is apt to find again more success than anticipated. In 1892, forty years after Pugin's death, the apostate Goth Richard Norman Shaw visited St. Augustine's, Ramsgate, the only church with which Pugin was wholly satisfied, and gave this account:

> There is a charming little church here (Roman Catholic), built by the great Pugin, some 45 years ago, for himself. He designed and *paid* for the whole thing, and it is beautiful, so full of interest all through. Hideous stained glass, but in spite of that serious drawback, a most delightful and interesting work, and done *so* long ago. I am afraid we have not advanced much. Such a work makes one feel small, *very* small.[2]

Today we have advanced much in some respects, although we are little less in sympathy with Pugin's aims than was Shaw, yet

Fig. 32. St. Augustine's, Ramsgate, by Welby Pugin, 1845–51.

we too can look back with admiration and approval, even if little awesome remains to us, upon the finer achievements of the Revival. And what will be the assessment of the inevitable New Zealander, that haunting image of the future? We must suppose him now to have come from a distant planet and to use a camera or some other more sophisticated device for his archaeological fieldwork, and we may suppose as well that all *Contrasts, True Principles*, and issues of the *Builder* are lost to him either through destruction or through the unintelligibility of their yet undeciphered language so that he knows nothing of the buildings before him but what he sees. Might he not find as much of interest and of beauty in the river front of the Houses of Parliament as in the dome of St. Paul's, or as in the elevation of the National Westminster Bank building?

In saying these things I do not mean to be unnecessarily apologetic about the Gothic Revival since it is no longer fashionable, at least among knowledgeable people, to decry it as a foolish and vain monument to tastelessness even though those who have no special interest in Victorian architecture do sometimes need to be reminded of its immediate and lasting importance. My point, rather, is that other methods than the one I have adopted are capable of revealing the importance of the Revival both then and now. I repeat, however, that to consider the theory of the Revival by itself, and in so doing to assume a perspective more basically in accord with the nineteenth-century outlook, discloses certain features of the Revival that seem to have remained obscure, or at least insufficiently appreciated, up till now. One such feature, which it has been the main purpose of this study to demonstate, is the aesthetic motivation and character of the Revival. The proponents of neo-Gothic were undoubtedly influenced in their course by religious, political, and social causes; but in addition they were driven by aesthetic motives no less compelling, and at times even more forcibly so. They sought a reformation of the art of architecture, and they based this reformation upon artistic principles, principles that they shared with contemporary artists in other areas. If we but recall how often these men referred to themselves as artists and to architecture as an art, we might be more aware of the importance of aesthetics to the movement.

A second feature has more to do with the men than with the movement, and this is that by concentrating on the writings of these architects one comes to see them as nothing less than prophets, a view that so far as I know is not commonly taken. Pugin, naturally, comes first to mind, and it seems hardly accidental that Robert Kerr should have eulogized him with an analogy to Elijah:

> Take him [Pugin] with all his faults, he was one of those rare spirits— Nature could not afford to produce many of them—in whom the very power of intellect was its own destruction. The common record of such men was that they were eccentric, visionary, impracticable; but what cared they for common record? If they lived in turmoil, in storm and cloud, such was the destiny of the heroic: if they even perished in despair, it was genius passing away in a chariot of fire.[3]

"Bring me my chariot of fire!" calls Blake in the preface to *Milton*, and who is more deserving the name of prophet than these two, poet and architect? Uncompromising, single-minded, utterly dedicated to the causes in which they believed, totally and fearlessly opposed to wrong as they saw it, convinced of their mission to build a new Jerusalem—they no less than Elijah were swept along in chariots of fire.

And if Pugin shares a prophetic role with Blake, then he and his followers in the movement—Scott, Street, Waterhouse, Butterfield, and others—might also be cast in the role so long reserved for writers like Carlyle, Ruskin, and Arnold, that of the Victorian Sage. At least it is true that these architects, like their literary contemporaries, delivered verdicts against the shallow materialism of their age while asserting the value of ideals. Here, for example, are two statements, the first by Pugin and the second by Arnold. Pugin concludes *The True Principles* with the exhortation, "Let then the Beautiful and the True be our watchword for future exertions in the overthrow of modern paltry taste and paganism, and the revival of Catholic art and dignity." Similarly, Arnold wrote of Oxford's battle against modern liberalism: "This our sentiment for beauty and sweetness, our sentiment against hideousness and rawness, has been at the bottom of our attachment to so many beaten causes, of our opposition to so many triumphant movements" (*Culture and Anarchy*, chap. 1). It is tempting to carry the parallel to the end and claim ultimate victory for the Revival as Arnold did for the Oxford movement, but this is hardly possible.

Instead one must seek another analogy, which presents itself as the title of this book. "Cities built to music" is intended to mean primarily that Gothic Revival buildings were erected from aesthetic motives and according to artistic standards, but the title carries another meaning as well, which is that the Gothic Revival rose from the ideals of Pugin, Scott, and others, even as Camelot was built on ideals, the chivalric ideals of the Round Table. Tennyson once said that he wrote the *Idylls* to demonstrate the need for ideals in modern society, and one may say that the leaders of the Revival wrote and built with a similar motive.

If, then, a consideration of the idealistic intentions of these men leads us to regard them as prophets and sages, we should perhaps be no more entitled to fault them with failing to realize these intentions than to blame Blake for not building the new Jerusalem, to indict Arnold for his inability to make sweetness and light prevail, or to reprove Arthur for the collapse of Camelot. Their prophetic task it was to lead others to the truth as revealed to them, and if the end was never gained, the aspirations that guided them remain enduring inspirations to those who come after. Thus it is that although the cities envisioned by Gothic Revival architects were never built at all, the ideals upon which the cities were to be built—truth and beauty for the buildings themselves, integrity for the builders, and a love of good architecture for the society at large—retain a permanent value for all time.

> For an ye heard a music, like enow
> They are building still, seeing the city is built
> To music, therefore never built at all,
> And therefore built for ever.

NOTES

INTRODUCTION

1. Some notable exceptions are Peter Collins, *Changing Ideals in Modern Architecture 1750–1950*; George L. Hersey, *High Victorian Gothic: A Study in Associationism*; Robert Macleod, *Style and Society: Architectural Ideology in Britain 1835–1914*; Nikolaus Pevsner, *Some Architectural Writers of the Nineteenth Century*; and S. Lang, "The Principles of the Gothic Revival in England." The first of these has been most helpful for my particular purposes. As might be expected, studies of Ruskin deal almost entirely with theory. See especially Kristine Ottesen Garrigan, *Ruskin on Architecture: His Thought and Influence*; and John Unrau, *Looking at Architecture with Ruskin*.

2. An exception is Phoebe B. Stanton's "Pugin: Principles of Design versus Revivalism." Professor Stanton's thesis is that the main purpose of the Gothic Revival was "the discovery of a definition of art and the establishment of rules, principally of design, which could be used to reform England's impoverished taste in architecture and the arts of decoration" (p. 20). In other words, she believes that the Revival's motive was more aesthetic than religious, and she offers as support the buildings themselves, while speculating that contemporary architectural theory would confirm her findings. The evidence presented in the following pages seems to do just that.

CHAPTER ONE

1. A. Welby Pugin, *An Apology for the Revival of Christian Architecture in England*, pp. 1–2.

2. Edward Lacy Garbett, *Rudimentary Treatise on the Principles of Design in Architecture as Deducible from Nature and Exemplified in the Works of the Greek and Gothic Architects*, p. 249.

3. William Burges, *Art Applied to Industry*, pp. 7–8.

4. Quoted in Nikolaus Pevsner, *High Victorian Design: A Study of the Exhibits of 1851*, p. 50.

5. Ralph Adams Cram, *The Ministry of Art*, p. 23.

6. Ibid., p. 15.

7. Ibid., p. xii. Cf. F. W. Cornish's comment: "And if our age, from its circumstances or its nature, wants material for art, if all our work must be more or less a Renaissance, not the new birth of a new creature, we must be content if our chief work should be to store up material for a future age. . . . A generation may yet arise in whom a knowledge of past beauty may be the begetter of a new beauty, a living growth, not an imitation" ("Greek Beauty and Modern Art," pp. 335–36).

8. Collins, pp. 131–32.

9. T. Mellard Reade, "A New Style: How Can It Be Found?", p. 537.

10. A. Welby Pugin, *The Present State of Ecclesiastical Architecture in England*, p. 7.

11. John Ruskin, *The Seven Lamps of Architecture*, in *The Works of John Ruskin*, 8:248–49. Cf. Alfred Austin's remark: "The decay of authority is one of the most marked features of our time. Religion, politics, art, manners, speech, even morality, considered in its widest sense, have all felt the waning of traditional authority, and the substitution for it of individual opinion and taste, and of the wavering and contradictory utterances of publications ostensibly occupied with criticism and supposed to be pronouncing serious judgments. By authority I do not mean the delivery of dogmatic decisions, analogous to those issued by a legal tribunal from which there is no appeal, that have to

be accepted and obeyed, but the existence of a body of opinion of long standing, arrived at after due investigation and experience during many generations, and reposing on fixed principles or fundamentals of thought. This it is that is being dethroned in our day, and is being supplanted by a babel of clashing, irreconciliable utterances, often proceeding from the same quarters, even the same mouths" (*The Bridling of Pegasus: Prose Papers on Poetry*, p. 1).

12. James Fergusson, *An Historical Inquiry into the True Principles of Beauty in Art, More Especially with Reference to Architecture*, p. 168; Samuel Huggins, *The Course and Current of Architecture: Being an Historical Account of the Origin, Successive and Simultaneous Developments, Relations, Periods, and Characteristics of Its Various Known Styles*, p. 184.

13. George Gilbert Scott, *Remarks on Secular and Domestic Architecture, Present and Future*, p. 279.

14. "English Architecture: Present Questions," pp. 24–25.

15. Alice Chandler, *A Dream of Order: The Medieval Ideal in Nineteenth-Century English Literature*, p. 1.

16. Charles L. Eastlake, *A History of the Gothic Revival*, p. 115.

17. Collins, pp. 38–39.

18. Cram, *Ministry*, p. 22.

19. R. G. Collingwood, *The Idea of History*, p. 82.

20. For discussions of this subject, see Morse Peckham, "Afterword: Reflections on Historical Modes in the Nineteenth Century"; and Jerome Hamilton Buckley, *The Triumph of Time: A Study of the Victorian Concepts of Time, History, Progress, and Decadence*, chap. 0.

21. The change from this condescending attitude is described as follows by a Victorian writer: "Whereas in these our actual times there is an ever wakeful sympathy with the past of history and society, a feeling sometimes reverential, sometimes regretful, sometimes compassionate, always keen and sensitive, an interest not only in the great actions, but in the every-day lives . . . in the standard writings of the eighteenth century, on the other hand, this interest is entirely mute, as though a whole department of intellectual curiosity had been as yet unopened. The style in which the writers of the 'Augustan age' of our literature looked back on the England of the past was that of immeasurable and self-satisfied superiority. Nothing, it seemed to them, was to be learned from those epochs of twilight civilization; then why waste time in deciphering their paltry riddles? These were the authorities who voted Shakespeare an inspired barbarian, and would only endure his genius in the travesties of Dryden" ([Louisa A. Merivale,] "On the 'Gothic' Renaissance in English Literature," p. 467).

22. Reprinted in Pevsner, *Some Architectural Writers*, p. 291.

23. For discussions of this subject, see John Gaunt, *Victorian Olympus*; Richard Jenkyns, *The Victorians and Ancient Greece*; and Frank M. Turner, *The Greek Heritage in Victorian Britain*.

24. Walter E. Houghton, *The Victorian Frame of Mind, 1830–1870*, pp. 2–3.

25. W. Jackson Bate, *The Burden of the Past and the English Poet*, p. 22. Cf. Peacock's statement in "The Four Ages of Poetry": "Then comes the age of brass, which, by rejecting the polish and the learning of the age of silver, and taking a retrograde stride to the barbarisms and crude traditions of the age of iron, professes to reurn to nature and revive the age of gold." Compare, also, a comment by Letitia E. Landon: "We ourselves are standing on the threshold of a new era, and we are already hastening to make as wide a space, mark as vast a difference as possible, between our own age and its predecessor. Whatever follies we may go back upon, whatever opinions we may re-adopt, they are never those which have gone *immediately* before us. Already there is a

wide gulph between the last century and the present" ("On the Ancient and Modern Influence of Poetry," p. 466).

26. John Mason Neale and Benjamin Webb in the "Introduction" to William Durandus, *The Symbolism of Churches and Church Ornaments: A Translation of the First Book of the Rationale Divinorum Officiorum*, p. cxxvii.

27. Benjamin Ferrey, *Recollections of A. W. N. Pugin and His Father Augustus Pugin*, p. 226.

28. Ecclesiological late Cambridge Camden Society, *A Hand-Book of English Ecclesiology*, p. 35.

29. *Builder* 8 (1850): 122. J. P. Seddon makes the same point: "It was, then, the unfortunate discovery, galvanizing, and deification, of the exhumed bones of the *Classic*, or, to speak strictly, *Roman* art, which was the veritable Gorgon's head that paralyzed true and healthy art. Its influence was doubly fatal; first, by substituting precedent for thought; and secondly, by substituting second-hand Paganism for Christianity" ("The Dark Ages of Architecture," pp. 269–70). Like Pugin, Seddon turns the tables by calling the Renaissance the Dark Ages. It should be pointed out, however, that a number of members present at the reading regarded Seddon's views as extreme.

30. Arthur Edmund Street, *Memoir of George Edmund Street, R. A., 1825–1881*, p. 78.

31. G. G. Scott, *Remarks*, pp. 191–92. Scott makes similar comments in "Copyism in Gothic Architecture."

32. T. G. Jackson, *Modern Gothic Architecture*, p. 20. This is further proof of Phoebe Stanton's thesis in "Pugin: Principles of Design" that the Revival was aesthetically motivated by a wish to restore art broadly, not Gothic specifically, or at least Gothic only insofar as it was a means to a larger end. I disagree with her thesis only in refusing to exclude the moral and religious motives, which I believe to be inextricable from the aesthetic in all art before Art-for-Art's-Sake made the separation.

33. Cram, *Ministry*, p. 45.

34. Ibid., p. 62. Here is an earlier version of the same figure of speech: "*Reculer pour mieux sauter*: the proverb implies that the forward spring must be preceded by a backward motion. There is no way of recovering first principles when obscured or lost but by the intelligent study of the past. It is just because men had become disgusted with traditions that had lost all their vitality, and conventionalisms that were fairly worn out, that they began to retrace their steps in search of truth, reality, and nature" ([Benjamin Webb,] "The Prospects of Art in England," p. 147).

35. This comment by John Gloag is fairly typical: "The architecture produced by the Gothic revivalists was intrinsically reactionary; those who created it looked back, never forward, so in an age of fantastic material progress, architecture was out of step with science, engineering, commercial enterprise and industrial expansion" (*Victorian Taste: Some Social Aspects of Architecture and Industrial Design, from 1820–1900*, p. xv).

36. Paul Thompson, *William Butterfield*, p. 82.

37. "The Practical Study of Gothic Architecture," p. 267.

38. G. G. Scott, *Remarks*, p. 269.

39. Ruskin, *Works*, 8:195.

40. A. E. Street, p. 123.

41. Jackson, *Modern Gothic*, pp. 94–95.

42. Alfred Barry, *The Life and Works of Sir Charles Barry*, p. 79.

43. *Builder* 3 (1845): 299. A dedication to historical accuracy in adopting Gothic architecture often entailed an intolerance of other styles. The architect J. Henry Stevens reacted with impatience to such prejudice in his reply to an article by George

Gilbert Scott: "It is evident that all who cannot at once turn up *preterpluperfect Goths*, and sign the pledge, must be accessories before or after the fact, to the debasing of the current architecture of her Majesty's realm" (*Builder* 15 [1857]: 638). T. G. Jackson discovered the same sort of prejudice when he first began his career: "In 1858, then, nothing would pass muster with the young enthusiasts among whom I found myself in Scott's office but severe Geometrical Decorated, or, better still, the severer Transitional. . . . The five orders of classic architecture were scoffed at. . . . Anything modern, if not condemned outright, was regarded with suspicion" (Thomas Graham Jackson, *Recollections of Thomas Graham Jackson*, p. 56).

44. Geoffrey Scott, *The Architecture of Humanism: A Study in the History of Taste*, p. 52.

45. Roy Strong, *Recreating the Past: British History and the Victorian Painter*, pp. 47, 64.

46. Burges, p. 13n.

47. A. E. Street, pp. 121–22, 188.

48. Pevsner, *High Victorian*, p. 116.

49. W. J. Lawrence, for example, made this argument against absolute realism in historical drama: "Managers are apt to forget that playgoers are not all as pedantically censorious as the author of *The Plant-Lore of Shakespeare*, who wrote to Mr. Irving after seeing the early Lyceum revival of *Much Ado about Nothing*, pointing out that Leonato's garden presented an anachronism in the shape of a cedar, that species of tree being unknown in Messina at the period of the play" ("Realism on the Stage: How Far Permissible?", p. 286).

50. Jackson, *Modern Gothic*, p. 29.

51. A. W. N. Pugin, *Contrasts*, p. 43.

52. Charles Spooner, "House and Church Furniture," in *The Arts Connected with Building*, ed. T. Raffles Davison, p. 165.

53. James Fergusson, *History of the Modern Styles of Architecture*, 2:102n.

54. Pugin, *Contrasts*, p. 57.

55. Pugin, *Apology*, p. 22.

56. Jackson, *Modern Gothic*, pp. 40, 32, 22.

57. Owen Jones, *The Grammar of Ornament*, p. 8

58. Barry, p. 78.

59. *Builder* 15 (1857): 81.

60. Quoted in W. R. Lethaby, *Philip Webb and His Work*, p. 76.

61. Pugin, *Apology*, p. 38. The *Ecclesiologist* has also been frequently charged with narrow-mindedness in its advocacy of faithful reproduction of the old forms, but consider the liberality of this reply to Alexander Thomson's "A Protest against Gothic": "When Mr. Thompson [*sic*] speaks of Gothic as an imperfect art, we consider that he is really speaking in its favour. If it was so far perfected as to be incapable of further improvement and development we should rank it with the Athenian. We fully believe that it never did reach the perfection of which it is capable, and for this reason we hope that it may be left to us and our successors to carry it on, and, by making it our own, and honestly adapting it to all the multitudinous wants and comforts of such an age as this, to enlarge its already vast scope" ("Architectural Fitness and Originality," p. 239).

62. Ruskin, *Seven Lamps*, in *Works*, 8:196.

63. Scott, *Remarks*, p. vi. At the risk of belaboring the point, I again repeat that none of the important figures of the Revival recommend any other method. But I think it necessary to repeat the point because so many charges of rigid copyism have been brought against the Revival. One explanation for this contradiction is that practice did not always follow theory, as we see in an article in the *Builder* that approves Scott's

notions about the adaptability of Gothic and then asks, "Are these the principles on which the revival *has* been conducted? And the answer must be in the negative. Precedent, and precedent alone, has governed: the most slavish adherence to prescribed forms has been insisted on, and any architect who ventured on a departure from these, who dared to try the effect of a new combination, or sought to display a spark of invention, was hounded down in the most virulent and contemptuous manner" ("Present Condition of Architecture," p. 1). On the other hand, this remark obviously suggests, too, that some opposed the principle of freedom in theory as well as practice; but the leaders were not in this group and, indeed, regarded such opposition as a positive hindrance. Consider, for example, this comment by G. E. Street: "I know but one reason for the long predominance of this Classic style, and that is, that men in attempting to imitate Gothic art have copied, and no more; have not adapted it, and used it according to the necessities of the times; and so have raised an unnecessary and baseless prejudice against it, which it is difficult to overcome" ("A Plea for the Revival of True Principles of Architecture in the Public Buildings of Oxford," p. 403).

64. Ruskin, *Works*, 10:314.

65. Jackson, *Modern Gothic*, pp. 47–48.

66. Arthur O. Lovejoy, *The Great Chain of Being: A Study in the History of an Idea*, p. 297.

67. Robert Kerr, *The Gentleman's House; or, How to Plan English Residences, from the Parsonage to the Palace*, p. 342.

68. "Position and Progress of Architecture," p. 584.

69. Kerr, *Gentleman's House*, p. 342.

70. Ibid., pp. 340–41

71. Quoted in Collins, p. 119.

72. Mark Girouard, *Sweetness and Light: The "Queen Anne" Movement, 1860–1900*.

73. Jackson, *Recollections*, p. 56.

74. A. E. Street, p. 86. See Roger A. Kindler's "Periodical Criticism, 1815–40: Originality in Architecture" for a recent discussion of this subject.

75. Ruskin, *Works*, 11: 70.

76. A. E. Street, p. 83.

77. G. G. Scott, *Remarks*, p. 271. Cf. Walter Crane's use of the organic simile to express the same idea: "Whereas art in past ages seems to have germinated and to have been continually evolved in new forms,—to be alive, and spontaneous, as it were, growing like a thing of nature, and expanding with man's ideas of nature, beauty, and life,—in our day this sense of spontaneity, this natural growth, is scarcely felt. Conscious and laborious effort takes the place of spontaneous invention, and originality is crushed by the weight of authority and precedent. The student is confounded and abashed by the mass of examples,—the dry bones in the strata of museums and books of what were once living and breathing organisms in the world of beauty. No form of architecture or art seems to spring naturally and unaffectedly out of the actual necessities and demands of daily life" ("The Architecture of Art," p. 313). See chap. 4 below for a discussion of the organic analogy used in this way.

78. G. G. Scott, *Remarks*, p. 18.

79. Burges, p. 8. Frederick J. Crowest made the fanciful wish for music: "Cannot we call upon the gods to favour us with, say, an earthquake, that shall rid us of everything that serves as style, model, foundation, or what not, in our musical creations? . . . [The English composer] is quite unable to throw off the taint and to free himself from trammels which effectually preclude him from striking out a path for himself . . . " ("Wanted—An English Musical Style," p. 209).

80. John Sedding, *Art and Handicraft*, p. 150.

81. Cram, *Ministry*, p. 217.

82. Henry Van Brunt, "On the Present Condition and Prospects of Architecture," pp. 375–76.

83. T. Blashill, "Originality of Style," p. 467.

84. Reade, p. 537; Guillaume G. Huskisson, "The Architecture and Art of the Present," p. 369. The opening statement of purpose in the *Architect and Building Operative* focuses on the disparity between the stagnation of art, especially architecture, and the remarkable progress in all other areas of life ("Address to our Readers," p. 5).

85. Fergusson, *Historical Inquiry*, p. 71. Although he accepted evolutionary change in art, Fergusson was not prepared in 1849 to affirm "the strange hypothesis that one species could be developed out of another" (p. 68).

86. Ibid., p. 70.

87. Huggins, p. 186.

88. William Richard Lethaby, *Architecture: An Introduction to the History and Theory of the Art of Building*, p. 194.

89. W. R. Lethaby, *Architecture, Nature, and Magic*, p. 16; Barnes quoted by C. J. P. Beatty in his introduction to *The Architectural Notebook of Thomas Hardy*, p. 32.

90. Ruskin, letter to *Pall Mall Gazette*, 16 March 1872, in *Works*, 10: 459.

91. Eastlake, p. 1.

CHAPTER TWO

1. Plutarch attributes the idea to Simonides, but Horace is the popular source. Among the many studies on this subject are W. Rennselaer Lee, "Ut Pictura Poesis: The Humanistic Theory of Painting"; Jean H. Hagstrum, *The Sister Arts: The Tradition of Literary Pictorialism and English Poetry from Dryden to Gray*; and James S. Malek, *The Arts Compared: An Aspect of Eighteenth-Century British Aesthetics*.

2. In this respect my approach to nineteenth-century architecture is like Hugh Honour's to eighteenth-century art: "When we try to understand the art of the late eighteenth century it does not matter very much which aspects seem most appealing now or which seem true or false by present-day standards. What matters is whether our conception of the whole, and hence the definition of our term, corresponds to what the artists thought and believed themselves" (*Neo-classicism*, p. 15).

3. Ruskin, *Lectures on Architecture and Painting*, in *Works*, 12: 89.

4. Jackson, *Modern Gothic*, p. 143.

5. Jones, p. 5.

6. Jackson, *Modern Gothic*, p. 143.

7. A. E. Street, pp. 328, 316.

8. Ibid., p. 92.

9. Sir Uvedale Price, *On the Picturesque*, p. 329.

10. A. E. Street, p. 124.

11. Ibid., p. 318.

12. Sedding, pp. 163, 164, 161.

13. G. G. Scott, *Remarks*, p. 19.

14. Sir John Soane observed that the idea derives from classical times: "The ancient writers . . . recommended the study of music to form part of an architect's education,

conceiving, perhaps, that a relish for the harmonies of tone would induce, by a sort of sympathy, a corresponding taste for those of proportion" ("Lecture on Architecture at the Royal Academy, 1832," p. 452).

15. "Architecture and Music," p. 197.

16. A. E. Street, p. 345. William Burges similarly identifies rhythm with proportion in his comments on the recently completed Houses of Parliament: "There is one great thing to praise in that not very satisfactory building, the New Houses of Parliament, and that is its rhythm. Each part balances the other, and you can see at once that the man who designed it was, at all events, master of the great principles of his art" (Burges, p. 113).

17. G. G. Bodley, "Architectural Study and the Examination Test," in *Architecture: A Profession or an Art*, ed. R. Norman Shaw and T. G. Jackson, p. 57.

18. Typical of this attitude is the following comment made in the *Ecclesiologist*: "But, like many other signs of hope in the present day, we are disposed to trace the progress [of the Gothic Revival] which has of late been made in a considerable degree to the writings of Sir Walter Scott: and whatever be his place among the chiefs of English Literature, he will we believe earn from posterity a higher praise than is ever the lot of any mere literary man, from the purity of his writings, and the lessons which his readers could not fail to draw from the truthful and attractive pictures he has given of those times which the grossness of a later age had treated with unmixed contempt" ("The French Académie and Gothic Architecture," p. 83).

19. Kenneth Clark, *The Gothic Revival: An Essay in the History of Taste*, p. 9. As an example of how literary changes not only accompanied but preceded architectural ones, Clark claims that Shakespeare's defiance of Aristotelian precepts paved the way for a disregard of Vitruvian laws later on.

20. Fergusson, *History of the Modern Styles*, 2:2.

21. The correspondence between philosophy and art, the theories of the latter reflecting those of the former, is made clear when the same metaphor describes both. Goethe somewhere says that nature is "the garment of life which the Deity wears," and Carlyle says that nature is "the Living Garment of God." A late nineteenth-century writer describes the artistic union of physical and spiritual with the same metaphor: "Art is the protean vesture that clothes in divers fashions the eternal, unchanging spirit of poetry whose unveiled purity is the poet's secret vision" (Martin Morris, "The Philosophy of Poetry," p. 509).

22. Cf. Ruskin's remark that "no man can be an architect, who is not a metaphysician" (*The Poetry of Architecture*, in *Works*, 1:5).

23. Frances Power Cobbe explains the two definitions of poetry in this way: "Poetry stands in a double position towards all forms of Art. It is *an* art—and, for many reasons, to be ranked the first of arts; but it is also the pervading spirit of all the other arts, in which the element of poetry has the largest and most important share. Poetry, expressed through the medium of language (to which we rightly give the name *par eminence*, because by language can it be most widely and perfectly expressed), is only one form of poetry. There is a poetry expressed in architecture, a poetry expressed in sculpture, in painting, and in music; and all these deserve to be estimated according to their value as poetry. Deduct the element of poetry from any art, and a mere *Caput mortuum*—a body without a soul—will remain" ("The Hierarchy of Art," pp. 98–99). A broad definition of poetry similar to this one had, of course, been in use for some time, although it had never been so widely employed.

24. Ruskin, *The Stones of Venice*, in *Works*, 10:206 and 9:60.

25. Ibid., 10:269.

26. Ibid., 10:112.

CHAPTER THREE

1. The importance of the inner, spiritual quality is evident in such a comment as this: "Landscape painting's great object as an art ought to be the faithful rendering of the spirit and character of natural scenery and interesting localities. . . . Everything in landscape art ought to contribute to render with the most striking fidelity, not merely the scene, but that which is far deeper and more divine, the *spirit* of the scene" (Philip Gilbert Hamerton, "The Place of Landscape Painting amongst the Fine Arts," p. 211).

2. Arthur Tilley, "The Poetic Imagination," p. 188.

3. Ibid., p. 189. This is what Ruskin calls the contemplative imagination. Tilley, seeing no difference between Ruskin's categories of contemplative and associative, combines them into what he calls the constructive imagination.

4. Gotthold Ephraim Lessing, *Laocoön: An Essay on the Limits of Painting and Poetry*, p. 106. A few years later Dr. Johnson was to make a similar distinction in evaluating the merits of Homer and Virgil: "We must consider (said he) whether Homer was not the greatest poet, though Virgil may have produced the finest poem. Virgil was indebted to Homer for the whole invention of the structure of an epick poem, and for many of his beauties" (*Life*, 22 September 1777).

5. Ruskin, *Works*, 11:201. In "The Art of Fiction" (1888), Henry James writes that "the deepest quality of a work of art will always be the quality of the mind of the producer"; and for John Sedding "the singular attractiveness of a work of art—poem, building, painting—is borrowed from the personality of its creator" (Sedding, p. 161).

6. Sedding, p. 2.

7. The idea has continued in our own century, and in *Space, Time and Architecture*, Siegfried Giedion presents this version of it: "However much a period may try to disguise itself, its real nature will still show through its architecture, whether this uses original forms of expression or attempts to copy bygone epochs. We recognize the character of the age as easily as we identify a friend's handwriting beneath attempted disguises" (p. 19). As recently as 1978 Roger Dixon and Stefan Muthesius wrote in the first sentence of the "Introduction" to *Victorian Architecture*, "Victorian architecture is the reflection of unprecedented social, intellectual and technological change" (p. 8).

8. Pugin, *Contrasts*, pp. 2–3.

9. Pugin, *Apology*, p. 38

10. *Builder* 17 (1859):516.

11. E. D. H. Johnson has dealt with the literary aspect of the artist's separation from society in *The Alien Vision of Victorian Poetry: Sources of the Poetic Imagination in Tennyson, Browning, and Arnold*.

12. A. E. Street, p. 319. Cf. Viollet-le-Duc's comment that in the Middle Ages artists were "les enfants du peuple" (quoted in Nikolaus Pevsner, *Ruskin and Viollet-le-Duc: Englishness and Frenchness in the Appreciation of Gothic Architecture*, p. 18); and Ralph Adams Cram's remark that English parish churches "are all a kind of material expression of society itself, not the self-conscious product of very specialized artists, but a precipitation in visible form of the character of the people that raised them in every hamlet of every county in England" (*The Significance of Gothic Art*, p. 6). David Watkin has recently attacked this idea, which he calls "an art-historical belief in the all-dominating *Zeitgeist*" and which he blames for a failure to appreciate "the imaginative genius of the individual" (*Morality and Architecture: The Development of a Theme in Architectural History and Theory from the Gothic Revival to the Modern Movement*, p. 115).

13. Here is a late Victorian statement of the idea: Evolution has shown that "there is no order of phenomena which is not conditioned by its environment, which does not depend on circumstances outside itself; and of this great rule poetry is a signal ex-

ample. The greatness or the littleness of the poetry of any given period depends to some extent on the faculties of the poets themselves; but to some extent also, and far more than was once thought, it depends on the social conditions into which the poets have been born . . . " (W. H. Mallock, "The Conditions of Great Poetry," p. 156). See also John Addington Symonds, "On the Application of Evolutionary Principles to Art and Literature," in *Essays: Speculative and Suggestive*, pp. 27–52. Herbert Spencer and Hippolyte Taine are yet better known exponents of the idea.

14. Lethaby, *Philip Webb*, p. 119; *Architecture: An Introduction*, p. 192.

15. Pugin, *Apology*, p. 4. The survival of this attitude in modern times is apparent from John Gloag's recent comment that "buildings cannot lie; they tell the truth directly or by implication about those who made and used them and provide veracious records of the character and quality of past and present civilizations" (*The Architectural Interpretation of History*, p. 1).

16. Edward A. Freeman, *The Preservation and Restoration of Ancient Monuments*, p. 15.

17. Geoffrey Scott, *The Architecture of Humanism*, p. 51.

18. Pugin, *Apology*, p. 4; Jackson, *Recollections*, p. 121.

19. Cram, *Ministry*, p. 27.

20. Lethaby, *Philip Webb*, p. 64.

21. Jackson, *Recollections*, p. 121

22. Pugin, *Apology*, p. 5.

23. Cram, *Ministry*, pp. 38–39.

24. Herbert Read, *The True Voice of Feeling: Studies in English Romantic Poetry*, p. 10.

25. Fergusson, *Historical Inquiry*, pp. 165–66. Cf. George Henry Lewes's belief that "unless a writer has Sincerity, urging him to place before us what he sees and believes *as* he sees and believes it, the defective earnestness of his presentation will cause an imperfect sympathy in us. He must believe what he says, or we shall not believe it. Insincerity is always a weakness; sincerity even in error is strength ("The Principles of Success in Literature," p. 95).

26. Jackson, *Modern Gothic*, p. 126.

27. Durandus, pp. xxii, xxvi.

28. A. E. Street, p. 58.

29. Barry, p. 238.

30. Quoted in Georg Germann, *Gothic Revival in Europe and Britain: Sources, Influences, and Ideas*, p. 9.

31. A. E. Street, pp. 334, 34.

32. Ruskin, *The Queen of the Air*, in *Works*, 19:389. Similarly a reviewer commends A. F. Rio for showing in *The Poetry of Christian Art* that "to execute a great and good work, a man must first make himself great and good; that genius itself must take its inspiration from a still higher source; and that the man who would decorate the Temple, must in the same Temple sanctify his thoughts and ways" ("The Poetry of Christian Art," p. 353).

33. Christopher Dresser, *Principles of Decorative Design*, p. 15.

34. Clark, p. 149.

35. Van Brunt, p. 379.

36. Eastlake, pp. 271–72.

37. Samuel Huggins explains the causal relationship between function and expression in this way: "Exact adaptation of form to purpose is the most direct element of expression, and assists more largely than is generally supposed in characterising the

structure. It is an essential,—nay, the foundation of all artistic expression. Utility or necessity called for the building, and the building, if the architect has faithfully responded to that call, will, in the absence of artistic expression, generally hint at the purpose. In most cases where fitness is thus attended to, the expression is in a great measure given,—the character of the edifice is half formed" ("Expression in Architecture," p. 325).

38. Pugin, *Contrasts*, p. 1. A. E. Street tells us that his father designed the plan of the Law Courts before the elevation in order "to make his exterior not merely contain the interior, but explain it and express its uses" (A. E. Street, pp. 166–67).

39. A. Welby Pugin, *The True Principles of Pointed or Christian Architecture*, p. 27.

40. G. G. Scott, "English Architecture: Present Questions," p. 24.

41. Vitruvius, *The Ten Books on Architecture*, pp. 14–15. In the eighteenth century the suitability of style to subject was usually known as decorum. A poet used an elevated style for an epic, a familiar style for a verse epistle; a painter similarly employed one style for a historical picture and another for a portrait. The genre dictated the treatment in poetry and painting just as the type of building determined the style appropriate to it.

42. *Architecture, Essai sur l'art*, rpt. and trans. in Helen Rosenau, *Boullée and Visionary Architecture*, pp. 98, 100.

43. Huggins, "Expression," p. 384.

44. Thompson, p. 118.

45. J. Hall Richardson, "Scotland Yard," p. 8.

46. Ruskin, "Academy Notes," in *Works*, 14:236.

47. Basing his remarks upon a belief that "it is not the form of a work of art that gives it value, but the thought that is bestowed upon it," James Fergusson asserted that many Dutch pictures "attempted, and with wonderful success, to reproduce nature by patient, painstaking fidelity, but with about the same quantity of mind as is required by a camera obscura to produce a daguerrotype. On the other hand, we possess certain sketches by Raphael and Michael Angelo, made with a pen or piece of chalk, without, if I may use the expression, any labour at all; but these few hurried, careless scratches do express an idea sometimes of the highest quality, and which now reproduce an emotion of beauty which all the art of a Mieris or a Metzu never could pretent to" (*Historical Inquiry*, p. 149).

48. Ibid., p. 152. C. F. A. Voysey also subordinated the mechanics of building to what he calls "ideas in things": "All art is the expression or manifestation of thought and feeling; therefore a technical knowledge of any craft by itself is but a language with which to express thought and feeling" ("Ideas in Things," in Davison, p. 105).

49. Ruskin, *The Stones of Venice* 2, in *Works*, 10:202.

50. Harris, "The Life and Work of William Butterfield," *Architect* 83 (1910): quoted in Thompson, p. 63; Pugin quoted in Ferrey, p. 260.

51. Fergusson, *Modern Styles*, p. 103.

52. Cram, *Ministry*, p. 144.

53. Clark, pp. 206–7.

54. Ecclesiological Society, p. 185.

55. Kerr, *Gentleman's House*, pp. 368–69; Voysey, p. 104; Collins, p. 109; Summerson, *Heavenly Mansions*, pp. 172–73; Clark, p. 191.

56. Lessing, p. 17.

CHAPTER FOUR

1. This account is from the *Ecclesiologist* 21 (1860):250.

2. Lethaby, *Philip Webb*, p. 1.

3. Garbett, p. 109; Jackson, *Modern Gothic*, p. 126.

4. In the eighteenth century Warburton had mentioned the concept in a note on Pope's *Moral Essays*, and in our own century Spengler repeated it in *The Decline of the West*. Sir James Hall provided a variation on the idea by proposing that Gothic originated as an imitation of wicker work (*Essay on the Origin, History, and Principles of Gothic Architecture*), and Sir Walter Scott cited Hall as his source for the following description in *The Lay of the Last Minstrel*:

> The moon on the east oriel shone
> Through slender shafts of shapely stone,
>   By foliaged tracery combined;
> Thou would'st have thought some fairy's hand
> 'Twixt poplars straight the ozier wand,
>   In many a freakish knot, had twined;
> Then framed a spell, when the work was done,
> And changed the willow-wreaths to stone.

2. 11

5. Ruskin, *The Two Paths*, in *Works*, 16:322; G. G. Scott, *Recollections*, pp. 204–5.

6. Dresser, p. 24.

7. A. E. Street, pp. 89, 182.

8. Garbett, p. 68.

9. Huggins, p. 3.

10. Baillie Scott, p. 149. Cf. Frank Lloyd Wright's comment, "Let our Universities realize and teach that *the law of organic change is the only thing that mankind can know as beneficent or as actual!*" (*An Organic Architecture*, p. 45).

11. Sedding, p. 10.

12. A. E. Street, p. 86.

13. Cram, *Ministry*, p. 29.

14. A good illustration of organic form used to support subjective expressionism in architecture is this comment: "As the convolutions of a shell, the spiny processes that guard its mouth, or the rich and delicate colours that bespeak its character as the home of life, convey to the naturalist positive information as to the nature of the animal which, in the dim laboratory of the sea, surrounded its soft flesh with a cuirass of porcelin; so do structural fabrics [buildings] reveal very much of the nature of the race that reared them" ([Francis R. Couder,] "Modern Architecture and Its Assailants," p. 386).

15. Samuel Huggins uses the analogy to organic form in arguing for objective expressionism in architecture: "True works of architecture speak to us just as nature does. In nature form exists by and through the essence—the spirit creates the form, and the idea of its use must create the building—its qualities must be represented on the same principles as in the works of creation" ("Expression in Architecture," p. 326).

16. A. E. Street, p. 342

17. Baillie Scott, p. 146. Thirteen years earlier (1896) Louis H. Sullivan had written, "It is the pervading law of all things organic, and inorganic, of all things physical and

metaphysical, of all things human and superhuman, of all true manifestations of the head, of the heart, of the soul, that the life is recognizable in its expression, that form ever follows function. This is the law" (*Kindergarten Chats and Other Writings*, p. 208).

18. Warren Hunting Smith, *Architecture in English Fiction*, p. 209.

19. A. E. Street, p. 79.

20. Jackson, *Modern Gothic*, p. 119.

21. Quoted in E. M. Dodd, "Charles Robert Cockerell," in *Victorian Architecture*, ed. Peter Ferriday, p. 109.

22. Arthur O. Lovejoy, "The First Gothic Revival and the Return to Nature," rpt. in *Essays in the History of Ideas*, pp. 152–53.

23. Pugin, *Apology*, p. 38.

24. Garbett, p. 45.

25. Barry, p. 20.

26. A. E. Street, p. 17; Stevenson, *An Inland Voyage* (1903).

27. Opposed to the eighteenth-century concept of uniform nature and belief in the beauty of general nature is the nineteenth-century idea that "of all the principles of beauty by which nature appears to move, one of the most striking seems to be variety. . . . Every natural appearance is varied, and to a much greater extent than cursory observers would imagine" ([John Zephaniah Bell,] "The Taste of the Day," p. 293). Carol T. Christ has discussed the artistic implications of this change in *The Finer Optic: The Aesthetic of Particularity in Victorian Poetry*.

28. Heinrich Wölfflin, *Principles of Art History: The Problem of the Development of Style in Later Art*, p. 159.

29. Quoted in Phoebe B. Stanton, "Architecture, History, and the Spirit of the Age," p. 151.

30. Jones, p. 5. The novel, according to Henry James, is organically unified as well: "A novel is a living thing, all one and continuous, like any other organism, and in proportion as it lives will it be found, I think, that in each of the parts there is something of each of the other parts" (*The Art of Fiction*).

31. William Gilpin, *Observations, Relative Chiefly to Picturesque Beauty, Made in the Year 1772, on Several Parts of England; Particularly the Mountains, and Lakes of Cumberland and Westmoreland*, 1:xiv.

32. Ibid., 2:188.

33. Dream houses, such as the one to which the poet and Emily will elope in Shelley's *Epipsychidion*, could be as organically conceived as Gilpin's ruins or Wordsworth's cottages:

> It scarce seems now a wreck of human art,
> But, as it were, Titanic; in the heart
> Of Earth having assumed its form, then grown
> Out of the mountains, from the living stone,
> Lifting itself in caverns light and high:
> For all the antique and learned imagery
> Has been erased, and in the place of it
> The ivy and the wild vine interknit
> The volumes of their many-twining stems.

A modern version of this idea is Eero Saarinen's comment, "The conviction that a building cannot be placed on a site, but that a building grows from its site, is another principle in which I believe" (*Eero Saarinen on His Work*, p. 6).

34. Pevsner, *Pioneers of Modern Design from William Morris to Walter Gropius*, p. 132. Cf. Wright's ideas about building the new house: "My sense of wall was not a side of a box. It was enclosure to afford protection against storm or heat when this was needed. But it was also increasingly to bring the outside world into the house, and let the inside of the house go outside. In this sense I was working toward the elimination of the wall as a wall to reach the function of a screen, as a means of opening up space . . . " (*An Autobiography*, p. 139). Wright, however, was not prepared for Philip Johnson's Glass House; upon entering it Wright expressed his uncertainty as to whether he should remove his hat, not knowing if he was inside or out. Ellen E. Frank has discussed the relationship between buildings and nature in "The Domestication of Nature: Five Houses in the Lake District," pp. 68–92. As my remarks should make clear, what she calls the domestication of nature I prefer to think of as the naturalization of architecture.

CHAPTER FIVE

1. M. H. Abrams, *The Mirror and the Lamp: Romantic Theory and the Critical Tradition*, p.15.

2. Price, *On the Picturesque*, p. 510. Christopher Hussey's *The Picturesque: Studies in a Point of View* remains the standard work on the subject. Chapter 6 deals specifically with architecture.

3. Price, p. 82.

4. A. E. Street, p. 331.

5. Barry, p. 21. Corresponding to the rising popularity of the picturesque and the change in taste from regularity to irregularity is the liking for odd numbers over even numbers. Boileau at the age of forty-six had in a poem reckoned his age at forty to satisfy the requirement of art to admit no odd numbers over nine. Presumably Wordsworth is within the bounds of this rule in "We Are Seven" but careless of it when he sets Matthew's age at seventy-two and Simon Lee's at thirty-five. Indeed, even before Wordsworth, Hogarth had written that "it is a constant rule in composition in painting to avoid regularity" and that "odd numbers have the advantage over the even ones, as variety is more pleasing than uniformity . . . " (*The Analysis of Beauty*, chaps. 3, 4). It was, however, Jane Austen who associated odd numbers directly with the picturesque. When, in *Pride and Prejudice*, Darcy invites Elizabeth to join himself and two others in a walk, Elizabeth banters, "'No, no; stay where you are. The picturesque would be spoilt by admitting a fourth.'"

6. A. E. Street, p. 331.

7. Price, p. 83. Sir James Hall, Price's contemporary, makes the same point: "The Grecian style excels in all those qualities of *elegance* and *grace*, which depend upon the nice adjustment and masterly execution of details. Whereas the Gothic style, which, with great truth, has been compared to the genius of Shakespeare, is lively, picturesque, and sublime, qualities which are derived from the bold variety, and often from the wild irregularity of its forms" (p. 147).

8. Hardy, *Architectural Notebook*, p. 33.

9. Kerr, "The Battle of the Styles," p. 294; *Gentleman's House*, p. 344.

10. Lethaby, *Philip Webb*, p. 121. On the assimilation of the picturesque into the beautiful, see Robert Kerr's remark: "I have always considered Burke to be egregiously in error when he draws a distinction between beauty and the sublime, and Price or Gilpin, or whoever it is, when he draws a distinction between beauty and the picturesque. Such distinctions are philosophically false. You may distinguish between the

picturesque beautiful and the non-picturesque beautiful; but the picturesque itself is only one province of the beautiful" ("Remarks on Professor Donaldson's 'Architectural Maxims and Theorems,'" p. 267). There is an interesting parallel between the breakdown of distinctions separating the beautiful, the sublime, and the picturesque; the breakdown of distinctions separating genres within art forms; and the breakdown of distinctions separating art forms themselves that was the subject of chapter 2. One is tempted as well to view the gradual acceptance of Gothic from a sociological perspective and to consider Gothic as rising from lowly status to middle-class respectability despite opposition by the classical aristocracy.

11. Barry, p. 241.

12. Henry-Russell Hitchcock, *Early Victorian Architecture in Britain*, 1:72.

13. Macleod, p. 25.

14. Sedding, p. 164.

15. Hitchcock, 1:25.

16. Pugin, *True Principles*, pp. 71–72.

17. Quoted in Barry, p. 60.

18. G. G. Scott, *Remarks*, p. 258. There seems to be complete agreement on this matter. Samuel Huggins rejected the picturesque for its own sake ("Expression," p. 325), and J. L. Petit, arguing that the builders of the original Gothic never consciously attempted it, criticizes modern architects because "now we *aim* at picturesqueness; we discover in it a great source of beauty, and therefore endeavour to obtain it by every means in our power.... But an artifical picturesqueness, as we have observed, is all but valueless ..." ("Utilitarianism in Architecture," p. 58).

19. Petit, p. 37. Petit was somewhat extreme for his time, though less so for later in the century, in citing furnaces and fortifications as examples of picturesque beauty gained by a utilitarian approach to building. More moderate and typical is Samuel Huggins's statement five years earlier (1851) that "truthfulness of treatment in design will assist us to originate it [the picturesque]; nay, will itself suggest or produce it" ("Expression," p. 325).

20. E. Trotman, "On the Comparative Value of Simplicity in Architecture," p. 107.

21. Cf. Archibald Alison's comment that "our admiration attaches itself only to those greater productions of the art, in which one pure and unmingled character is preserved, and in which no feature is admitted, which may prevent it from falling upon the heart with one full and harmonious effect" (*Essays on the Nature and Principles of Taste*, 1:130. The first edition was published in 1790. In America, Edgar Allan Poe was the most famous proponent of unity of feeling.

22. John Evelyn, *An Account of Architects and Architecture*, pp. 9, 10. The first edition is dated 1664.

23 Trotman, p. 107.

24. Ruskin, *The Poetry of Architecture*, in *Works*, 1:8.

25. Ruskin, *Modern Painters* 1, in *Works*, 3:336.

26. Jackson, *Modern Gothic*, p. 119.

27. Quoted in Thompson, p. 305.

28. Voysey, p. 121.

29. Ruskin, letter to the *Times*, 25 May 1854, in *Works*, 12:334.

30. W. F. Axton, "Victorian Landscape Painting: A Change in Outlook," pp. 304–5.

31. Lethaby, *Philip Webb*, p. 131.

32. Pugin, *True Principles*, p. 72.

33. Ibid., p. 74.

34. Alison, 1:4–6. George L. Hersey's *High Victorian Gothic: A Study in Associationism* is the most thorough discussion of the influence of associationism on architecture.

35. Thomson, "Enquiry into the Appropriateness of the Gothic Style for the Proposed Buildings for the University of Glasgow," quoted in Pevsner, *Some Architectural Writers*, p. 184. For those, like Thomson, who were unable to give up the traditional concept of beauty as harmony of form, a new category, similar in purpose to those of the picturesque and unity of feeling, was established to accommodate pleasures derived from the association of ideas, and this was generally labeled "poetic." (See above, chap. 2.) W. H. Scott, for example, makes this distinction between the beautiful and the poetical: "We shall venture to include all that is properly called beautiful under the definition of *harmony*, and to refer the beautiful, improperly so called, or what we now name the poetical, to the head of *association*. We are not saying, it will be observed, that the Beautiful and Poetical never meet and intermingle in the same subject; nothing, on the contrary, is more common: but we say that the two are always distinguishable in idea, and may be separate in fact. Harmony, then, is the philosophy of the Beautiful, and association its poetry" ("The Theory of the Picturesque," p. 4).

36. Here is a late Victorian version of the idea: "Not only is imagination necessary for the production of a work of art, but it is also necessary for the understanding of it. The conception which is born of imagination can only be apprehended by imagination. Hegel indeed makes a distinction between the active or productive imagination of the artist, and the passive or receptive imagination of the beholder of a work of art, and calls them by different names; but in reality the difference between them is one of degree and not one of kind. The impression which is made upon the beholder of a work of art, though doubtless far less intense, is no doubt similar in kind to that which the artist himself had when he conceived it" (Arthur Tilley, "The Poetic Imagination," p. 185).

37. Ruskin, *The Poetry of Architecture*, in *Works*, 1:5. For arguments that Ruskin believed beauty to exist independently of associations, see George P. Landow, *The Aesthetic and Critical Theories of John Ruskin*, pp. 89–110; and Robert Hewison, *John Ruskin: The Argument of the Eye*, pp. 54–64.

38. Alison, 1:11–12.

39. Sedding, p. 4.

40. J. C. Loudon, "Architecture Considered as an Art of Imagination," p. 146.

41. J. E., "Grecian and Gothic Architecture," p. 511. Clough was to maintain, on the contrary, that centuries of classical education had provided sufficient familiarity for an appreciation of Greek architecture:

> 'Tis not, these centuries four, for nought
> Our European world of thought
> Hath made familiar to its home
> The classic mind of Greece and Rome.

Dipsychus, 4

Wordsworth implies in "The world is too much with us," however, that belief, not just knowledge, is the prerequisite. Those who argued for modern subjects in painting and poetry did so largely because such subjects were more familiar, and therefore more evocative, than historical subjects.

42. Price, p. 482.

43. Jones, p. 5.

44. Lessing, pp. 19–20.

45. Christopher Ricks, *Tennyson*, p. 49.

46. [Coventry Patmore,] "Architects and Architecture," p. 656.

47. Baillie Scott, p. 144.

48. "The Philosophy of Gothic Architecture," p. 65.

49. J. M. Capes, "Music and Architecture," p. 708.

50. Fergusson, *History of the Modern Styles*, 2:164. The poet to whom Fergusson refers is Milton:

> But let my due feet never fail
> To walk the studious Cloysters pale,
> And love the high embowed Roof,
> With antick Pillars massy proof,
> And storied Windows richly dight,
> Casting a dimm religious light.
>
> *Il Penseroso*

But compare Clough's lines:

> Maturer optics don't delight
> In childish dim religious light,
> In evanescent vague effects
> That shirk, not face, one's intellects.
>
> *Dipsychus*, 1

See also his "Epi-strauss-ium" for a similar idea. As for external lighting, Ruskin was not the first to recommend viewing buildings in darkness when he said Westminster Abbey should be seen at five in the morning. Walter Scott had earlier advised the observer of Melrose Abbey to

> Go visit it by the pale moonlight;
> For the gay beams of lightsome day
> Gild, but to flout, the ruins grey.
>
> *The Lay of the Last Minstrel*, 1. 2

51. Ruskin, *The Stones of Venice* 2, in *Works*, 10:214.

52. Garbett, p. 75.

53. Ibid., p. 229.

54. Voysey, p. 121. Cf. Dresser, p. 14; and Ralph Nicholson Wornum, "The Exhibition as a Lesson in Taste," p. VI***.

55. An early discussion of polychromy in Greek art is Kugler's *Ueber die Polychromie der Griechischen Architektur, und Sculptur und ihre Grenzen* (Berlin, 1835).

56. "The Late William Butterfield, F.S.A.," *Journal of the R.I.B.A.* 7 (1900):244.

57. Voysey, p. 114.

58. Jackson, *Modern Gothic*, pp. 81–82. Ingress E. Bell also commented on "that tendency observable in contemporary architecture to bestow too much care on the accessories, and too little on the general design, inducing a quality which I cannot better describe in a single word than by the title I have chosen for this paper [unrest]" ("'Unrest' in Architecture," p. 536).

59. George Wightwick, *The Palace of Architecture: A Romance of Art and History*, p. 14.

CHAPTER SIX

1. Fergusson, *Historical Inquiry*, p. 173.

2. Cram, *Ministry*, p. viii.

3. Wornum, p. II***.

4. Cram, *Ministry*, p. 127. Cf. Vernon Lee's comment that "art is at the same time two very different things: it is the product of a given mental condition, and it is the producer of another mental condition . . . " ("Comparative Aesthetics," p. 300).

5. Eastlake, p. 265.

6. Esmé Wingfield-Stratford, *Those Earnest Victorians*, p. 239.

7. Quoted in Phoebe Stanton, *Pugin*, p. 52.

8. A. E. Street, p. 62.

9. Cram, *Ministry*, pp. 61–62.

10. A. E. Street, p. 74.

11. Cram, *Ministry*, pp. 245–46.

12. J. W. Mackail, *The Life of William Morris*, 1:162.

13. Vernon F. Storr, *The Development of English Theology in the Nineteenth Century, 1800–1860*, p. 269; James F. White, *The Cambridge Movement: The Ecclesiologists and the Gothic Revival*, p. 204.

14. Collins, p. 109.

15. *Ecclesiologist* 20 (1859):185.

16. Sedding, p. 29.

17. A. Welby Pugin, *A Reply to Observations Which Appeared in "Fraser's Magazine," for March 1837, on a Work Entitled "Contrasts,"* p. 4.

18. Cram, *Ministry*, pp. 234–35.

19. Ibid., p. 113.

20. Durandus, p. 1. Cf. Friedrich Schlegel's remark, "All architecture is symbolical, but none so much as the Christian architecture of the middle age" (*Lectures on the History of Literature*, 1).

21. Durandus, p. xxvii.

22. Pugin, *Contrasts*, p. 3. In 1860 a Dr. Barlow read a paper before the R.I.B.A. in which he commented that "the very designs of sacred edifices—their forms, arrangements, and ornamentation,—all have their origin in a significant symbolism, and were conceived and carried out in accordance with it" ("Symbolism in Reference to Art," p. 97).

23. Ruskin, *Works*, 9:186. See also *Lectures on Architecture and Painting*, in *Works*, 12:36–43.

24. Jackson, *Modern Gothic*, pp. 95–98. So did G. G. Scott; see his comment made during the discussion following Dr. Barlow's "Symbolism in Reference to Art" (note 22, above).

25. Robert Kerr, *The Newleafe Discourses on the Fine Art Architecture*, p. 145. Some, however, argued that one need not be consciously aware of symbolism for it to have effect. A Mr. White, Fellow of the R.I.B.A., responded to Dr. Barlow's "Symbolism in Reference to Art" by saying that symbolism's "presence and influence was felt, even although those who felt it had no knowledge of that which was represented. Thus-. . . porch, font, nave, choir, chancel, sanctuary, altar, etc., simply and solely symbolical as they were, had an effect on those entering the building, though their attention had never been called to the symbolism itself" (*Papers Read at the R.I.B.A.* 4 [1857–60]:109).

26. Otto von Simson, *the Gothic Cathedral: Origins of Gothic Architecture and the Medieval Concept of Order*, p. 135. See also Erwin Panofsky, *Gothic Architecture and Scholasticism*.

CHAPTER SEVEN

1. Lethaby, *Philip Webb*, p. 68.

2. Quoted in Ferrey, pp. 106–7.

3. G. G. Scott, *Remarks*, p. 242.

4. Jackson, *Recollections*, p. 56.

5. *Building News*, 9 May 1873, p. 524, quoted in Girouard, p. 58.

6. Joseph Gwilt, *An Encyclopaedia of Architecture: Historical, Theoretical, and Practical*, p. 792. First published in 1842. This anecdote has elsewhere been attributed to Chesterfield although I have not been able to find it. It recalls Francis Bacon's remark, "Houses are built to live in, and not to look on . . . " ("Of Building").

7. A. E. Street, p. 59. Sham fronts were treated humorously in M'Cann's "Song on Pugin's *Contrasts*":

> Some raise a front up to the street,
>   Like ould Westminster Abbey;
> And then they think the Lord to cheat,
>   And build the back part shabby.
> For stuccoed bricks, and sich like tricks,
>   At present all the rage is,
> They took no one in! those fine ould min!
> In the "pious Middle Ages!!!
>
>   Quoted in Ferrey, p. 116

Consider also Longfellow's lines:

> In the elder days of Art,
>   Builders wrought with greatest care
> Each minute and unseen part;
>   For the Gods see everywhere.
>
>   "The Builders"

8. Kerr quoted by Beatty in his introduction to *The Architectural Notebook of Thomas Hardy*, p. 2; Shaw quoted in Andrew Saint, *Richard Norman Shaw*, pp. 270–71.

9. John Brandon-Jones, "C. F. A. Voysey," in Ferriday, p. 273.

10. Ferrey, p. 120.

11. Pugin, *Present State*, pp. 61, 18.

12. Barry, pp. 60–61.

13. A. E. Street, p. 77.

14. Burges, p. 113.

15. Kerr, "The Battle of the Styles," p. 292.

16. John Mason Neale, *A Few Words to Church-Builders*, p. 5.

17. Quoted in Thompson, p. 128.

18. Dresser, p. 68.

19. Pugin, *True Principles*, p. 6.

20. Gwilt, p. 792. Pugin seems to have been right about the exterior wall serving no structural function and acting only as a screen to conceal the flying buttresses, but both he and Gwilt were wrong about the dome. Harold Dorn and Robert Mark have recently shown that there is a third, conical dome between the outer and inner ones, and that the combination of the three domes makes for a much stronger structure than the

single dome of St. Peter's, which has cracked and had to be wrapped with ten iron chains ("The Architecture of Christopher Wren").

21. A. E. Street, p. 342.

22. Ruskin, *Seven Lamps*, in *Works*, 8:61; G. G. Scott, *Remarks*, p. 260.

23. Lethaby, *Architecture: An Introduction*, p. 194.

24. Pugin, *True Principles*, p. 1.

25. Dresser, p. 65.

26. Thompson, p. 168.

27. Pugin, *True Principles*, p. 1.

28. Ibid., p. 34.

29. Garbett, p. 126.

30. Kerr, *Gentleman's House*, pp. 368–69.

31. Dresser, pp. 21–22.

32. Pevsner, *High Victorian Design*, p. 98.

33. Alf Bøe, *From Gothic Revival to Functional Form: A Study in Victorian Theories of Design*, p. 148.

34. Ruskin, *The Stones of Venice* 1, in *Works*, 9:72.

35. Ruskin, *Lectures on Architecture and Painting*, in *Works*, 12:84.

36. J. T. Micklethwaite, "Architecture and Construction," in Shaw and Jackson, pp. 26–27.

37. Rpt. in *Kindergarten Chats and Other Writings*, p. 187.

38. Pugin, *Apology*, p. 39.

39. Garbett, p. 129.

40. Jones, p. 5.

41. Bruno Taut, *Modern Architecture*, p. 9.

42. Germann, p. 125.

43. Pugin, *Contrasts*, p. 1; *True Principles*, p. 12. Cf. James Gowans's statement, "If a thing has the look of fitness and true structural proportion, it will please the eye without further adornment" ("The Useful, Structural, and Beautiful, in Architecture," p. 945).

44. Ruskin, *Lectures on Architecture and Painting*, in *Works*, 12:25.

45. Dresser, p. 19.

46. Lethaby, *Architecture, Nature, and Magic*, p. 146; *Philip Webb*, p. 123.

47. Lethaby, *Architecture: An Introduction*, p. 192.

48. Pugin, *Present State*, p. 31; Baillie Scott, pp. 150–51.

49. Lethaby, *Philip Webb*, p. 125.

50. Ruskin, *Lectures on Architecture and Painting*, in *Works*, 12:72.

51. Burges, p. 92.

52. A. E. Street, p. 113.

CONCLUSION

1. A. Welby Pugin, *Some Remarks on the Articles Which Have Recently Appeared in the "Rambler," Relative to Ecclesiastical Architecture and Decoration*, p. 11.

2. Shaw, letter to Mrs. Foster, 18 October 1892, quoted in Saint, p. 290.

3. Kerr, "The Battle of the Styles," p. 294.

BIBLIOGRAPHY

A., W. "A Speculation, Whether Architecture Be Not Rather an Invention of Art, Than an Imitation of Nature." *Annals of the Fine Arts* 1 (1817):295–300.

Abrams, M. H. *The Mirror and the Lamp: Romantic Theory and the Critical Tradition.* New York: Oxford University Press, 1953.

Addison, Agnes. *Romanticism and the Gothic Revival.* New York: Richard R. Smith, 1938.

Addleshaw, G. W. O., and Frederick Etchells. *The Architectural Setting of Anglican Worship.* London: Faber & Faber, 1948.

"Address to our Readers." *Architect and Building Operative* 1 (1849):5–6.

Alison, Archibald. *Essays on the Nature and Principles of Taste.* 2 vols. 5th ed. Edinburgh: Archibald Constable & Co., 1817.

Allen, B. Sprague. *Tides in English Taste (1619-1800): A Background for the Study of Literature.* 2 vols. 1937. Reprint. New York: Rowman & Littlefield, 1969.

"Architectural Fitness and Originality." *Ecclesiologist* 27 (1866):234–39.

"Architecture among the Poets." *Builder* 44 (1883):491–92, 526–28, 558–59, 628–29, 696–98, 764–66.

"Architecture and Music." *Builder* 29 (1871):197–98. Also printed in *Church-Builder*, no. 39 (1871), pp. 103–7.

"Architecture in England as Affected by the Taste and Feelings of Past and Present Times." *Builder* 12 (1854):543–44.

Arnold, Matthew. *The Complete Prose Works of Matthew Arnold,* 11 vols. Edited by R. H. Super. Ann Arbor: University of Michigan Press, 1960–77.

"As to Expression in Architecture." *Builder* 29 (1871):340–41.

Ashton, Alex. Fred. "Architectural Reflections." *Builder* 6 (1848):447–48, 458–59.

Austin, Alfred. *The Bridling of Pegasus: Prose Papers on Poetry.* London: Macmillan & Co., 1910.

Axton, W. F. "Victorian Landscape Painting: A Change in Outlook." In *Nature and the Victorian Imagination*, pp. 281–308. Edited by U. C. Knoepflmacher and G. B. Tennyson. Berkeley: University of California Press, 1977.

B., E. I. "On the Ethical Value of the Gothic Revival." *Architectural Review: For the Artist and Craftsman* 5 (1898–99):272.

Babbitt, Irving. *The New Laokoon: An Essay on the Confusion of the Arts.* Boston: Houghton Mifflin Co., 1910.

Barlow, Dr. "Symbolism in Reference to Art." *Papers Read at the Royal Institute of British Architects* 4 (1857–60):97–110.

Barry, Alfred. *The Life and Works of Sir Charles Barry.* London: John Murray, 1867.

291

Bate, W[alter] Jackson. *The Burden of the Past and the English Poet*. Cambridge, Mass.: Harvard University Press, Belknap Press, 1970.

———. *From Classic to Romantic: Premises of Taste in Eighteenth-Century England*. Cambridge, Mass.: Harvard University Press, 1946.

Bell, Ingress E. "'Unrest' in Architecture." *Builder* 38 (1880):536–38.

[Bell, John Zephaniah.] "The Taste of the Day." *Fraser's Magazine* 56 (1857):288–96.

Blashill, T. "Originality of Style." *Builder* 19 (1861):467.

Bloxam, Matthew Holbeche. *The Principles of Gothic Ecclesiastical Architecture*. 11th ed. London: George Bell & Sons, 1882.

Boase, T. S. R., ed. *The Oxford History of English Art*. Oxford: Clarendon Press, 1949–. Vol. 10, *English Art, 1800–1870*, 1959.

Bøe, Alf. *From Gothic Revival to Functional Form: A Study in Victorian Theories of Design*. Oslo Studies in English, no. 6. Oslo: Oslo University Press, 1957.

Bosanquet, Bernard. *A History of Aesthetic*. 2d ed. 1904. Reprint. London: Allen & Unwin, 1966.

Bradbury, Ronald. *The Romantic Theories of Architecture of the Nineteenth Century, in Germany, England, and France (Together with a Brief Survey of the Vitruvian School)*. New York: Dorothy Press, 1934.

Briggs, Martin S. *Goths and Vandals: A Study of the Destruction, Neglect, and Preservation of Historical Buildings in England*. London: Constable & Co., 1952.

Bright, Michael. "A Reconsideration of A. W. N. Pugin's Architectural Theories." *Victorian Studies* 22 (1979):151–72.

"The British School of Architecture." *Blackwood's Edinburgh Magazine* 40 (1836):227–38.

Brunt, Henry Van. "On the Present Condition and Prospects of Architecture." *Atlantic Monthly* 57 (1886):374–84.

Buckley, Jerome Hamilton. *The Triumph of Time: A Study of the Victorian Concepts of Time, History, Progress, and Decadence*. Cambridge, Mass.: Harvard University Press, 1966.

Burges, William. *Art Applied to Industry*. Oxford and London: John Henry and James Parker, 1865.

———. "Why We Have So Little Art in Our Churches." *Ecclesiologist* 28 (1867):150–56.

Burke, Edmund. *A Philosophical Enquiry into the Origin of Our Ideas of the Sublime and Beautiful*. Edited by J. T. Boulton. London: Routledge & Kegan Paul, 1958.

C. "The True School for Architects." *Fraser's Magazine* 86 (1872):743–50.

A Cambridge Graduate. "As to a New Style." *Builder* 30 (1872):31.

Capes, J. M. "Music and Architecture." *Fortnightly Review* 8 (1867):703–10.

Carlyle, Thomas. *The Works of Thomas Carlyle*. 30 vols. Centenary Edition. Edited by Henry Duff Traill. London: Chapman and Hall, 1896–99.

Casson, Hugh. *An Introduction to Victorian Architecture*. New York: Pellegrini & Cudahy, 1948.

Chambers, Frank P. *The Hisory of Taste: An Account of the Revolutions of Art Criticism and Theory in Europe*. New York: Columbia University Press, 1932.

Chandler, Alice. *A Dream of Order: The Medieval Ideal in Nineteenth-Century English Literature*. Lincoln: University of Nebraska Press, 1970.

Christ, Carol T. *The Finer Optic: The Aesthetic of Particularity in Victorian Poetry*. New Haven, Conn.: Yale University Press, 1975.

Clark, Kenneth. *The Gothic Revival: An Essay in the History of Taste*. 3d ed. London: John Murray, 1962.

Clarke, Basil F. L. *Church Builders of the Nineteenth Century: A Study of the Gothic Revival in England*. London: Society for Promoting Christian Knowledge, 1938.

Cobbe, Frances Power. "The Hierarchy of Art." *Fraser's Magazine* 71 (1865):97–108.

Cole, David. *The Work of Sir Gilbert Scott*. London: Architectural Press, 1980.

Coleridge, Samuel Taylor. *Biographia Literaria*. 2 vols. Edited by John Shawcross. Oxford: Clarendon Press, 1907.

Collingwood, R. G. *The Idea of History*. Oxford: Clarendon Press, 1946.

Collins, Peter. *Changing Ideals in Modern Architecture, 1750–1950*. Montreal: McGill University Press, 1965.

Cornish, F. W. "Greek Beauty and Modern Art." *Fortnightly Review* 20 (1873):326–36.

[Couder, Francis R.] "Modern Architecture and Its Assailants." *Edinburgh Review* 141 (1875):386–416.

Cram, Ralph Adams. *The Ministry of Art*. 1914. Reprint. Freeport, N.Y.: Books for Libraries Press, 1967.

———. *The Significance of Gothic Art*. Boston: Marshall Jones Co., 1918.

Crane, Walter. "The Architecture of Art." *Builder* 52 (1887):313–14. Also printed in *Architect's Register* 2 (1887):20–30.

Crichton, Fenella. "Revivalism and Ritualism: Victorian Church Art at the V. and A." *Apollo* 95 (January 1972):53–55.

Crook, J. Mordaunt. *William Burges and the High Victorian Dream*. Chicago: University of Chicago Press, 1981.

Crowest, Frederick J. "Wanted—An English Musical Style." *National Review* 9 (1887):208–13.

Curl, James Stevens. *Victorian Architecture: Its Practical Aspects*. Rutherford, N.J.: Fairleigh Dickinson University Press, 1973.

Davis, Terence. *The Gothick Taste*. Rutherford, N.J.: Fairleigh Dickinson University Press, 1975.

Davison, T. Raffles, ed. *The Arts Connected with Building*. London: B. T. Batsford, 1909.

De Zurko, Edward Robert. *Origins of Functionalist Theory*. New York: Columbia University Press, 1957.

Dixon, Roger, and Stefan Muthesius. *Victorian Architecture*. New York: Oxford University Press, 1978.

Donaldson, Thomas L. "On the Origin and Progress of Expression in the Monuments of Architecture." *Builder* 16 (1858):39–42.

Dorn, Harold, and Robert Mark. "The Architecture of Christopher Wren." *Scientific American*, July 1981, pp. 160–73.

Dresser, Christopher. *Principles of Decorative Design*. 1873. Reprint. New York: St. Martin's Press, 1973

Durandus, William. *The Symbolism of Churches and Church Ornaments: A Translation of the First Book of the Rationale Divinorum Officiorum*. Introduced by John Mason Neale and Benjamin Webb. London: Gibbings & Co., 1893.

E., J. "Grecian and Gothic Architecture." *Arnold's Magazine of the Fine Arts and Journal of Literature and Science* 1 (1833):510–11.

Eastlake, Charles L. *A History of the Gothic Revival*. London: Longmans, Green & Co., 1872.

Ecclesiological late Cambridge Camden Society. *A Hand-Book of English Ecclesiology*. London: Joseph Masters, 1847.

Edwards, Tudor. "Victorian Castles." *History Today* 19 (1969):225–31.

Elmes, James. *Lectures on Architecture, Comprising the History of the Art from the Earliest Times to the Present Day*. 1821. Reprint. New York: Benjamin Blom, 1971

"English Architecture: Present Questions." *Builder* 32 (1874):24–25.

Evelyn, John. *An Account of Architects and Architecture*. 3d ed. London: n.p., 1723.

Fawcett, Jane, ed. *Seven Victorian Architects*. University Park: Pennsylvania State University Press, 1977.

Fergusson, James. *An Historical Inquiry into the True Principles of Beauty in Art, More Especially with Reference to Architecture*. London: Longman, Brown, Green & Longmans, 1849.

———. *History of the Modern Styles of Architecture*. Vol. 2. 3d ed. Edited by Robert Kerr. New York: Dodd, Mead & Co., 1891.

Ferrey, Benjamin. *Recollections of A. W. N. Pugin and His Father Augustus Pugin*. 1861. Reprint. London: Scolar Press, 1978.

Ferriday, Peter, ed. *Victorian Architecture*. London: Jonathan Cape, 1963.

Frank, Ellen E. "The Domestication of Nature: Five Houses in the Lake District." In *Nature and the Victorian Imagination*, pp. 68–92. Edited by U. C. Knoepflmacher and G. B. Tennyson. Berkeley: University of California Press, 1977.

Freeman, Edward A. *The Preservation and Restoration of Ancient Monuments*. Oxford: John Henry Parker, 1852.

"The French Académie and Gothic Architecture." *Ecclesiologist* 6 (1846):83.

Garbett, Edward Lacy. *Rudimentary Treatise on the Principles of Design in Architecture as Deducible from Nature and Exemplified in the Works of the Greek and Gothic Architects*. London: John Weale, 1850.

Garrigan, Kristine Ottesen. *Ruskin on Architecture: His Thought and Influence.* Madison: University of Wisconsin Press, 1973.

Gaunt, John. *Victorian Olympus.* Rev. ed. London: Jonathan Cape, 1975.

Gent, Margaret. "'To Flinch From Modern Varnish': The Appeal of the Past to the Victorian Imagination." In *Victorian Poetry,* pp. 11–35. Edited by Malcolm Bradbury and David Palmer. Stratford-Upon-Avon Studies, no. 15. London: Edward Arnold, 1972.

Germann, Georg. *Gothic Revival in Europe and Britain: Sources, Influences, and Ideas.* Translated by Gerald Onn. London: Lund Humphries with the Architectural Association, 1972.

Giedion, Siegfried. *Space, Time, and Architecture.* 5th ed. Cambridge, Mass.: Harvard University Press, 1967.

Gilbert, Katharine Everett, and Helmut Kuhn. *A History of Esthetics.* Rev. ed. Bloomington: Indiana University Press, 1954.

Gilpin, William. *Observations, Relative Chiefly to Picturesque Beauty, Made in the Year 1772, on Several Parts of England; Particularly the Mountains, and Lakes of Cumberland and Westmoreland.* 2d ed. London: R. Blamire, 1788.

Girouard, Mark. *The Return to Camelot: Chivalry and the English Gentleman.* New Haven, Conn.: Yale University Press, 1981.

———. *Sweetness and Light: The "Queen Anne" Movement, 1860–1900.* Oxford: Clarendon Press, 1977.

Gloag, John. *The Architectural Interpretation of History.* London: Adam and Charles Black, 1975.

———. *Victorian Taste: Some Social Aspects of Architecture and Industrial Design, from 1820–1900.* London: Adam and Charles Black, 1962.

Goodchild, Thomas. Letter. *Builder* 15 (1857):81.

Goodhart-Rendel, H. S. *English Architecture since the Regency: An Interpretation.* London: Constable & Co., 1953.

Gowans, James. "The Useful, Structural, and Beautiful, in Architecture." *Builder* 28 (1870):944–45.

Griffith, W. Pettit. "A Natural System of Architecture *versus* a New Style." *Builder* 24 (1866):880–82.

Gwilt, Joseph. *An Encyclopaedia of Architecture: Historical, Theoretical, and Practical.* Revised by Wyatt Papworth. London: Longmans, Green & Co., 1872.

Gwynn, Denis. *Lord Shrewsbury, Pugin, and the Catholic Revival.* London: Hollis & Carter, 1946.

Hagstrum, Jean H. *The Sister Arts: The Tradition of Literary Pictorialism and English Poetry from Dryden to Gray.* Chicago: University of Chicago Press, 1958.

Hall, Sir James. *Essay on the Origin, History, and Principles of Gothic Architecture.* London: John Murray, 1813.

Hamerton, Philip Gilbert. "The Place of Landscape Painting amongst the Fine Arts." *Fortnightly Review* 3 (1865):197–216.

Hardy, Thomas. *The Architectural Notebook of Thomas Hardy.* Introduced by C. J. P. Beatty. Dorchester: Dorset Natural History and Archaeological Society, 1966.

———. *A Laodicean: A Story of To-Day.* London: Macmillan & Co., 1968.

Hawthorne, Nathaniel. *Our Old Home.* Centenary Edition of the Works of Nathaniel Hawthorne, vol. 5. Edited by William Charvat (1905–1966), Roy Harvey Pearce, Claude M. Simpson (1910–1976), and Thomas Woodson; Fredson Bowers, textual editor, L. Neal Smith, associate textual editor. Columbus: Ohio State University Press, 1970.

Hersey, George L. *High Victorian Gothic: A Study in Associationism.* Baltimore: Johns Hopkins University Press, 1972.

Hewison, Robert. *John Ruskin: The Argument of the Eye.* Princeton, N.J.: Princeton University Press, 1976.

Hipple, Walter John, Jr. *The Beautiful, the Sublime, and the Picturesque in Eighteenth-Century British Aesthetic Theory.* Carbondale: Southern Illinois University Press, 1957.

Hitchcock, Henry-Russell. *Early Victorian Architecture in Britain.* 2 vols. New Haven, Conn.: Yale University Press, 1954.

———. "G. E. Street in the 1850s." *Journal of the Society of Architectural Historians* 19 (1960):145–71

Hogarth, William. *The Analysis of Beauty.* Edited by Joseph Burke. Oxford: Clarendon Press, 1955.

Honour, Hugh. *Neo-classicism.* Rev. ed. Harmondsworth: Penguin Books, 1977.

Hope, Thomas. *An Historical Essay on Architecture.* 3d ed. 2 vols. London: John Murray, 1840.

Houghton, Walter E. *The Victorian Frame of Mind.* New Haven, Conn.: Yale University Press, 1957.

Huggins, Samuel. *The Course and Current of Architecture: Being an Historical Account of the Origin, Successive and Simultaneous Developments, Relations, Periods, and Characteristics of Its Various Known Styles.* London: John Weale, 1863.

———. "Expression in Architecture." *Builder* 9 (1851):324–26, 384–85, 401–2, 428–29.

Huskisson, Guillaume G. "The Architecture and Art of the Present." *Builder* 31 (1873):369.

Hussey, Christopher. *The Picturesque: Studies in a Point of View.* London: G. P. Putnam's Sons, 1927.

Jackson, Thomas Graham. "Architecture—A Profession or an Art." *Nineteenth Century* 33 (1893):405–15.

———. *Modern Gothic Architecture.* London: Henry S. King & Co., 1873.

———. *Recollections of Thomas Graham Jackson.* Edited by Basil H. Jackson. London: Oxford University Press, 1950.

James, Henry. *The Art of Fiction, and Other Essays*. Introduced by Morris Roberts. New York: Oxford University Press, 1948.

Jenkyns, Richard. *The Victorians and Ancient Greece*. Cambridge, Mass.: Harvard University Press, 1980.

Johnson, E. D. H. *The Alien Vision of Victorian Poetry: Sources of the Poetic Imagination in Tennyson, Browning, and Arnold*. Princeton Studies in English, no. 34. Princeton, N.J.: Princeton University Press, 1952.

Johnson, Edwin. "Gothic and Saracen Architecture." *Westminster Review* 136 (1891):643–49.

Jones, Owen. *The Grammar of Ornament*. 1856. Reprint. New York: Van Nostrand Reinhold Co., 1972.

Jordan, Robert Furneaux. *Victorian Architecture*. Baltimore: Penguin Books, 1966.

Kaye, Barrington. *The Development of the Architectural Profession in Britain: A Sociological Study*. London: Allen & Unwin, 1960.

Kerr, Robert. "The Battle of the Styles." *Builder* 18 (1860):292–94

———. *The Gentleman's House; or, How to Plan English Residences, from the Parsonage to the Palace*. 2d ed. London: John Murray, 1865.

———. *The Newleafe Discourses on the Fine Art Architecture*. London: J. Weale, 1846.

———. "Remarks on Professor Donaldson's 'Architectural Maxims and Theorems.'" *Builder* 6 (1848):265–67.

Kindler, Roger A. "Periodical Criticism, 1815–40: Originality in Architecture." *Architectural History: Journal of the Society of Architectural Historians in Great Britain* 17 (1974):22–37.

Kornwolf, James D. "High Victorian Gothic; or, The Dilemma of Style in Modern Architecture." *Journal of the Society of Architectural Historians* 34 (1975):37–47.

[Landon, Letitia E.] "On the Ancient and Modern Influence of Poetry." *New Monthly Magazine* 35 (1832):466–71.

Landow, George P. *The Aesthetic and Critical Theories of John Ruskin*. Princeton, N.J.: Princeton University Press, 1971.

Lang, S. "The Principles of the Gothic Revival in England." *Journal of the Society of Architectural Historians* 25 (1966):240–67.

"Late Mr. Pugin, The." *Ecclesiologist* 13 (1852):352–57.

"Late William Butterfield, F. S. A., The." *Journal of the R.I.B.A.* 7 (1900):241–48.

Lawrence, W. J. "Realism on the Stage: How Far Permissible?" *Westminster Review* 135 (1891):273–88.

Lee, Vernon. "Comparative Aesthetics." *Contemporary Review* 38 (1880):300–326.

Lee, W. Rennselaer. "Ut Pictura Poesis: The Humanistic Theory of Painting." *Art Bulletin* 22 (1940):197–269.

Leeds, W. H. "Architectural Revivalism and Puginism." *Fraser's Magazine* 28 (1843):593–605.

Lessing, Gotthold Ephraim. *Laocoön: An Essay on the Limits of Painting and Poetry.* Translated by Edward Allen McCormick. Indianapolis: Bobbs-Merrill, 1962.

Lethaby, William Richard. *Architecture: An Introduction to the History and Theory of the Art of Building.* 3d ed. Preface and Epilogue by Basil Ward. London: Oxford University Press, 1955.

———. *Architecture, Nature, and Magic.* London: Duckworth & Co., 1956.

———. *Philip Webb and His Work.* London: Oxford University Press, 1935.

Letter in reply to "The Practical Study of Gothic Architecture." *Builder* 3 (1845):299.

Lewes, George Henry. "The Principles of Success in Literature." *Fortnightly Review* 1 (1865):85–95. Reprinted in *The Principles of Success in Literature,* edited by T. Sharper Knowlson. London: Walter Scott, n.d.

Loudon, J. C. "Architecture Considered as an Art of Imagination." *Architectural Magazine* 1 (1834):145–47.

———. "Forms, Lines, Lights, Shades, and Colours, Considered with Reference to the Production of an Architectural Whole." *Architectural Magazine* 1 (1834):249–55.

———. "On the Difference between Common, or Imitative, Genius, and Inventive, or Original, Genius, in Architecture." *Architectural Magazine* 1 (1834):185–88.

———. "On those Principles of Composition, in Architecture, Which Are Common to all the Fine Arts." Architectural Magazine 1 (1834):217–22.

Lovejoy, Arthur O. "The First Gothic Revival and the Return to Nature." MLN 47 (1932):419–46. Reprinted in *Essays in the History of Ideas.* Baltimore; Johns Hopkins Press, 1948.

———. *The Great Chain of Being: A Study of the History of an Idea.* Cambridge, Mass.: Harvard University Press, 1936.

Macaulay, James. *The Gothic Revival, 1745–1845.* Glasgow: Blackie & Son, 1975.

Mackail, J. W. *The Life of William Morris,* 2 vols. London: Longmans, Green & Co., 1911.

Macleod, Robert. *Style and Society: Architectural Ideology in Britain, 1835–1914.* London: RIBA Publications, 1971.

Malek, James S. *The Arts Compared: An Aspect of Eighteenth-Century British Aesthetics.* Detroit: Wayne State University Press, 1974.

Mallock, W. H. "The Conditions of Great Poetry." *Quarterly Review* 192 (1900):156–82.

Maynadier, Howard. *The Arthur of the English Poets.* Boston: Houghton Mifflin Co., 1907.

[Merivale, Louisa A.] "On the 'Gothic' Renaissance in English Literature." *North British Review* 43 (1865):461–86.

Mill, John Stuart. *Essays on Politics and Culture*. Edited by Gertrude Himmel-farb. New York: Doubleday & Co., 1963.

Mitchell, W. M. "The Present Position of Gothic Architecture." *Builder* 31 (1873):383–405.

Morris, Martin. "The Philosophy of Poetry." *Nineteenth Century* 46 (1899):504–13.

Morris, William. *The Collected Works of William Morris*. Edited by May Morris. 24 vols. 1910–15. Reprint. New York: Russell & Russell, 1966.

Munro, Thomas. *The Arts and Their Interrelations*. 2d ed. Cleveland: Press of Western Reserve University, 1967.

Muthesius, Stefan. *The High Victorian Movement in Architecture, 1850–1870*. London: Routledge & Kegan Paul, 1972.

Neale, John Mason. *A Few Words to Church-Builders*. 3d ed. Cambridge: At the University Press, 1844.

"On the Principles of Taste." *Magazine of the Fine Arts* 1 (1821):321–28, 401–19.

Panofsky, Erwin. *Gothic Architecture and Scholasticism*. New York: Meridian Books, 1957.

"Past and Future Developements of Architecture." *Ecclesiologist* 5 (1846):52.

Patrick, James. "Newman, Pugin, and Gothic." *Victorian Studies* 24 (1981):185–207.

[Patmore, Coventry.] "Architects and Architecture." *Fraser's Magazine* 46 (1852):653–59.

Peckham, Morse. "Afterword: Reflections on Historical Modes in the Nineteenth Century." In *Victorian Poetry*, pp. 277–300. Edited by Malcolm Bradbury and David Palmer. Stratford-Upon-Avon Studies, no. 15. London: Edward Arnold, 1972.

Petit, J. L. "Utilitarianism in Architecture." *Builder* 14 (1856):37–38, 58–60.

Pevsner, Nikolaus. *High Victorian Design: A Study of the Exhibits of 1851*. London: Architectural Press, 1951.

———. *Pioneers of Modern Design from William Morris to Walter Gropius*. 2d ed. New York: Museum of Modern Art, 1949.

———. *Ruskin and Viollet-le-Duc: Englishness and Frenchness in the Appreciation of Gothic Architecture*. London: Thames & Hudson, 1969.

———. *Some Architectural Writers of the Nineteenth Century*. Oxford: Clarendon Press, 1972.

"Philosophy of Gothic Architecture, The." *Ecclesiologist* 4 (1845):65.

Picton, J. A. "An Attempt to Explain the Elements and Principles of Gothic Architecture to the General Reader." *Architectural Magazine* 1 (1834):328–33.

"Poetry of Christian Art, The." *Blackwood's Edinburgh Magazine* 80 (1856):350–64.

"Pope and Blackstone's Gothic Comparisons." *Builder* 32 (1874):508.

"Position and Progress of Architecture." *Builder* 31 (1873):584.

"Practical Study of Gothic Architecture, The." *Builder* 3 (1845):266–67.

"Present Condition of Architecture." *Builder* 16 (1858):1–2.

Price, Martin. "The Picturesque Moment." In *From Sensibility to Romanticism: Essays Presented to Frederick A. Pottle*, pp. 259–92. Edited by Frederick W. Hilles and Harold Bloom. London: Oxford University Press, 1965.

Price, Sir Uvedale. *On the Picturesque*. Edited by Sir Thomas Dick Lauder. Edinburgh: Caldwell, Lloyd & Co., 1842.

"Principles of Gothic Architecture." *Quarterly Review* 69 (1841):111–49.

Pugin, A. Welby. *An Apology for the Revival of Christian Architecture in England*. London: John Weale, 1843.

——. *Contrasts: or, A Parallel between the Noble Edifices of the Middle Ages and Corresponding Buildings of the Present Day; Shewing the Present Decay of Taste. Accompanied by Appropriate Text*. 2d ed. 1841. Reprint. New York: Humanities Press, 1969.

——. *The Present State of Ecclesiastical Architecture in England*. 1843. Reprint. Oxford: St. Barnabas Press, 1969.

——. *A Reply to Observations Which Appeared in "Fraser's Magazine," for March 1837, on a Work Entitled "Contrasts."* London: James Moyes, 1837.

——. *Some Remarks on the Articles Which Have Recently Appeared in the "Rambler," Relative to Ecclesiastical Architecture and Decoration*. London: Charles Dolman, 1850.

——. *The True Principles of Pointed or Christian Architecture*. 1841. Reprint. London: Academy Editions, 1973.

Quiney, Anthony. *John Loughborough Pearson*. New Haven, Conn.: Yale University Press, 1979.

Read, Herbert. *The True Voice of Feeling: Studies in English Romantic Poetry*. London: Faber & Faber, 1947.

Reade, T. Mellard. "A New Style: How Can It Be Found?" *Builder* 20 (1862):537.

[Redding, Cyrus.] "The Good Old Times." *New Monthly Magazine* 8 (1823):428–33.

Reynolds, Sir Joshua. *Discourses on Art*. 2d ed. Edited by Robert R. Wark. New Haven, Conn.: Yale University Press, 1975.

Richardson, J. Hall. "Scotland Yard." *Murray's Magazine* 8 (1890):7–8.

Ricks, Christopher. *Tennyson*. New York: Macmillan Co., 1972.

Rope, H. E. G. *Pugin*. Hassocks, Surrey: Pepler & Sewell, 1935.

Rosenau, Helen. *Boullée and Visionary Architecture*. London: Academy Editions, 1976.

Ruskin, John. *The Works of John Ruskin*. Library Edition. Edited by E. T. Cook and Alexander Wedderburn. 39 vols. London: George Allen, 1903–12.

Saarinen, Eero. *Eero Saarinen on His Work*. Edited by Aline B. Saarinen. New Haven, Conn.: Yale University Press, 1962.

Saint, Andrew. *Richard Norman Shaw*. New Haven, Conn.: Yale University Press, 1976.

Schlegel, Friedrich. *Lectures on the History of Literature, Ancient and Modern*. 2 vols. Edinburgh: William Blackwood, 1818.

Scott, Geoffrey. *The Architecture of Humanism: A Study in the History of Taste*. 2d ed. 1924. Reprint. Gloucester, Mass.: Peter Smith, 1965.

Scott, Sir George Gilbert. "Copyism in Gothic Architecture." *Builder* 8 (1850):169–70.

———. "English Architecture: Present Questions." *Builder* 32 (1874):24–25.

———. *Personal and Professional Recollections*. Edited by G. Gilbert Scott. London: Sampson Low, Marston, Searle & Rivington, 1879.

———. *Remarks on Secular and Domestic Architecture, Present and Future*. 2d ed. London: John Murray, 1858.

Scott, W. H. "The Theory of the Picturesque." *Atlantis* 5 (1860):1–23.

Sedding, John D. *Art and Handicraft*. 1893. Reprint. New York: Garland Publishing, 1977.

Seddon, J. P. "The Dark Ages of Architecture." *Papers Read at the Royal Institute of British Architects* 5 (1860–62):266–79.

Shaw, R. Norman, and T. G. Jackson, eds. *Architecture: A Profession or an Art*. London: John Murray, 1892.

Shiells, W. G. "Nature the Standard of Truth in Architecture." *Builder* 25 (1867):7–8.

Simson, Otto von. *The Gothic Cathedral: Origins of Gothic Architecture and the Medieval Concept of Order*. 2d ed. New York: Pantheon Books, 1962.

Smith, Warren Hunting. *Architecture in English Fiction*. New Haven, Conn.: Yale University Press, 1934.

Soane, Sir John. "Lecture on Architecture at the Royal Academy, 1832." *Library of the Fine Arts* 3 (1832):450–54.

———. *Lectures on Architecture*. Edited by Arthur T. Bolton. London: Sir John Soane's Museum, 1929.

Stanton, Phoebe B. "Architecture, History, and the Spirit of the Age." In *The Mind and Art of Victorian England*, pp. 146–58. Edited by Josef L. Altholz. Minneapolis: University of Minnesota Press, 1976.

———. *Pugin*. London: Thames & Hudson, 1971.

———. "Pugin: Principles of Design versus Revivalism." *Journal of the Society of Architectural Historians* 13, no. 3 (1954):20–25.

———. "The Sources of Pugin's *Contrasts*." In *Concerning Architecture*, pp. 120–39. Edited by Sir John Summerson. London: Penguin Books, 1968.

Steegman, John. *Victorian Taste: A Study of the Arts and Architecture from 1830 to 1870*. Cambridge, Mass.: MIT Press, 1971.

Stevens, J. Henry. Letter in reply to G. G. Scott. *Builder* 15 (1857):638.

Stevenson, Robert Louis. *An Inland Voyage*. Vol. 1, *The Works of Robert Louis Stevenson*. 26 vols. Edited by L. Osbourne and F. Van de G. Stevenson. New York: Charles Scribner's Sons, 1921–23.

Storr, Vernon F. *The Development of English Theology in the Nineteenth Century, 1800–1860*. London: Longmans Green & Co., 1913.

Street, Arthur Edmund. *Memoir of George Edmund Street, R. A. 1824–1881*. 1888. Reprint. New York: Benjamin Blom, 1972.

Street, George Edmund. "On the Future of Art in England." *Ecclesiologist* 19 (1858):232–40.

―――. "A Plea for the Revival of True Principles of Architecture in the Public Buildings of Oxford." *Builder* 11 (1853):403–4.

―――. "The True Principles of Architecture, and the Possibility of Development." *Ecclesiologist* 13 (1852):247–62.

Strong, Roy. *Recreating the Past: British History and the Victorian Painter*. London: Thames & Hudson, 1978.

Sullivan, Louis H. *Kindergarten Chats and Other Writings*. New York: George Wittenborn, 1947.

Summerson, Sir John. *The Architecture of Victorian London*. Charlottesville: University Press of Virginia, 1976.

―――, ed. *Concerning Architecture*. London: Penguin Books, 1968.

―――. *Heavenly Mansions*. New York: Norton, 1963.

―――. *Victorian Architecture: Four Studies in Evaluation*. New York: Columbia University Press, 1970.

Symonds, John Addington. *Essays: Speculative and Suggestive*. 3d ed. London: Smith, Elder & Co., 1907.

―――. *Italian Byways*. London: Smith, Elder & Co., 1883.

T., E. L. "Style in Architecture." *Builder* 27 (1869):489.

Taut, Bruno. *Modern Architecture*. London: Studio, 1929.

"The Tendencies of Praeraffaelitism, and Its Connection with the Gothic Movement." *Ecclesiologist* 21 (1860):248–50.

Thompson, Paul. *William Butterfield*. Cambridge, Mass.: MIT Press, 1971.

Tilley, Arthur. "The Poetic Imagination." *Macmillan's Magazine* 53 (1886):184–92.

Trappes-Lomax, Michael. *Pugin: A Mediaeval Victorian*. London: Sheed & Ward, 1932.

Trotman, E. "On the Comparative Value of Simplicity in Architecture." *Architectural Magazine* 1 (1834):103–8.

Turner, Frank M. *The Greek Heritage in Victorian Britain*. New Haven, Conn.: Yale University Press, 1981.

Unrau, John. *Looking at Architecture with Ruskin*. Toronto: University of Toronto Press, 1978.

―――. "A Note on Ruskin's Reading of Pugin." *English Studies* 48 (1967): 335–37.

"Urban Architecture versus Street Architecture." *Builder* 39 (1880):65–66.

Vitruvius. *The Ten Books on Architecture.* Translated by Morris Hicky Morgan. 1914. Reprint. New York: Dover Publications, 1960.

Warren, Alba H., Jr. *English Poetic Theory 1825–1865.* Princeton, N.J.: Princeton University Press, 1950.

Waterhouse, Paul. "The Life and Work of Welby Pugin." *Architectural Review: For the Artist and Craftsman* 3 (1897–98):167–75, 211–21, 264–73; 4 (1898):23–27, 67–73, 115–18, 159–65.

Watkin, David. *Morality and Architecture: The Development of a Theme in Architectural History and Theory from the Gothic Revival to the Modern Movement.* Oxford: Clarendon Press, 1977.

[Webb, Benjamin.] "The Prospects of Art in England." *Bentley's Quarterly Review* 1 (1859):143–82.

"Welby Pugin and the 'Bristol and West of England Archaeological Magazine.'" Builder 2 (1844):165–66.

Wellek, René. *A History of Modern Criticism, 1750–1950.* Vols. 1–3. New Haven, Conn.: Yale University Press, 1955, 1965.

Whewell, W. "Of Certain Analogies between Architecture and the Other Fine Arts." *Papers Read at the Royal Institute of British Architects* 6 (1862–63):175–89.

Whistler, James Abbott McNeill. *The Gentle Art of Making Enemies.* London: William Heinemann, 1890.

White, James F. *The Cambridge Movement: The Ecclesiologists and the Gothic Revival.* Cambridge: At the University Press, 1962.

White, William H. "On 'The Hope of English Architecture.'" *Builder* 32 (1874):1044–46, 1065–67.

Wightwick, George. *The Palace of Architecture: A Romance of Art and History.* London: James Fraser, 1840.

Wilde, Oscar. *The Artist as Critic: Critical Writings of Oscar Wilde.* Edited by Richard Ellmann. New York: Random House, 1968.

Wimsatt, William K., Jr., and Cleanth Brooks. *Literary Criticism: A Short History.* New York: Alfred A. Knopf, 1957.

Wingfield-Stratford, Esmé. *Those Earnest Victorians.* New York: William Morrow & Co., 1930.

Wölfflin, Heinrich. *Principles of Art History: The Problem of the Development of Style in Later Art.* 7th ed. Translated by M. D. Hottinger. New York: Dover Publications, n.d.

Wornum, Ralph Nicholson. "The Exhibition as a Lesson in Taste." In *The Crystal Palace Exhibition Illustrated Catalogue,* pp. I***–XXII***. 1851. Reprint. New York: Dover Publications, 1970.

Wright, Frank Lloyd. *An Autobiography.* London: Longmans, Green & Co., 1938.

———. *An Organic Architecture.* 2d ed. 1941. Reprint. Cambridge, Mass.: MIT Press, 1970.

Yvon, Paul. *Le Gothique et la Renaissance Gothique en Angleterre (1750–1880).* Caen: Jouan & Bigot, 1931.

INDEX